A WORLD BANK COUNTRY STUDY

India
Sustaining Rapid Economic Growth

The World Bank
Washington, D.C.

World Bank Country Studies are among the many reports originally prepared for internal use as part of the continuing analysis by the Bank of the economic and related conditions of its developing member countries and of its dialogues with the governments. Some of the reports are published in this series with the least possible delay for the use of governments and the academic, business and financial, and development communities. The typescript of this paper therefore has not been prepared in accordance with the procedures appropriate to formal printed texts, and the World Bank accepts no responsibility for errors. Some sources cited in this paper may be informal documents that are not readily available.

The World Bank does not guarantee the accuracy of the data included in this publication and accepts no responsibility whatsoever for any consequence of their use. The boundaries, colors, denominations, and other information shown on any map in this volume do not imply on the part of the World Bank Group any judgment on the legal status of any territory or the endorsement or acceptance of such boundaries.

The material in this publication is copyrighted. Requests for permission to reproduce portions of it should be sent to the Office of the Publisher at the address shown in the copyright notice above. The World Bank encourages dissemination of its work and will normally give permission promptly and, when the reproduction is for noncommercial purposes, without asking a fee. Permission to copy portions for classroom use is granted through the Copyright Clearance Center, Inc., Suite 910, 222 Rosewood Drive, Danvers, Massachusetts 01923, U.S.A.

ISSN: 0253-2123

Library of Congress Cataloging-in-Publication Data

India : sustaining rapid economic growth / World Bank.
     p. cm. — (A World Bank country study)
   ISBN 0-8213-3992-3
   1. India—Economic policy—1980-   2. India—Economic conditions—1947-   3. Structural adjustment (Economic policy)—India.   4. Sustainable development—India.   I. World Bank.
II. Series.
HC435.2.I539   1997
338.954—dc21

                                          97-30310
                                          CIP

Contents

List of tables

List of boxes

List of figures

ABSTRACT

India's economic performance over 1996-97 has continued to be strong, a result of the past six years of macroeconomic adjustment and structural reforms. Real GDP is estimated to have grown by over 6 percent for the fourth successive year; private saving and investment rates have risen well above their historical averages; inflation is moderate and the external accounts remain strong. Private capital inflows are expected to continue to boost international reserves.

Despite these favorable developments, a slowdown in investment and growth during 1996-97--due to both world demand factors and domestic capacity constraints, notably infrastructure--raised apprehension on the economy's capacity to sustain the rates of growth of the last few years without further and faster reforms. Chief among these reform priorities is the reduction of fiscal imbalances which remain the major source of macroeconomic strains. Lower fiscal deficits would not only help reduce the high real interest rates that have prevailed in the past and increase investment but would also provide favorable conditions for an acceleration of banking and public enterprise reforms, would help sustain the growth-inflation mix of the past few years, and would help correct the severe price distortions and misguided sector policies which are preventing private investment and hampering development in India today.

The report stresses that, in addition to the macro-and-micro-economic dimensions of fiscal adjustment, a third and very important reason for stronger fiscal adjustment is that of expenditure composition, particularly at the state level. Reversing the severe deterioration of India's infrastructure and accelerating the development of India's human resources would depend to a large extent on states' willingness to correct their pricing and sector policies and their associated implied subsidies which continue to absorb a large share of their budgets, crowding-out growth enhancing expenditure.

ACKNOWLEDGMENTS

This report was prepared by a team led by Zoubida Allaoua. It draws on contributions from Mona Haddad, William McCarten, V.J. Ravishankar (state issues, fiscal), Miria Pigato and Uri Dadush (external sectors), Dina Umali-Deininger (agriculture), Joelle Chassard, Kari Nyman, Djamal Mostefai, Mudassar Imran (energy), Harald Hansen (transport). Roberto Zagha (Lead Economist) contributed to the report and provided guidance. Rui Coutinho who participated in the discussions with the government also provided invaluable assistance. The report benefited from comments from John Williamson (Chief Economist), Luis Serven (reviewer), Colin Bruce, Sanjay Kathuria, Benoit Blarel, Keith Hinchliff, James Hanson, and Dimitri Tzanninis and Martin Muhleisen (IMF). Primary statistical and computational assistance was received from Bhaskar Naidu and Rajni Khanna. The report benefitted from Luis Ernesto Derbez (Division Chief) continuous support.

The report benefitted from and reflects discussions held with the Indian authorities in May 1997. We gratefully acknowledge the cooperation of government officials, the RBI, and members of the business community for their valuable time and assistance.

Arrangements for mission to India were made by Padma Gopalan and Sheni Rana. The report was desktoped by Lin Chin.

ABBREVIATIONS AND ACRONYMS

BE	Budget Estimates	MPBF	Maximum Permissible Bank Finance
BOLT	Build-Operate-Lease-Transfer	MTM	Mark to Market
BOP	Balance of Payments	MTO	Multimodal Transport services
BOO	Build-Own-Operate	MUV	Manufactures Unit Value
BOT	Build-Operate-Transfer	MW	Megawatt
BSE	Bombay Stock Exchange	NBFCs	Non Bank Financial Companies
CEA	Central Electricity Authority	NCAER	National Council of Applied Economic Research
CEM	Country Economic Memorandum		
CERC	Central Electricity Regulatory Commission	NFA	Net Financial Assets
CFS	Container Freight Station	NHAI	National Highways Authority of India
CGE	Computable General Equilibrium	NPV	Net Present Value
CMNAP	Common Minimum National Action Plan	NRER(A)	Non-Resident External Rupee Account
CMP	Common Minimum Program	NSE	National Stock Exchange
CONCOR	Container Corporation of India	NTB	Non-Tariff Barriers
CRR	Cash Reserve Requirement	NTPC	National Thermal Power Corporation
CSO	Central Statistical Organization	O&M	Overhaul and Maintenance
DOT	Department of Telecommunications	OCC	Oil Coordination Committee
DRS	Debt Reporting System	OECD	Organization for Economic Cooperation and Development
EAS	Employment Assurance Scheme		
ECB	Euro-Convertible Bond	OTCEI	Over-the-Counter Exchange
EU	European Union (formerly the EC)	ONGC	Oil and Natural Gas Corporation
FCI	Food Corporation of India	PD	Primary Dealers
FCNRA	Foreign Currency (Non-Resident) Accounts	PDS	Public Distribution System
FDI	Foreign Direct Investment	PE	Public Enterprise/
FII	Foreign Institutional Investor	PLF	Plant Load Factor
FIPB	Foreign Investment Promotion Board	PLR	Prime Lending Rate
GATT	General Agreement on Tariffs and Trade	POL	Petroleum, Oil and Lubricants
GDP	Gross Domestic Product	PPP	Purchasing Power Parity
GDR	Global Depository Receipts	PRI	Panchayati Raj Institutions
GNFS	Goods and Non-factor Services	PWD	Public Works Department
GNP	Gross National Product	R&D	Research and Development
GOI	Government of India	RBI	Reserve Bank of India
HSEB	Haryana State Electricity Board	RE	Revised Estimates
HUDCO	Housing and Urban Development Corporation	REB	Regional Electricity Board
		RER	Real Exchange Rate
HYV	High Yielding Varieties	REER	Real Effective Exchange Rate
ICD	Inland Container Depot	RLDC	Regional Load Dispatch Center
ICDS	Integrated Child Development Scheme	RRB	Rural Regional Bank
ICICI	Industrial Credit and Investment Corporation of India	SAIL	Steel Authority of India Ltd.
		SBI	State Bank of India
IDBI	Industrial Development Bank of India	SC	Scheduled Castes
IDF	Indian Development Forum	SCICI	Shipping Credit and Investment Corporation of India
IDFC	Infrastructure Development Finance Company		
		SDP	State Domestic Product
IFCI	Industrial Financial Corporation of India	SDR	Special Drawing Rights
IGIDR	Indira Gandhi Institute for Development Research	SEB	State Electricity Board
		SEBI	Security and Exchange Board of India
IIP	Index of Industrial Production	SERC	State Electricity Regulatory Commission
IMF	International Monetary Fund	SICA	Sick Industrial Companies Act
IOC	Indian Oil Corporation	SIL	Special Import License
IPP	Independent Power Producers	SITC	Standard Industrial Trade Classification
IRDP	Integrated Rural Development Program	SLR	Statutory Liquidity Requirements
ISO	International Standards Organization	SSA	Sub-Saharan Africa
JRY	Jawahar Rozgar Yojana	SSI	Small Scale Industry
Kwh	Kilowatt-hour	ST	Scheduled Tribes
LAC	Latin America and the Caribbean	STCI	Securities Trading Corporation of India
MAT	Minimum Alternative Tax	TFC	Tenth Finance Commission
MFA	Multifiber Agreement	TOT	Terms of Trade
MFIL	Mahindra Ford India Limited	TRAI	Telecom Regulatory Authority of India
MMMF	Money Market Mutual Fund	TRIPS	Traded Intellectual Property Rights
MODVAT	Modified Value Added Tax	UP	Uttar Pradesh
MOF	Ministry of Finance	UT	Union Territory
MOP	Ministry of Power	VAT	Value Added Tax
MOST	Ministry of Surface Transport	WPI	Wholesale Price Index
MOU	Memorandum of Understanding	WTO	World Trade Organization

Currency

Currency	Rs/ US$		
	Official	Unified	Market [a]
Prior to June 1966	4.76		
June 6, 1966 to mid-December 1971	7.50		
Mid-December 1971 to end-June 1972	7.28		
1971-72	7.44		
1972-73	7.71		
1973-74	7.79		
1974-75	7.98		
1975-76	8.65		
1976-77	8.94		
1977-78	8.56		
1978-79	8.21		
1979-80	8.08		
1980-81	7.89		
1981-82	8.93		
1982-83	9.63		
1983-84	10.31		
1984-85	11.89		
1985-86	12.24		
1986-87	12.79		
1987-88	12.97		
1988-89	14.48		
1989-90	16.66		
1990-91	17.95		
1991-92	24.52		
1992-93	26.41		30.65
1993-94		31.36	
1994-95		31.40	
1995-96		33.46	
1996-97		35.50	

Note: The Indian fiscal year runs from April 1 through March 31.
Source: IMF, International Finance Statistics (IFS), line "rf"; Reserve Bank of India.

[a] A dual exchange rate system was created in March 1992, with a free market for about 60 percent of foreign exchange transactions. The exchange rate was reunified at the beginning of March 1993 at the free market rate.

Economic Development Data

GNP Per Capita (US$, 1995-96): 350 [a]

Gross Domestic Product (1995-96)

	US$ Bln	% of GDP	Annual Growth Rate (% p.a., constant prices)					
			70-71-75-76	75-76-80-81	80-81-85-86	85-86-90-91	91-92	92-93-95-96
GDP at Factor Cost	294.6	89.7	3.4	4.2	5.4	5.9	0.8	6.4
GDP at Market Prices	328.3	100.0	3.3	4.2	5.6	6.2	0.4	6.3
Gross Domestic Investment	86.1	26.2	5.3	3.7	5.7	9.5	-11.0	12.5
Gross National Saving	80.4	24.5	4.4	2.6	3.5	8.7	-0.3	13.2
Current Account Balance	-5.8	-1.8	--	--	--	--	--	--

Output, Employment and Productivity (1990-91)

	Value Added		Labor Force [b]		V. A. per Worker	
	US$ Bln	% of Tot	Mill.	% of Tot.	US$	% of Avg.
Agriculture	82.5	31.0	186.2	66.8	443	46.4
Industry	78.0	29.3	35.5	12.7	2198	230.2
Services	105.7	39.7	57.2	20.5	1849	193.7
Total/ Average	266.2	100.0	278.9	100.0	955	100.0

Government Finance

	General Government [c]			Central Government		
	Rs. Bln.	% of GDP		Rs. Bln.	% of GDP	
	95-96	95-96	90-91-95-96	95-96	95-96	90-91-95-96
Revenue Receipts	2118.7	19.3	19.4	1101.3	10.0	10.1
Revenue Expenditures	2539.4	23.1	23.3	1398.6	12.7	13.2
Revenue Surplus/ Deficit (-)	-420.7	-3.8	-3.9	-297.3	-2.7	-3.1
Capital Expenditures [d]	416.2	3.8	4.2	305.1	2.8	3.4
External Assistance (net) [e]	3.2	0.0	0.6	3.2	0.0	0.6

Money, Credit, and Prices

	89-90	90-91	91-92	92-93	93-94	94-95	95-96
	(Rs. billion outstanding, end of period)						
Money and Quasi Money	2309	2658	3170	3668	4344	5314	6040
Bank Credit to Government (net)	1172	1402	1583	1762	2039	2224	2574
Bank Credit to Commercial Sector	1517	1718	1880	2201	2378	2927	3409
	(percentage or index numbers)						
Money and Quasi Money as % of GDP	50.6	49.6	51.4	52.0	53.6	55.7	55.0
Wholesale Price Index (1981-82 = 100)	165.7	182.7	207.8	228.7	247.8	274.7	294.8
Annual Percentage Changes in:							
Wholesale Price Index	7.4	10.3	13.7	10.1	8.4	10.9	7.3
Bank Credit to Government (net)	20.3	19.7	12.9	11.4	15.7	9.1	15.7
Bank Credit to Commercial Sector	14.4	13.2	9.4	17.1	8.0	23.1	16.5

a. The per capita GNP estimate is at market prices, using World Bank Atlas methodology. Other conversions to dollars in this table are at the prevailing average exchange rate for the period covered.

b. Total Labor Force from 1991 Census. Excludes data for Assam and Jammu & Kashmir.

c. Transfers between Centre and States have been netted out.

d. All loans and advances to third parties have been netted out.

e. As recorded in the government budget.

Balance of Payments (US$ Millions)

Merchandise Exports (Average 1990-91-1995-96)

	1993-94	1994-95	1995-96
Exports of Goods & NFS	27,947	32,796	40,181
Merchandise, fob	22,683	26,857	32,433
Imports of Goods & NFS	29,798	38,150	48,788
Merchandise, cif	25,069	31,840	41,721
of which Crude Petroleum	3,407	3,285	3,442
of which Petroleum Products	2,244	2,396	4,105
Trade Balance	-2,386	-4,983	-9,288
Non Factor Services (net)	535	-371	681
Resource Balance	-1,851	-5,354	-8,607

	S$ Mil	% of Tot.
Tea	404	1.8
Iron Ore	487	2.2
Chemicals	1,891	8.6
Leather & Leather products	1,439	6.5
Textiles	2,708	12.3
Garments	2,731	12.4
Gems and Jewelry	3,753	17.0
Engineering Goods	2,832	12.8
Others	5,803	26.3
Total [e]	22,047	100.0

	1993-94	1994-95	1995-96
Net factor Income[a]	-3,775	-3,621	-4,157
Net Transfers[b]	3,825	6,200	7,000
Balance on Current Account	-1,801	-2,775	-5,764
Foreign Investment	4,235	4,895	4,143
Official Grants and Aid	368	472	416
Net Medium & Long Term Capi	3,122	1,153	-1,036
Gross Disbursements	7,150	5,982	5,744
Principal Repayments	4,027	4,828	6,780
Other Capital Flows[c]	419	1,476	-1,654
Non-Resident Deposits	1,097	818	945
Net Transactions with IMF	189	-1,174	-1,719
Overall Balance	8,538	6,858	-2,005
Change in Net Reserves	-8,727	-5,684	3,724
Gross Reserves (end of year)[d]	15,476	21,160	17,436

External Debt, March 31, 1996

	US$ Mill.
Public & Publicly Guaranteed	79,725
Private Non-Guaranteed	6,618
Total (Including IMF and Short Term)	93,766

Debt Service Ratio for 1995-96

	% curr receipts
Public & Publicly Guaranteed	21.0
Private Non-Guaranteed	1.4
Total (Including IMF and Short Term)	27.2

IBRD/ IDA Lending, March 31, 1996 (US$ Mill)

	IBRD	IDA
Outstanding and Disbursed	9,849	17,499
Undisbursed	4,034	4,583
Outstanding incl. Undisb.	13,883	22,082

Rate of Exchange

End-March 1997	US$ 1.00 = Rs. 34.80

-- Not available.

a. Figures given cover all investment income (net). Major payments are interest on foreign loans and charges paid to IM and major receipts is interest earned on foreign assets.

b. Figures given include workers' remittances but exclude official grant assistance which is included within official loan and grants, and non-resident deposits which are shown separately.

c. Includes short-term net capital inflow, changes in reserve valuation and other items.

d. Excluding gold.

e. Total exports (commerce); net of crude petroleum exports.

Sources : National Accounts Statistics; Ministry of Commerce; Union Budget Documents;
Reserve Bank of India; 1991 Census; World Bank Debt Reporting System.

India Social Indicators

	Latest single year			Some region/income group	
	1970-75	**1980-85**	**1990-95**	**South Asia**	**Low-income**
POPULATION					
Total population, mid-year (millions)	613.5	765.2	929.4	1,243.00	3,179.90
Growth rate (% annual average)	2.3	2.1	1.7	1.9	1.6
Urban population (% of population)	21.3	24.3	26.8	26.4	28.6
Total fertility rate (births per women)	5.6	4.8	3.2	3.5	3.2
POVERTY					
(% of population)					
National headcount index*	..	..	35.0	..	..
Urban headcount index	..	..	30.5	..	..
Rural headcount	..	..	36.7	..	..
INCOME					
GNP per capita (US$)	180	280	350	350	430
Consumer price index (1990=100)	36	70	165	..	..
Food price index (1990=100)	..	66	174	..	..
INCOME/CONSUMPTION DISTRIBUTION					
(% of income or consumption)					
Lowest quintile	5.9	8.1	8.5	..	..
Highest quintile	49.4	41.4	42.6	..	..
SOCIAL INDICATORS					
Public expenditure					
(% of GDP)					
Health	..	..	0.7	..	..
Education	2.1	2.5	2.9	..	..
Social security and welfare	..	..	..	..	..
Access to safe water					
(% of population)					
Total	31	54	63	63.2	53
Urban	..	..	..	..	..
Rural	..	..	..	..	..
Immunization rate					
(% under 12 months)					
Measles	..	..	84	80	77
DPT	..	41	92	84	80
Child malnutrition (% under 5 years)	..	..	63	61	42
Life expectancy at birth					
(years)					
Total	50	55	62	61	63
Male	51	56	62	61	62
Female	49	55	63	62	64
Mortality					
Infant (per thousand live births)	132	108	68	75	69
Under 5 (per thousand live births)	..	..	95	106	104
Adult (15-59)					
Male (per 1,000 population)	..	..	229	239	244
Female (per 1,000 population)	..	..	219	230	211
Maternal (per 100,000 live births)	..	460	437	..	..

* Data for 1993-94

Sources: World Development Indicators CD-ROM, World Bank, February 1997 and India: Achievements and Challenges in Reducing Poverty, May 1997.

EXECUTIVE SUMMARY

A number of reports issued in 1996-97 (the Ministry of Finance's Economic Survey; the Reserve Bank of India's (RBI) Annual Report; the RBI Report on Currency and Finance; the RBI Report on Trend and Progress of Banking in India; the India Development Report (IGIDR); the government appointed Expert Group Report on Infrastructure; the 1997-98 Budget speech; the RBI April Credit Policy; and the May 1997 Ministry of Finance's discussion paper on government subsidies) document comprehensively India's past and recent performance, articulate the governments' development objectives, and provide an accurate picture of the policy challenges the country faces. Because of the comprehensiveness and depth of this documentation to which interested readers are referred, this report comments only on salient recent economic and policy developments.

The Economy is Stronger and More Competitive

The reforms of the past six years brought about an unprecedented strong economic performance. For the third year in a row, GDP is estimated to have grown by about 7 percent in the fiscal year 1996-97 ending on March 31, placing India among the world's best performing economies. Unlike similar episodes in the past, this expansion has been driven by private investment (which reached the historically high level of 18 percent of GDP out of a total investment of 26 percent in the last two years), and has not put pressure on the balance of payments. In spite of the persistent poor performance of public savings, national savings have risen (from 23 percent of GDP in 1991-92 to 26 percent of GDP in 1996-97). The country's external position is strong. The current account deficit was 1.1 percent of GDP in 1996-97; the country's US$94 billion external debt declined to 27 percent of GDP in 1996-97 from 34 percent in 1991-92, and the debt service to 24 percent of current account receipts from 29 percent. In spite of the reduction of the central government fiscal deficit, consolidated fiscal

imbalances remain serious, however, and excessively slow progress is being made to correct them. A May 1997 government paper shows that implicit and explicit subsidies for "non-merit" goods absorb an alarming 11 percent of GDP and are a major factor behind India's chronically high fiscal deficits. Inflation has increased moderately (from below 5 percent in May 1996 to 6 percent in May 1997, point-to-point), partly the result of a more expansionary monetary stance (broad money growth accelerated from 13.7 percent to 15.6 percent).

Underlying the economy's strong economic performance are important *structural transformations*. The declining role of the public sector since the start of the reform program in 1991, both as producer of goods and services and economic regulator, is one of India's most fundamental structural change since Independence. The liberalization of the economy has opened to the private sector areas previously the exclusive domain of the public sector--such as heavy manufacturing, banking, civil aviation, telecommunications, power generation and distribution, ports, and roads. Equally important, the liberalization of the economy has reduced distortions and increased external and internal competition.

In *agriculture*, the sector's terms of trade have improved. As a result, agricultural commodities have been one of India's fastest growing exports, and commercial crops are expanding rapidly. In *industry*, firms are restructuring and entering into joint ventures and alliances with foreign firms. Productivity has increased and consumers have a wider range of better quality goods from which to choose. Important legislative changes, deregulation, and foreign investors are improving corporate governance of industrial and financial firms. The regulatory and institutional framework of the *financial sector* has been strengthened considerably. In the *banking system*, although still vulnerable, the financial health of the public banks has improved and 19 out of the 27 public sector banks reached the capital adequacy ratio of 8 percent in 1995-96. The entry of new private banks and the mainstreaming of Non-Bank Finance Companies (NBFCs) in a financial sector still dominated by public banks (which control 85 percent of the system's assets) have increased competition and forced the latter to reduce costs, and improve quality of service. Similar developments have taken place in *civil aviation*. In *infrastructure*, while much too slowly to address India's infrastructure crisis, private investment is taking place in ports, power, and toll bridges. A new financial institution (IDFC) has been established to facilitate the development of a long-term rupee bond market for infrastructure financing. Last but not least, increased competition in product markets has led to an improvement in industrial relations with a consequent decline in labor disputes.

Reforms have continued during 1996-97 in spite of political uncertainty. The positive effects of the reforms have demonstrated the extent to which India stands to gain from deregulation and better fiscal management, and have helped create some consensus on the need to continue liberalizing the economy and correcting fiscal imbalances. This may explain why, notwithstanding three changes of government of very diverse political backgrounds, reforms have continued in 1996-97 and expanded into some new areas, albeit at a rate that can be seen as excessively gradual.

The *investment regime* has been liberalized further, with particular emphasis on foreign investment-- approval procedures have been simplified and restrictions on end-use relaxed. Announced a few years ago, the independent *Telecom Regulatory Authority of India* has started its operations. In the case of *major ports* (regulated by the central government), an independent Tariff Authority was established, guidelines have been issued for private investment through BOT-type contracts. Several private investments in *minor ports* (under the states' jurisdiction) have already taken place. In *roads*, while there is awareness in India that this is an area where the public sector will retain a major role, attempts have been made nonetheless to facilitate private sector entry with some degree of success, particularly in bridges. Also, legislative changes have been announced to facilitate land acquisition--an important impediment to private investment in roads. In *power*, where the need

is the greatest, private sector interest to invest the strongest, and action by state governments essential to transform this interest into concrete investments, a conference of state Chief Ministers reached agreement on a *Common Minimum National Action Plan for Power* (CMNAP) reforms, issued by the Ministry of Power in December 1996. Much of the CMNAP has been inspired by the pioneering reforms Orissa started a few years ago. The CMNAP envisages changes in legislation to enable the states to have their own independent power regulatory agencies, with authority to grant licenses including for distribution, and fix tariffs. *This would remove the main impediments to large scale private investment in a sector that needs it urgently.* Some states are giving the CMNAP's recommendations serious consideration and taken steps towards their implementation. In *coal*, major reforms have freed imports from licensing restrictions, reduced tariffs to 5-10 percent, pursued the liberalization of private investment in the sector, lifted price controls on high grade coal and will lift the remaining restrictions over the next 2-3 years. Also, a decision was taken to divest shares in Coal India's subsidiaries.

This progress notwithstanding, it is evident that the induction of private capital in areas which for decades have been under public sector monopoly has been slower than anticipated, and so have its results. Unless investment in infrastructure expands significantly, India's emerging infrastructure crisis may prevent the country from sustaining the high levels of growth that the last few years have shown to be within reach. In particular, remarkably little progress has been made in addressing the fundamental policy and institutional changes (most of which under the exclusive purview of state authorities) needed to expand *urban infrastructure* and alleviate the tremendous problems of India's fast growing cities. *Water supply systems*-- rural and urban--continue to be poorly managed by state-government institutions at a high cost to the economy (the subsidy for irrigation alone is close to 2 percent of GDP) and insufficient efforts are being made to attract private investment.

The liberalization of the *trade regime* has continued. Tariff reductions announced in the 1997-98 Budget presented to Parliament in February 1997 brought the maximum rate down to 40 percent and the average import-weighted rate to 20 percent. The Finance Minister announced its intention to reduce it further to East Asian levels. The new Exim Policy eliminated licensing requirements for about one-sixth of consumer goods (essentially, the only imports still restricted) and India has indicated its readiness to eliminate gradually the remaining licensing restrictions.

Several measures were taken also to strengthen the banking system, increase banks' operational autonomy, and improve the functioning of financial markets. Of particular importance, banks are now required to mark to market 60 percent of their portfolios. Virtually all interest rates are now market determined with the exception of interest rates on lending for amounts below Rs. 200,000, and on deposits of below one year. Cash reserve requirements were reduced from 14 percent of deposits in April 1996 to 10 percent in January 1997; reserve requirements on inter-bank liabilities have been abolished; regulations governing loan syndication and amounts of credit for working capital purposes have been eliminated; and prudential regulations were tightened further. The elimination of CRR on inter-bank liabilities coupled with the RBI's rationalization of its refinance rates into a single rate is expected to help establish a reference interest rate which would help develop a yield curve and improve RBI's ability to manage monetary and exchange rate policies.

Regarding *capital markets*, the Depositories Act was passed to provide the legal framework for the dematerialization of securities and their secure transfer through electronic book entry. The establishment of the modern electronic securities exchange system, the National Stock Exchange (NSE), transformed the functioning of the stock markets in India by increasing their transparency through scripless trading. The NSE has promoted the National Securities Depository Limited (NSDL) to facilitate scripless trading and the National Clearing Corporation Limited (NCCL) to guarantee all trade done on the NSE. Screen-based trading has now been generalized to other exchanges. All transactions in debt securities, previously handled by brokers in an unregulated telephone market, are now done solely through the NSE which has emerged as the premier exchange for scripless trading in debt as

well as stock instruments. Finally, SEBI, the securities and exchange board of India, is strengthening its oversight capacity and the transparency of capital markets. It has introduced *inter alia* new and more effective guidelines for public issues and takeovers.

A key objective of the *tax reform* pursued by the Center since 1991 has been to simplify and broaden the base of the tax system by lowering rates, streamlining the rate structure, and improving tax administration. Some of the most severe distortions of the tax system have been corrected. The 1997-98 Budget maintains the overall direction of tax reforms. In particular, it simplified India's tax system further, reduced import tariffs, and brought corporate and personal rates in line with those of East Asia. In the process, the budget also seeks to improve the rules governing tax sharing between the central government and the states and strengthen compliance.

There was also some progress in deregulating agriculture. The strong response of agriculture to reforms created favorable conditions for the government to re-introduce--after a 31-year hiatus--futures trading in cotton lint, jute and jute goods and partially lift restrictions on commodity trading such as those on storage, credit and movement controls, particularly for *cotton and oilseeds*. Export quotas on cotton and cotton yarn were raised and the number of yarn quota exemptions expanded. Sugar exports (subject to quotas) were decanalized in January 1997. To boost rice exports, the government removed the minimum export price but declining government stocks led to the reimposition of the levy on rice mills exporting non-basmati rice. Recent liberalization measures notwithstanding, agriculture continues to be highly regulated by both central and state governments at a high cost to the economy and the poor.

There was less progress in reforming public enterprise (PEs), however. While public enterprises are now more exposed to competition, their autonomy remains limited and this has reduced the ability of their managers to introduce essential restructuring. Thus, with a few exceptions, the financial performance of PEs has failed to improve. A Disinvestment Commission which was established in 1996 to examine options for reducing central government equity in central public enterprises has since submitted an approach paper and two reports articulating a strategy--which was amply debated by the public at large and experts in the privatization field--for reforming PEs on the basis of which the Commission recommended the full or partial privatization of nine public enterprises. While these are positive steps, there are no signs yet that its recommendations will be adopted by the government and that a rapid process of disinvestment will take place.

Economic Management Issues

Possible slowdown in investment and growth. During 1996-97, a number of developments raised apprehension on the future course of the economy and on its capacity to sustain the rates of growth of the last three years. In particular, declines in the rates of growth of imports of capital goods (which declined by 7 percent), of corporate profits (5 percent), of lending commitments by specialized long-term financial institutions (30 percent), and of primary equity issues (17 percent) gave rise to the perception that *investment and growth* might have declined. The reasons were believed to be a tepid stock market which led corporations to delay security issues; high real interest rates; and commercial banks' heightened aversion to risk (largely a result of tighter enforcement of prudential regulations and the Indian Bank debacle), all of which made it difficult to reach financial closure on investment projects, leading many firms to postpone investment decisions. Political uncertainty was an obvious additional factor.

The authorities responded to this situation through a number of measures taken at different points in time. *First,* there was a relaxation of monetary policies which led to a decline in short-term real interest rates. *Second,* a number of measures were introduced to encourage private investment--particularly FDI. These were the removal of entry barriers (reservation policy) to a number of industries--mostly selected agro-industries--and relaxation of scale limitations. *Third,* important regulatory changes were introduced to facilitate private investment in infrastructure. *Finally,* a pro-reform budget aimed at boosting confidence was presented to Parliament on February 28, 1997.

The 1997-98 budget: a creative but fiscally risky supply-side initiative. The main objective of the 1997-98 Budget is to reactivate private investment. Towards this objective, several measures were taken to revive the stock market. Corporate taxation was sharply reduced (from 43 percent to 35 percent) and is now in line with that in East Asia. Dividend taxation at the individual income tax level was repealed and replaced by a 10 percent final withholding on corporate distributions. Other measures (such as allowing share buy-backs, announcing the reform of the Company's Act, and increasing the cap on ownership by foreign institutional investors in Indian companies from 24 percent of paid-up capital to 30 percent) were intended to improve the business climate, increase private investment, and sustain growth. *Combined with improvements in tax administration, the reactivation of private investment is critical to achieve the 1997-98 fiscal deficit target of 4.5 percent of GDP and represents the main downside risks of an otherwise credible budget forecast.* The budget also reduced the maximum marginal personal income tax rate to 30 percent from 40 percent and the lowest rate to 10 percent from 15 percent; further simplified the excise tax structure; and introduced measures to strengthen compliance. Also, tariff reductions for capital goods were more pronounced than for the rest.

Fiscal adjustment in the 1996-97 and 1997-98 budgets. Deferred pay adjustments associated with the Fifth Pay Commission's recommendations (for which 0.3 percent of GDP had been budgeted) into 1997-98 and other minor expenditure adjustment offset the impact of a shortfall in privatization (0.4 percent of GDP) proceeds, allowing the government to meet its fiscal deficit target of 5 percent of GDP in 1996-97 (from 5.5 percent of GDP in 1995-96). The 1997-98 budget projects a 0.5 percent fiscal correction to 4.5 percent of GDP in 1997-98 to be achieved mainly by maintaining tax revenue at its current share of GDP, and modestly accelerating privatization. However, this fiscal deficit target may be difficult to achieve without additional measures. In particular, the budget relies upon improved compliance to offset the impact of the sharp cuts in taxation and maintain tax revenue at its current share of GDP.

Changing States' Development Policies

India's pre-1991 development strategy and inter-governmental transfers have shaped the states' development and fiscal policies. The Indian Constitution gives the states considerable autonomy to define their development policies. The states are responsible for the provision and regulation of key infrastructure and social services, including primary education and basic health. They defined their development policies at a time when national policies excluded private investment from key sectors of the economy. Where permitted, central licensing authorities, not the enabling environment, determined the volume and composition of private investment. Consequently, across India, states' development policies focused on expanding public investment, often in areas which are not the public sector's comparative advantage. For this expansion, they relied on transfers recommended by the Finance and Planning Commissions, two institutions which command considerable respect in India, and whose recommendations are generally accepted by the central government.

Driven mainly by the objective of equalizing the availability of infrastructure and social services across India, Finance Commissions make recommendations: on how to share with each state taxes collected by the central government, on the amounts of central government grants to each state and, until the 1996 Tenth Finance Commission which discontinued this practice, on unconditional debt forgiveness for highly indebted states. Driven mostly by the objective of mobilizing finance for the investment plans of the states, the Planning Commission makes recommendations on central government loans and grants to the states, and on the amounts of states' borrowings from captive sources: "market borrowings" from commercial banks, insurance companies and pension funds, all of which must invest a share of their resources in "designated securities", such as state bonds.

Starting in the early 1970s, both the Finance and the Planning Commissions recommended gradually but persistently increasing transfers to the states. These developments built expectations that the states needed not be overly concerned with mobilizing resources since ever-expanding and politically more expedient financing would be forthcoming. As a result, throughout the 1970s and 1980s, the states rapidly expanded investments in physical infrastructure (power, irrigation, ports, roads), and provision of social services, without establishing mechanisms for cost recovery and for maintaining these assets and programs in the long run. Prices charged for power, water, irrigation and other services declined to levels equivalent to a small fraction--in some cases zero--of production costs.

The states face three crises--fiscal, infrastructure, and human resource development. By the second half of the 1980s, it became evident that the states were experiencing considerable fiscal difficulties. Implicit and explicit subsidies for goods and services which are not of a public nature rose to reach about 7 percent of GDP. They also expanded public employment to the point that in most states wages and pensions absorb between 4-5 percent of the state GDP, and 9-10 percent is not infrequent. They contracted debt without establishing the financial base for its servicing. As a result, fiscal stress became evident. In particular, there was a deterioration in the quality of spending. While the states' fiscal deficit remained relatively stable at around 3 percent of GDP, capital, education, health and operations and maintenance expenditure started to decline from the mid-1980s, and interest expenditure to increase. Resources for operations and maintenance became insufficient and infrastructure begun to exhibit signs of decay. These trends were exacerbated by the reforms started in 1991 when growth of central government transfers declined and eventually became negative, and interest payments increased. Most states found themselves unable to play their central role in India's development: to provide key infrastructure, health, and education.

State Reforms: Priorities and Progress

The reforms underway since 1991 have radically changed the framework within which states' development policies are implemented. States can attract private capital in such sectors as power, irrigation, ports, roads, and all areas of manufacturing--

and it is its ability to attract private capital which now determines a state's growth performance. Development spending therefore needs to be more narrowly focused on the state's areas of comparative advantage, where it complements rather than substitutes for the private sector. This is a radical departure from the pre-1991 period, when the volume of public development spending was a key determinant of a state's growth performance.

Attracting private capital requires states to provide an enabling and investor-friendly environment. That is, good quality and abundant infrastructure, an educated labor force, a business-friendly public administration, and moderate levels of taxation. Significant reforms are needed to bring this about in India's states. In particular, it requires: (i) policy, pricing, institutional, and regulatory reforms to translate private sector interest to invest in infrastructure into commercially viable ventures--and improvements in the states' capacity to manage commercially enforceable contracts; (ii) an environment conducive to efficient public investment in areas where the public sector will remain important such as roads and urban services; (iii) public expenditure restructuring (such as privatization, freeze on employment, and reduction of consumption subsidies) to eliminate wasteful spending and make room for priority programs in public infrastructure, health and education; and (iv) tax reforms to provide stable sources of revenue at a low efficiency cost.

In many states, policy, pricing and institutional reforms of key sectors would bring about the needed fiscal restructuring. For example, power and irrigation sector reforms--particularly increases in power and water tariffs--would generate large fiscal gains in virtually all of India's 25 states. In some states, such reforms, alone, would be sufficient to restore fiscal sustainability. In others, putting the states' public finances on a sustainable path would require more comprehensive reforms of public expenditures, such as public enterprise reform, freeze on public employment, reduction in consumption subsidies and a rationalization and retargeting of the states' welfare programs. Finally, in highly indebted states, sectoral reforms and public expenditure restructuring may need to be complemented by debt refinancing.

Several states have already started to implement *sector reforms*, particularly *in power*--where about five states have taken the first steps towards increasing tariffs, establishing an independent regulatory agency, and privatizing generation and distribution in a process of reform that will take several years to be brought to its logical conclusion--*ports, roads,* and, to a lesser extent, *water and irrigation*, although a few states have already begun moderately adjusting water tariffs, and devolving maintenance to farmers' associations. Albeit extremely modest, some progress has also been made in *restructuring public expenditure* with a view to reducing unproductive expenditure. In particular, there is growing recognition of the need to control recruitment to reduce the wage bill, eliminate poorly targeted welfare programs, and privatize public enterprises. *On the revenue front*, reforms are needed to increase cost recovery (as an essential part of sector reform), broaden the base, improve the efficiency of taxation, and ensure tax harmonization across states. Some states have already taken significant steps in this direction, but much remains to be done.

Policy Priorities

India's overarching development objective during its Ninth Plan period (1997-02) is achieving and sustaining high annual rates of growth of 7-8 percent and ensuring that this growth benefits the poor. A broad consensus has emerged across India's political spectrum for this objective and for continuing the liberalization of the economy. At what speed this will be done remains however an unresolved--yet critical--issue because it will determine the country's growth performance.

The rapid growth of the last few years has shown how much India stands to gain from *deregulation* and *fiscal adjustment*. It has also shown that the economy is facing capacity constraints, most notably in *infrastructure*. High *real interest rates* are another indication of stress on domestic resources which has been at the origin of pressures put on the authorities to accelerate, perhaps prematurely, the opening of the capital account--a development that in all circumstances would need to be carefully synchronized with India's progress in structural reforms. Resources are also being strained in *agriculture* which has grown dependent on extremely large subsidies (power, water, fertilizer, to name just the main ones). These subsidies put an unsustainably large burden on central and state government budgets, and also are at the origin of microeconomic distortions and misuse of resources (of which overexploitation of groundwater resources and poor energy conservation policies are two important examples) which reduce productivity growth.

The centrality of fiscal adjustment. As it has for the past several years, reducing India's fiscal imbalances remains of central importance for the achievement of the country's development goals. While gains have been made in reducing the central government fiscal deficit, those have been offset in the recent past by a deterioration in the financial position of public enterprises, mostly because of the large cost (0.8 percent of GDP in 1996-97) of subsidizing oil products. As a result, the consolidated public sector deficit has remained at the relatively high level of 9 percent of GDP for the past few years, of which consolidated central and state governments deficit amounts to 6.8 percent of GDP at present. Yet, it is only with a more rapid decline in fiscal imbalances that the high real interest rates that have prevailed in the recent past will decline. A target of 4 percent of GDP for the consolidated central and state governments deficit may be a realistic goal to achieve in the next 3-4 years. Reducing central and state governments subsidies on "non-merit goods" which absorb 11 percent of GDP at present could provide the resources needed to reach, and perhaps exceed, this target. A more rapid privatization of public enterprises would enable the government to retire public debt and reduce interest costs. The benefits of a more rapid correction of fiscal imbalances go well beyond just lower interest rates and higher investment. Lower fiscal deficits and interest rates would provide favorable conditions for an acceleration of banking reform, would help improve the health of the financial system, would provide more flexibility to the RBI in the conduct of monetary policy, would reduce pressure for opening the capital account ahead of the structural reforms needed to make it a success, and would make it easier to manage surges in capital inflows, and possible external shocks. International experience shows that a strong fiscal position has a central role in managing effectively the capital and current accounts of the balance of payments.

Also, as highlighted in the May 1997 government paper on subsidies, central and state government deficits are linked to significant microeconomic distortions whose cost they bear. Again in this case, the benefits of fiscal corrections go beyond improvements in the macroeconomic framework--because they are tantamount to correcting severe price distortions and misguided sector policies which are preventing private investment and hampering development. Power is one well known case where the correction of price distortions would not only reduce state governments fiscal imbalances (by 2 percent of GDP), but would also lead to a more efficient use of resources, and provide the basis for private capital in power and the much needed capacity expansion. Similar situations exist in other sectors.

In addition to the macro-and micro-economic dimensions of fiscal adjustment, a third, and at least as important one, is that of expenditure composition, particularly at the level of the states. In most states, the cost of subsidies, of an excessively large labor force, and of government activities which are not of a development nature absorb a large share of state governments budgets. To a large extent, the deterioration of India's infrastructure, and the difficulties the country is experiencing to mobilize resources to accelerate the development of its human resources are the result of states' pricing and sectoral policies and the associated implied subsidies--and it is also with the states that lies their resolution. Recent declines in central government financial support to the states have provided some--but as yet insufficient--impetus to the states to start taking corrective actions.

Addressing the challenge of infrastructure. Much has been said and written on India's infrastructure problems. The recently completed report of an Expert Group on infrastructure provides a sobering review of India's tremendous infrastructure problems and makes three recommendations to address them. The *first* is *fiscal reforms* to strengthen state and local governments capacity to mobilize resources to invest in infrastructure. This is particularly important for infrastructure of a public nature where benefits are best captured through taxation. The *second* is *regulatory and pricing reforms* to translate India's immense infrastructure needs into viable commercial ventures, capable of attracting private capital. The *third* is *financial sector reforms* to enable the large pool of India's financial savings to flow to high returns infrastructure investments.

Banking reforms. Further banking and financial deregulation (reducing government equity in the capital of public banks and further reductions in the SLR) would reduce the influence of government on commercial banks' basic business decisions (such as on hiring, on pay scales, branch expansion or closure), and permit more vigorous competition from private banks. The RBI is gradually strengthening its oversight capabilities, and this provides the basis for a further deregulation of the banking system.

At the same time, to support agricultural reforms, it would be essential to bring rural credit reform to its logical conclusion. A coherent strategy for increasing flows to agriculture and other rural economic activities must address issues of access to financial services by the rural population in general, as well as the financial sustainability of the rural financial institutions themselves. Further measures are needed to encourage and facilitate an orderly re-orientation of India's rural financial system from the supply-led approach of concessional, targeted agriculture credit, to the systematic development of demand-oriented rural financial markets.

Deregulating agriculture. Deregulation would enable agriculture to achieve potentially large efficiency gains and provide a basis for the removal of subsidies. The 1997-98 Budget contains the first steps of a promising beginning of reforms at the level of the central government, which could provide impetus-- although it has not thus far--for similar reforms at the level of the states. Intimately related to the liberalization of agriculture is the deregulation of agro-industry where important segments are still regulated by industrial licenses or scale limitations that impose large costs to an industry characterized by economies of scale. Because the incomes of the poor are so closely associated with the fortunes of the agricultural sector, a liberalization of agriculture would not only

have positive growth effects, it would also help increase the incomes of the poor.

Completing the liberalization of the *trade and investment regimes* remains an important policy objective. India's import-weighted tariff has been reduced from 87 percent in 1991-92 to around 20 percent at present. The 1997-98 budget indicates that the process will continue, until India reaches the tariff levels of its East Asian neighbors. There are also indications that the government intends to eliminate restrictions on consumer goods in a phased manner. Implementation of this agenda would improve considerably the competitiveness of India's manufacturing, as would a further deregulation of the investment regime. The radical liberalization of the last six years notwithstanding, extremely costly regulations continue to restrict investment in areas reserved for small scale and agro-industries.

A prudent management of the capital account remains appropriate until fiscal consolidation has been achieved, the instruments and markets for indirect monetary control are more fully developed, the commercial banking system is strengthened, trade liberalization is complete and exports sufficiently diversified. Consistent with this objective, the pace of liberalization of restrictions on debt-related capital and short-term capital would need to be gradual, tailored to the pace of fiscal consolidation, progress in strengthening the domestic financial system, and export performance. Priority would be given to meeting the needs of long-term infrastructure financing as the government has indicated in its 1997-98 External Commercial Borrowing guidelines. Otherwise, there would be a danger of prompting volatile financial conditions and sharp cross-border surges in short-term funds that would be difficult to manage and could put serious stress on the domestic banking system.

External financing requirements

India will continue to need to rely on official development assistance, notwithstanding the growing role of private inflows. Besides India's low level of per capita GDP (US$350), official development assistance is also critically necessary for India to meet its enormous needs for infrastructure and human resource development. As indicated in the ***Poverty Assessment Report***, distributed to members of India Development Forum (IDF), India's poverty remains widespread and the lives of many of India's more than 300 million poor are burdened by poor health, illiteracy, and social inequalities. Prospects for improving their standards of living depend on India's ability to promote growth and invest in human resources development. While the private sector shows strong interest in investing in a number of infrastructure areas, particularly power and telecommunications, an important role remains for public sector investment in some key areas--such as roads, rural infrastructure and social services--which would need to be substantially increased. Such investments are crucial for sustaining rapid growth and ensuring that the poor participate in the growth process.

The Bank therefore recommends that the members of the IDF should aim for official development assistance that directly supports priority public investments in physical infrastructure and human capital development. This investment would also help crowd-in the necessary complementary private investment particularly in physical infrastructure. In addition to the financial flows, official development assistance is also crucial to build institutional capacity particularly at the level of the state and local governments. Therefore, as had last year's CEM, this report makes a case for India's continued access to long-term assistance, including a substantial concessional component. In view of its still current high debt burden, India would need to continue to prudently manage its external debt. With an expected modest current account deficit of 2 percent of GDP over the next few years and the necessary build-up of reserves, India would still require total gross financing of close to US$14 billion in 1997-98, and an average of about US$17 billion in each of the following four years. Bilateral and multilateral participants at last year's India Development Forum pledged about US$6.7 billion in official assistance to India's development efforts as a recognition of India's strong commitment to reform and need to accelerate growth and reduce poverty and a similar amount is expected for this year. Debt and non-debt commercial sources are expected to account for the country's remaining financing needs.

Chapter 1

RECENT ECONOMIC DEVELOPMENTS

A number of reports issued in 1996-97 (the Ministry of Finance's Economic Survey; the Reserve Bank of India's (RBI) Annual Report; the RBI Report on Currency and Finance; the RBI Report on Trend and Progress of Banking in India; the India Development Report (IGIDR); the government appointed Expert Group Report on Infrastructure; the 1997-98 Budget speech; the RBI April Credit Policy; and the May 1997 Ministry of Finance's discussion paper on government subsidies) document comprehensively India's past and recent performance, articulate the governments' development objectives, and provide an accurate picture of the policy challenges the country faces. Because of the comprehensiveness and depth of this documentation to which interested readers are referred to, this report comments only on salient recent economic and policy developments. A poverty assessment issued as a companion to this report discusses India's progress in human resource development and poverty alleviation over the last fifty years.

Recent Economic Developments

A strong supply response

The reforms of the past six years brought about an unprecedented strong economic performance. After growing at over 5 percent in 1992-93 and 6 percent in 1993-94, preliminary estimates suggest that real GDP grew at close to 7 percent for the third year in a row in the fiscal year ending March 31, 1997 (Figure 1.1). A good monsoon (agricultural output grew by 3.7 percent in 1996-97, led by continued record growth levels of commercial crops--particularly oilseeds and cotton) offset the impact of slower industrial growth, from 11.6 percent in 1995-96 to 8.7 percent in 1996-97 (Annex, Table 1). However, data made available after the CSO published its preliminary estimates for 1996-97, suggest that the decline in the growth rate of industrial production might be more pronounced than initially expected, thus leading to a lower 1996-97 GDP growth.

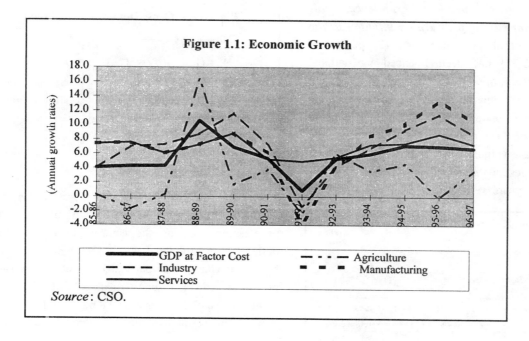

Figure 1.1: Economic Growth

Source: CSO.

The slowdown of industrial growth was due to production shortfalls of crude oil (following steadily declining output from Bombay High and Neelam fields, and sluggish implementation of enhanced recovery programs) and power (production grew by only 3.4 percent against a 10 percent rise in demand, reflecting inadequate levels of investment in the sector). Within manufacturing, the capital goods industry benefited from tariff cuts on essential inputs and experienced a strong recovery in 1995-96 and 1996-97--although more recent indicators suggest that the recovery may be tapering off (Figure 1.2, Annex, Table 2).

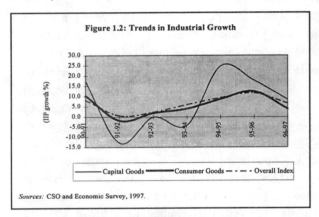

Sources: CSO and Economic Survey, 1997.

Strong saving and investment performance

Contrary to India's previous experiences, this expansion is not putting pressure on inflation or the external accounts. Higher investment (26 percent of GDP in 1996-97) has been financed by national savings (25 percent of GDP)--rising mainly on account of the good performance of private savings. Public savings remained low as a result of the poor financial performance from center and states governments and public enterprises (Figure 1.3, Annex, Table 3). Private savings and investment reached historically high levels in the last few years, respectively 24 percent of GDP

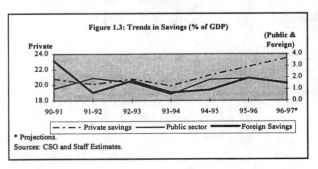

and 18 percent of GDP in 1995-96 (Figures 1.3 and 1.4), and that may explain times series analysis suggesting that India's long-term growth path is now around 6 percent, compared to 4 percent in the period preceding the 1991 reforms.

Fiscal developments remain a serious concern

Preliminary estimates indicate that the central government has met its fiscal deficit target of 5 percent of GDP for 1996-97. This was achieved not only as a share of GDP, but also in nominal rupees (with a fall in the primary deficit from 0.9 percent of GDP in 1995-96 to 0.4 percent) (Annex, Table 4). This outcome occurred despite large shortfalls in privatization proceeds (0.4 percent of GDP) and corporate tax receipts (0.1 percent of GDP) as well as an overrun in defense spending (0.3 percent of GDP). This was offset by delays in the implementation of the recommendations of the Fifth Pay Commission for which 0.3 percent of GDP had been allocated, by savings in interest payments (0.2 percent of GDP), and by a slight increase in income tax collections and lower than budgeted spending on education and nutrition (mostly on account of the mid-day meal program) which provided the remaining 0.3 percent of GDP.

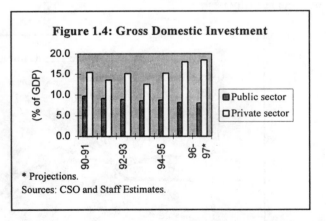

While there has been gradual but persistent progress in reducing the central government fiscal deficit, the consolidated public sector deficit remains broadly unchanged. In particular, the cost of subsidies on diesel and kerosene (financed out of the oil companies' cash flow) is now 0.8 percent of GDP. This is the main reason why the consolidated public sector

Table 1.1: Evolution of the Public Deficit, 1990-97 (percent of GDP)							
	1990-91	1991-92	1992-93	1993-94	1994-95	1995-96	1996-97[a]
Central Government							
Fiscal Deficit	8.3	5.9	5.7	7.4	6.1	5.5	5.0
Primary Deficit [b]	4.3	1.6	1.3	2.9	1.4	0.9	0.4
State Government							
Fiscal Deficit	3.3	2.9	3.0	2.6	2.9	3.4	3.1
Primary Deficit [b]	1.6	1.2	1.0	0.6	0.8	1.3	0.9
General Government [c]							
Fiscal Deficit	9.9	7.3	7.4	8.9	7.6	7.5	6.8
Primary Deficit [b]	5.1	2.3	2.16	3.5	2.2	2.2	1.2
Consolidated Nonfinancial Public Sector [d]							
Fiscal Deficit	12.3	9.6	9.5	10.7	9.0	8.9	9.2

a. 1996-97 is estimated.
b. Fiscal deficit minus interest payments.
c. Includes central and states government and excludes net lending from center to states.
d. The consolidated non-financial public sector comprises the Central Government (including the balance of the OCC), Central Public Enterprises, and State Governments. Excludes intra-govermental transfers.
Source: Budget documents; RBI; IMF; and staff estimates.

deficit (which excludes the deficit of state governments public enterprises), after falling to 8.9 percent of GDP in 1995-96, is estimated to have increased to 9.2 percent in 1996-97 (Table 1.1).

Moreover, the *quality of spending* has not improved. A recently released government report estimated that central and state governments subsidies account for a staggering 15 percent of GDP (Box 1.1), 11 percentage points of which (7 percent attributable to states and 4 percent to the central government) are absorbed in the provision of "non-merit" goods (goods whose consumption does not have strong externalities). While some efforts have been made to reduce subsidies, the magnitude of the problem suggests that firm actions on a broader front are urgently needed.

Monetary policy eased but inflation remains moderate

Monetary policy eased as concerns grew over a possible slowdown in the economy--particularly in the industrial sector. With inflation under control (below 5 percent), the RBI in its April 1996 Credit Policy announced measures to ease the "liquidity crunch" and also to deepen the money and foreign exchange markets. The monetary stance was relaxed through a series of CRR reductions that brought it from 14 percent in April 1996 to 10 percent in January 1997, and through other measures that lowered the pre-emption of NRI deposits. In addition, in its April 1997

Box 1.1: The High Cost of Government Subsidies

A path breaking discussion paper on *Government Subsidies* was tabled by the Ministry of Finance in Parliament in May 1997. The report brings to the forefront the massive cost to the Indian economy of the current extensive system of subsidies. These include explicit and implicit subsidies. The latter estimates unrecovered costs of publicly provided goods and services, rather than actual cash flows. Subsidies are estimated to be equivalent to a staggering 15 percent of GDP in 1994-95. Even if the concerns raised over the estimation methodology used in the report were to be taken into account and one would assume a margin of error of a few percentage points of GDP, the subsidies as inventoried in this report remain nevertheless very large. More importantly, the report shows that much of the subsidies are "probably appropriated by the middle to high income groups" resulting in wasteful consumption (especially for electricity, irrigation and diesel fuel). Confirming earlier analyses, the report adds that "a significant and increasing portion of the food subsidy does not reach consumers and it is captured by the increasing costs of handling and storing foodgrains".

Out of a total subsidy bill of about 15 percent of GDP, subsidies on "merit goods", such as primary education and immunization, account for less than 4 percent of GDP. Indicating "an unduly large and ill-directed subsidy regime", subsidies on "non-merit" goods account for the rest. The Central Government provides "non-merit" subsidies equivalent to 4 percent of GDP whereas state governments' "non-merit" subsidies are equivalent to 7 percent of GDP.

credit policy, the RBI reduced the cost of funds to banks by lowering the interest rate ceiling on deposits of more than 30 days and less than one year, and by deregulating interest rates on FCNR(B) deposits. Banks were also given more leeway in determining their risk exposure. To improve its liquidity management, the RBI reduced banks' access to automatic refinance of export credit from April 1996 and removed the refinance facility against government securities.

Broad money (M3) grew by 15.6 percent (Figure 1.5) compared with 13.7 percent in 1995-96 but remained within the target range of 15.5-16 percent for 1996-97 (15-15.5 percent for 1997-98). Banks' improved liquidity positions, combined with lower growth of RBI credit to the government (2.3 percent compared with 20 percent in 1995-96), helped offset the expansionary effect on reserve money of a 28 percent increase in RBI's foreign exchange assets (Annex, Table 5). However, inflation rose from 5 percent in March 1996 to 7.2 percent in March 1997 exceeding the government's 6-7 percent target for 1996-97 (Figure 1.6), before declining to around 6 percent in May 1997. In addition to the relaxation of monetary policy, the rise in inflation was fueled by the July 1996 adjustment in administered petroleum prices and increases in food prices that abated in the latter part of the fiscal year.

The relaxation of monetary policy reduced interest rates but the yield curve stiffened. While the interest rate on 91-day Treasury bills has fallen from 13 percent in March 1996 to 8 percent recently (March 1997), long-term rates remained almost unchanged at close to 14 percent (Annex, Table 6). This possibly reflects financial markets' perception that, with fiscal imbalances still high, the risk of an acceleration of inflation in the future remains significant. Despite the monetary easing, bank lending grew at slower rates than last year and the Prime Lending Rate (PLR)--the

"benchmark" interest rate for domestic and foreign banks lending--fell by less than two percentage points, remaining at 14.0-15.0 percent, with most lending taking place at 16.5-19.5 and higher rates for some borrowers. Because of its beneficial effects on corporate profitability and on bank's balance sheets, the easing of monetary policy will, however, have positive effects on banks' profitability.

Money and Foreign Exchange Markets have been more stable. Increased liquidity, resumption of repos by the RBI, banks' heightened aversion to risk (in the wake of the Indian Bank debacle following major losses associated with speculative lending which wiped out the Bank's entire net worth) and a slowdown of bank credit (from 18 percent in 1995-96 to 10.5 percent in 1996-97) reduced volatility in the call money and foreign exchange markets. Call money markets were stable with the rate falling from an average high of 35 percent during November 1995 to around 6 percent in November 1996. The rate fell further to around 2 percent during January 1997. Banks returned to risk-free government securities above and beyond what is required under the SLRs. This helped the government to reduce its reliance on the RBI credit line ("ad-hocs"). Consequently, net RBI credit to the government rose by 2.3 percent during 1996-97 compared with the 20 percent growth in 1995-96.

Exports and imports growth slowed down; the external accounts remain strong

In response to the sharp depreciation of the real exchange rate in 1991-93 and reduction of import tariffs since 1991, and thus of the anti-export bias implicit in the previous trade regime, *exports* grew at rates in excess of 20 percent during 1993-96. As growth and corporate restructuring gained momentum, *imports* grew by slightly over 20 percent in 1995-96, driven by capital goods imports.

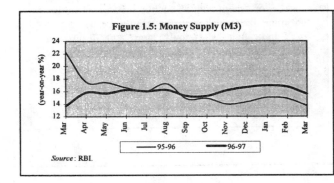

Figure 1.5: Money Supply (M3)

Source: RBI.

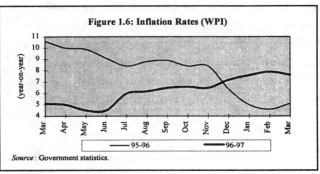

Figure 1.6: Inflation Rates (WPI)

Source: Government statistics.

However, during 1996-97, there was a significant slowing down of growth of external trade flows (Figure 1.7). India's exports in nominal US$ grew by only 4.1 percent in 1996-97 compared with 21 percent in 1995-96. Assuming that India's export growth is 40 percent higher than growth in world trade (the trend of the last few years), Table 1.2 summarizes the estimated contribution of different factors to the export slowdown. It shows that price effects, namely the appreciation of the US dollar, accounted for a large share of the decline in nominal exports (in SDR terms,

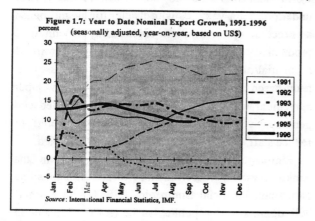

Figure 1.7: Year to Date Nominal Export Growth, 1991-1996
percent (seasonally adjusted, year-on-year, based on US$)

Source: International Financial Statistics, IMF.

the decline in export growth is much more modest: from 17.2 percent in 1995-96 to 9.3 percent in 1996-97) (Figure 1.8). The table also suggests that domestic factors played an important role in the slowdown of exports. Infrastructure constraints, the cost of credit, some appreciation of the real exchange rate (Figure 1.9 and Annex, Table 7), and sector specific developments are all believed to have played a role but it is difficult to specify the exact contribution of each. Supported by a small current account deficit combined with large capital inflows (the RBI has been accumulating reserves), the nominal exchange rate has remained stable at around Rs. 35-36/US$ since May 1996, leading to some real appreciation.

Table 1.2: Merchandise Export and Import Slowdown, 1995-1996

	Exports	Non-oil imports	Oil imports
Growth(value)			
1995	20.9	28.2	27.0
1996	4.1	-1.0	34.4
Change in Growth			
Rates	-16.8	-29.2	7.4
of which:[a]			
Price	-7.4	-14.5	15.3
Volume	-9.4	-14.7	-7.9
of which in percent:			
External demand	-3.3		
Domestic factors	-6.1		

a. The decomposition between volume and price effects is based on data for the first nine months of the year.
Source: Staff Estimates, IECAP

Two noteworthy sector specific developments were the decline in exports of gems and jewelry and in exports of leather products. The fall in the value of *cut and polished diamond* exports are explained by weaker demand in key markets such as Japan, and price declines due the failure of Argyle Diamond--one of India's largest suppliers--to renew its distribution contract with De Beer's Central Selling Organization in mid 1996. Following a Supreme Court decision that tightened regulations on environmental protection, the *leather* industry suffered a major fall in production and exports as a result of the closure of small scale tanneries due to their inability to set up effluent-treatment plants.

The growth of the dollar value of imports during 1995-1996 reflected the fluctuations of the US dollar. After growing by 30 percent in 1995-96, imports rose by only 7.4 percent in dollar terms over April to December 1996-97, in spite of a 34 percent increase in oil imports. Non-oil imports actually declined by 1 percent due to a fall in capital goods imports.

In 1996-97, increased private transfers helped offset a rise in the trade deficit (by US$500 million)

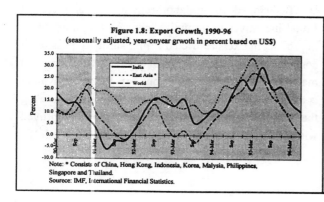

Figure 1.8: Export Growth, 1990-96
(seasonally adjusted, year-on-year grwoth in percent based on US$)

Note: * Consists of China, Hong Kong, Indonesia, Korea, Malysia, Philippines, Singapore and Thailand.
Source: IMF, International Financial Statistics.

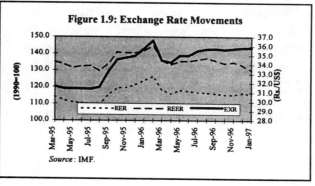

Figure 1.9: Exchange Rate Movements

Source: IMF.

and kept the current account deficit at 1.1 percent of GDP in 1996-97, from 1.8 percent in 1995-96--well below what the government considers sustainable (2 percent).

The capital account remains strong. As in previous years, foreign direct investment and portfolio investment flows contributed to a large surplus in the capital account. During 1996-97, India received private inflows of US$5.1 billion, about 24 percent higher than their corresponding level in 1995-96 (Figure 1.10, Annex, Table 8). These positive developments in the external accounts translated into foreign currency reserves of US$22.4 billion at the end of March 1997-- that is six months of imports (Annex, Table 9).

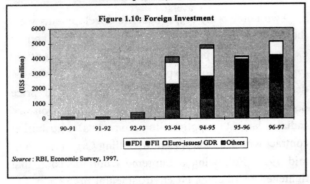

Figure 1.10: Foreign Investment

Source: RBI, Economic Survey, 1997.

Highlights of Structural Reforms

Increase in competition

Underlying positive developments in the real economy are important structural transformations. The declining role of the public sector since the start of the reform program in 1991, both as producer of goods and services and economic regulator, is one of India's most fundamental structural changes since Independence. The liberalization of the economy has opened to the private sector areas previously the exclusive domain of the public sector--such as heavy manufacturing, banking, civil aviation, telecommunications, power generation and distribution, ports, and roads. Equally important, the liberalization of the economy has reduced distortions and increased external and internal competition. Agriculture's terms of trade have improved. Led by commercial crops, agricultural commodities are one of India's fastest growing exports. In manufacturing,

Indian firms have restructured and upgraded their industrial basis, often through alliances with foreign firms. There is growing presence of multi-nationals. Indicative of improved product quality, the number of Indian firms receiving ISO9000 certifications has witnessed a ten-fold increase.

The restructuring of the automobile industry is an example of how large Indian firms have responded to liberalization. To face international competition, they had to bring their distribution and manufacturing up to world standards. To do so, firms in the sector undertook joint ventures with foreign firms and began a process of internal re-engineering to improve productivity, for example by moving from a sequential/functional mass production processes to team-based structure. In a particular case, a new labor agreement was signed, workers were reassigned and generous voluntary separation schemes offered to reduce staff. Labor productivity more than doubled.

Similar developments have taken place in the banking system, where the entry of private banks and Non Bank Financial Companies (NBFCs) in a sector still dominated by public banks (which control 85 percent of the sector's assets) forced the latter to significantly improve their services. Most public banks have retained the services of management consulting firms to restructure operations, cut costs, expand the menu of services and improve profitability (Box 1.2). Moreover, the opening up of bank capital to private shareholders and their participation in the banks boards have contributed to improve governance (Box 1.3).

India's liberalization and integration in the world market also had an effect on labor markets--as seen in firm level restructuring. Prior to 1991, investment and trade restrictions created high rents, particularly in the formal sector of the economy. This system enabled firms to pass on to consumers the cost of workers' benefits embedded in labor regulations, and eroded firms' incentives to minimize labor costs. Competition in product markets restricted firm's ability to pass on to consumers the cost of these labor regulations, and made workers more conscious of the employment consequences of their demands. In the years following the liberalization, industrial labor relations improved with consequent declines in labor disputes (Table 1.3).

Box 1.2: State Bank of India (SBI) Responds to Competition

India's public sector banks have had to change since economic liberalization exposed them to increasing competition with a phased deregulation of the financial market and the entry of new domestic and foreign private sector rivals. Few have managed the transition better than SBI, the country's oldest and largest commercial bank. Its share of loans and deposits is more than 20 percent (of the total). The bank, which also claims to have more than 87 percent of large companies as its clients, is still in a strong run of earnings growth which has made it a leading stock on the subcontinent.

SBI is reaping the benefits of a wide-ranging restructuring started in 1994 which led SBI to refocus its operations around a four-pillar structure: corporate banking, national banking for retail and small to mid-sized companies, international operations, and associated services such as the bank's investment banking operations. The aim was to streamline operations, decentralize decision-making, improve customer service and boost profitability.

To strengthen the bank's balance sheet, the bank is looking at ways of increasing earnings out of fee-based services from their current 14 percent of total income to about 25 percent at the turn of the century. The bank is also increasing its exposure to project finance, with infrastructure development expected to rise strongly over the next five years. Another potential area of future business is financing takeovers and acquisitions. In most countries, this would be uncontroversial, but in India such a concept is near revolutionary. Public banks traditionally have been very averse to funding takeovers, often taking a passive attitude in uncritically supporting company management. Earnings are also expected to benefit from a continued reduction in provisions for non-performing assets as its balance sheet is progressively cleaned up. Whether SBI's efforts will yield tangible results will depend however to a large extent on how autonomous it can be in managing its future operations since SBI is now 40 percent privately owned with the government still retaining a majority stake.

Structural reforms have continued in 1996-97

The liberalization of the *trade regime* has continued. The most recent round of tariff reform introduced in the 1997-98 Budget reduced maximum tariffs to 40 percent from 50 percent in 1996-97 (from over 200 percent in 1990-91) and the import weighted average tariff to 20.3 percent (Annex, Table 10) from 87 percent in 1990-91. The new Exim Policy eliminated licensing requirements for around one-sixth of consumer goods (basically, the only imports still restricted) and it is expected that India will agree with the WTO in June 1997 to a phased elimination of the remaining licensing restrictions. The new Exim Policy also took several measures to enhance exporters' access to imported inputs at international prices.

	Employment in the Organized Sector (million) [a]	Number of Disputes [b]			Number of Man-days Lost (million) [b]						
Years		**Strikes**	**Lockouts**	**Total**	**Strikes**		**Lockouts**		**Total**		**% of total employment [c]**
1981-85	24.6	1,862	420	2,282	29.9	(62)	18.7	(38)	48.7	(100)	0.85
1986-90	26.4	1,393	416	1,809	13.3	(42)	18.4	(58)	31.8	(100)	0.52
1990	26.4	1,459	366	1,825	10.6	(44)	13.4	(56)	24.1	(100)	0.38
1991	26.7	1,278	532	1,810	12.4	(47)	14.0	(53)	26.4	(100)	0.41
1992	27.1	1,011	703	1,714	15.1	(48)	16.1	(52)	31.3	(100)	0.48
1993	27.2	914	479	1,393	5.6	(28)	14.7	(72)	20.4	(100)	0.31
1994	27.4	--	--	--	--	--	--	--	19.2	(100)	0.29
1995	27.5	--	--	--	--	--	--	--	18.0	(100)	0.27

Table 1.3: India: Industrial Disputes: 1981-85 to 1995-96

Note: Figures in the parentheses indicate percent of total man-days lost.
a. End of period.
b. Average for the period.
c. Percent of employment in the organized sector assuming that each worker works 240 days.
Source: CMIE, India's Industrial Sector, January 1996, and Economic Survey 1996-97.

Box 1.3: Improving Corporate Governance in India

In the past few years corporate governance has received more attention throughout India. Traditionally, Indian shareholders tended to play a passive role in the management of corporations thus placing few constraints on management. The government through a series of actions directed to improve transparency and accountability, including revising the Company Law and the Takeover Code, has taken important steps to help making management more accountable to shareholders.

Foreign portfolio investment is also expected to contribute to changes in corporate governance One case is the Industrial Credit and Investment Corporation of India (ICICI), one of India's largest development-investment banks.[1] While foreign portfolio investors in developing countries are generally not considered demanding, and tend to vote with their feet rather than at board meetings, ICICI's experience probably presages the future. Indeed, the changes that are taking place at ICICI parallel those of a growing number of corporations in developed countries.

ICICI's ongoing experiment with corporate governance started with the issue of several GDRs in the early 1990s, which led to a change in the ownership structure of the company. Today, ICICI still has more than half a million shareholders, but some 34 percent of the shares are now held by foreigners, especially large institutional investors, and 41 percent by large domestic institutions, including the central government. Foreign investors were critical of the company's activities in several areas, including poor accountability and transparency and, more generally, little concern for managing the company to increase the value of shares. Foreign investors joined large domestic investors in voicing these concerns at Board meetings and were instrumental in having management accept sea changes in corporate governance. In turn, ICICI has pushed for similar changes in its many client companies.

The main reforms implemented at ICICI regard the role and composition of the Board of Directors, including having a distinct chairperson who is separate form the Chief Executive Officer. The reforms have created a more balanced, responsible, and independent Board, with greater participation by the independent external directors. To further increase the sense of responsibility toward shareholders, directors now have a fiduciary responsibility. Complementing these reforms at the Board level, the risk management and internal audit departments have been strengthened and made more independent, and a new key performance indicator for middle management is the impact of their work on shareholder value.

1. Information on ICICI is based on K.V. Kamath (1996) in "The Road to Financial Integration: Private Capital Flows to Developing Countries", World Bank, forthcoming.

The liberalization of the foreign investment regime has been significant particularly in ports, roads, coal mining and many activities previously reserved for small scale industry are now open for foreign direct investment. The government released its first-ever guidelines for the *Foreign Investment Promotion Board* (FIPB) in January 1997. The guidelines aim at simplifying the approval process and providing more transparent criteria for the decision-making process. With some exceptions, most projects will be approved now directly by the RBI. Similarly, Indian investments abroad up to US$4 million are eligible for automatic approval by the RBI and restrictions on issuing equity or debt abroad and on end-use have all been relaxed. The government removed most restrictions on the type of financial assets Foreign Institutional Investors (FIIs) can hold with FIIs now allowed to invest through dedicated debt funds 100 percent of their portfolio in Indian debt instruments including government

securities (but not treasury bills). With the exception of real estate and stocks, restrictions on end-uses of GDRs--put in place in 1993-94 to discourage capital inflows--have been removed. In addition, a number of important legislations (Foreign Exchange and Regulations Act, Companies Act, Income Act, Takeover Code, and various Banking Acts) are all under review. The government also announced the establishment of an expert group to examine the conditions under which India should seek capital account convertibility.

It is evident that the induction of private capital in areas which for decades have been under public sector monopolies has been slower than anticipated, and so have its results (Box 1.4). Unless stronger measures are taken, India will continue to face an increasingly serious infrastructure crisis that will prevent the country from sustaining the high levels of growth that the last few years have shown to be within reach. For example, addressing the labor-related issues in ports would help ensure that the current strong private interest in investing there materializes. The strong response to the JNPT tender was largely induced by the importance of this port for India's containerized trade, and the bidders were willing to accept unusual conditions--existing labor rules, and to charge for their services in local currency--and risks--even initial losses--because of JNPT's strategic position and the prospect of potential gains in the long-run. It is conceivable that participation in future tenders for new port facilities elsewhere may be weak because of the inhibiting conditions set by government. Also, despite the attractiveness of such investments to the private sector, it will be a complement to, but not a full substitute for, investments by the Port Trusts or other public funding. In this context, corporatizing the Major Port Trusts would help increase efficiency of existing assets as well as raise public investment. International experience with port systems reform has repeatedly demonstrated that divesting regulatory and institutional responsibility over ports to the local (state or municipal) level leads to major productivity improvements due to induced competition.

Box 1.4: Gradual but Persistent Progress in Infrastructure

For four decades after Independence, the public sector in India held a monopoly in the provision of most infrastructure. In 1991, when the reforms started, electricity, railways, ports, roads and telecommunications were among the sectors reserved for the public sector. Over the last six years, the government has been introducing reforms to break this monopoly and change the policy, legal, and administrative framework to attract private investment in the sector. Doing so brought new and tremendous challenges--to be expected in such dramatic restructuring which includes resolving conflicting vested interests through the judicial system--and there was an inevitable period of necessary experimentation and learning. While this may have lengthened the process of change, it nonetheless provided a more solid grounding. In 1996-97, a number of important regulatory changes were implemented. Announced a few years ago, the independent Telecom Regulatory Authority of India (TRAI) has started its operations in March 1997 and is exerting its authority as an independent regulator. The department of telecommunications, tax authorities, and financial institutions have reached an agreement on the tax treatment of the value of licenses. This will enable the financial closure of a number of cellular and basic telecom projects which are in abeyance pending a decision on this matter. Cellular services are expanding rapidly beyond the initial four non-metro areas and a few basic telecom projects are at an advanced stage of preparation.

Several measures have improved the policy and regulatory framework in ports. In the case of *major ports* (regulated by the central government), an independent Tariff Authority for regulating tariffs was established, guidelines have been issued for private investment through BOT-type contracts, and one contract (US$200 million) has already been awarded for the construction of a major extension to the existing container terminal at JNPT. This is a major breakthrough in private sector funding and management of port facilities in India. These reforms are expected to help relieve the acute capacity shortages and low productivity levels which have plagued Indian ports and upgrade cargo-handling technology thereby increasing efficiency in the shipping industry. However, gross overstaffing and restrictive labor practices remain a major issue. Similarly, states also initiated plans to develop and manage their ports through public-private partnerships (see chapter 2). The Ministry of Surface Transport has recently announced its plans to issue during the next two years tenders for 21 new projects throughout the country's waterfront sector, estimated to cost US$6.6 billion.

In *roads*, while there is awareness in India that this is an area where the public sector will retain a major role, attempts have been made nonetheless to facilitate private sector entry with some degree of success, particularly in bridges. Also, the government issued new guidelines and introduced legislative changes in January 1997 to encourage private investment in national highway projects. The guidelines allow automatic approval by the RBI for foreign investment up to 74 percent of equity in companies engaging in construction and maintenance of roads, bridges, tunnels, pipelines, ports, harbors and runways and railbeds. Foreign participation up to 51 percent also will be allowed in inter alia operation of highway bridges and toll roads. The Ministry of Industry further authorized the FIPB to approve higher foreign equity participation up to 100 percent in companies engaged in development of highways on a BOT basis. Land requirements for the construction and operation of the facilities will be acquired by the government and leased by the developer during the concession period. Investors will be permitted to collect tolls for specified periods and road funds will be set-up through earmarking of toll revenues and levy of tolls on national highways that are improved.

Finally, remarkably little progress has been made in addressing the fundamental policy and institutional changes (most of which under the purview of state authorities) needed to expand *urban infrastructure* and alleviate the tremendous problems of India's fast growing cities. *Water supply systems,* an area of potentially considerable interest to the private sector, continue to be poorly managed by state-government institutions at a high cost to the economy. Similarly, progress in restructuring public enterprises has been slow. A report prepared by the Disinvestment Commission has offered a menu of options for reform of public enterprises including privatization but todate no concrete action has been taken.

To liberalize the financial sector, the government has pursued a very gradual two-pronged strategy consisting of: (i) gradually relaxing controls that repress the market's ability to price risk and; (ii) developing institutional infrastructure to manage a de-regulated financial market. In terms of reducing this risk (the market's perception of macroeconomic instability due to the large fiscal deficit and banks' weak balance sheets), some progress was achieved this year with the RBI's move to indirect instruments for monetary policy management and the reduction of the central government fiscal deficit by 0.5 percent of GDP. The 1997-98 Budget announced a further 0.5 percent fiscal correction in 1997-98 and the substitution of a system of advances to the current government's automatic access to RBI credit. This system--known as ways and means advances--in addition to increasing the RBI's independence may improve the government and RBI's ability to better forecast and manage government's short-term cash flows and debt and may therefore reduce short-run interest rate volatility and money market instability.

To improve commercial banks' balance sheets, the guidelines issued in 1992 for income recognition, asset

---

Box 1.4: Gradual but Persistent Progress in Infrastructure (cont...)

In *power*, where the need is the greatest, private sector interest to invest the strongest, and action by state governments essential to transform this interest into concrete investments, a conference of state Chief Ministers reached agreement on a Common Minimum National Action Plan for Power (CMNAP) reforms, issued by the Ministry of Power in December 1996. The CMNAP envisages changes in legislation to enable the states to have their own independent power regulatory agencies, with authority to grant licenses, including for distribution, and fix tariffs. It also envisages gradual elimination of power subsidies. Implementing the CMNAP recommendations would provide a sound basis for private investment in a sector that needs it urgently. Some states are giving it serious consideration (Orissa, Gujarat, Haryana, Rajasthan, AP). Recent reforms in the *coal* sector are important and are expected to help facilitate private investment in power since they should--in the long term--significantly reduce the prevailing coal supply risks (an important deterrent to private sector investment in power).

In *coal*, private entry was extended in February 1997 to captive mines and ancillary activities while a decision was taken to divest shares in Coal India's subsidiaries. The government also deregulated the prices and distribution of high-grade coal with the result that about 40 percent of prices remain administered; they are expected to be freed by the year 2000. In the *hydrocarbons* subsector, reforms remain insufficient and have not succeeded in improving the financial performance of public enterprises or generating any significant demand or investment response. Private investors remain concerned about distorted pricing system, inadequate operational flexibility, potential unfair competition from public sector enterprises, lengthy delays in evaluating bids and lack of transparencies in the decision making process, and the quality of acreage offered--which is of small size and poor quality; and for which geological information is either inadequate or obsolete.

The dramatic improvements witnessed in *civil aviation* since the reforms began could be eroded by *the new aviation policy* which may lead to restrictions of competition to protect the domestic government-owned airline. The new policy limits the capacity expansion of a private airline to 20 percent of total additional capacity, does not allow equity participation by foreign airlines in India's domestic private airlines, although it permits up to 40 percent foreign equity participation by non-airline equity investors. These costs are expected to be further compounded by the *new airport policy* which, while allowing foreign investors majority equity in airports construction projects, limits them to a BOT rather than a BOO model. This change is expected to seriously reduce the prospects for airport capacity expansion to meet the growing demand of around 12 percent per year over the next five years.

classification and provisioning requirements were further tightened in 1996-97. The government provided over Rs. 16.5 billion (about 0.2 percent of GDP) during 1995-96 and 1996-97 in recapitalization to help the public banks meet the 8 percent capital adequacy ratio. As a result, the financial health of the public banks has improved and 19 out of the 27 public sector banks reached the capital adequacy ratio of 8 percent in 1995-96. While this is an improvement over a year ago when only 13 did, further and faster improvements are needed to ensure that all banks satisfy the prudential requirements. Several public banks (commercial and term lending institutions) have also sought to strengthen their capital base by accessing the capital market to raise funds either through equity or subordinated loans (Figure 1.11).

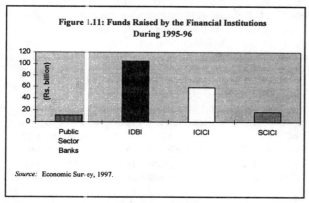

Figure 1.11: Funds Raised by the Financial Institutions During 1995-96

Source: Economic Survey, 1997.

The RBI is also expanding its supervisory scope to cover development finance institutions and non-bank financial companies. The latter have become very profitable because they occupy a niche traditionally not served by banks (consumer credit and small scale investments), but also because they escape many of the regulatory costs imposed on banks such as holding reserves, having a required equity-to-assets ratio, and paying deposit insurance premiums (Box 1.5). This is going to be a challenge for the RBI because while reforms are under-way to strengthen RBI's on-site inspection and, in particular, its off-site monitoring capacity to enforce the new prudential guidelines, this is admittedly one area where faster implementation of reforms is urgently needed to ensure the soundness of the financial system. India's current supervisory framework still tends to focus on enforcing statutory compliance (by financial intermediaries regarding their reserve requirements, credit targets particularly to priority sectors) and on cataloguing defects rather than on measuring and preventing undue risk-taking.

A number of measures were taken to help banks manage their liquidity, and increase the efficiency of the money market to allow a yield curve to develop. In its April 1997 credit policy, the RBI announced further measures aimed at reducing interest rates, giving banks more freedom in managing their asset portfolio, establishing a benchmark interest rate, deepening the foreign exchange market and encouraging further the development of the debt market by abolishing reserve and statutory requirements on inter-bank liabilities (a major impediment to the development of a yield curve). This comes in the sequel of measures taken in June 1996 when the RBI approved six primary dealers to deal in government securities. To develop a retail market for government securities and thus a secondary market, guidelines were also recently announced for setting up of satellite dealers (SDs) and SBI approved mutual funds dedicated to government securities.

Despite these improvements, many public banks remain vulnerable. Profits are low, reflecting still large reserve and statutory liquidity requirements, non-performing assets and high costs (Table 11 and Fig. 1.12). Moreover, pressures on public banks are likely to increase as competition increases in the financial sector. Increased competition will reduce spreads, helping depositors and borrowers but reducing the availability of funds for writing off non-performing assets. If credit and liquidity conditions were to tighten sharply, these problems would increase.

The *Tax reforms* of the 1997-98 Budget simplified India's tax system further and brought its rates in line with those of East Asia and developed countries. In addition to cutting across the board corporate and income taxation, taxes on investment income, and import duties, the budget also expanded the use of presumptive taxes on individuals and small retailers (see Box 1.6). However, lower compliance and weak administration remain a major weakness to increasing tax buoyancy.

Agriculture is becoming a focus of reform

The strong response of agriculture to reforms created favorable conditions for the government to re-introduce--after a 31-year hiatus--futures trading in cotton lint, jute and jute goods and partially lift restrictions on commodity trading such as those on storage, credit and movement controls, particularly for

cotton and oilseeds.. Export quotas on cotton and cotton yarn were raised and the number of yarn quota exemptions expanded. Sugar exports (subject to quotas) were decanalized in January 1997. To boost rice exports, the government removed the minimum export price but declining government stocks led to the reimposition of the levy on rice mills exporting non-basmati rice. Similarly, a shortfall in domestic wheat

---

Box 1.5: Non-Bank Financial Companies

With the progressive liberalization of India's financial system, non-bank financial companies (NBFCs) are taking on an increasingly vigorous role. The companies now prominent in the sector mostly date back to the early 1980s, when they emerged as "go-betweens" banks and small enterprises requiring finance for vehicles and machinery. They found it profitable to borrow from banks and lend the proceeds--through the modalities of hire-purchase and bill discounting--to firms that had difficulty borrowing from banks because they were regarded as risky.

Asset-based financing remains the NBFCs' core business. Their basic operations are loans of three to five years for commercial or industrial equipment, particularly vehicles. They fulfill a crucial role in financing small-scale capital investment. Because they are almost all privately-owned institutions, and subject to intense competition, they have tended to be particularly careful about loan recovery. Although no firm data is available, it has been estimated that the share of non-performing assets in the larger NBFCs is between 2 and 4 percent. In addition, the larger NBFCs have up-to-date computer systems, wide branch networks, better trained staff who operate under an incentives system to make sound loans and to ensure recovery.

There are about 40,000 NBFCs although only about 4650 function as deposit-taking intermediaries. Of these, about 100 have assets of Rs. 1 billion (US$30 million). The NBFCs have expanded in scope since the early 1980s, and now carry on a wide range of funded and unfunded activities. They are permitted to take deposits of one year or more at an interest rate fixed by the RBI generally at about 2 or 3 percentage points above the maximum deposit rate allowed for commercial banks. Some of the larger NBFCs have made a profitable business of brokering India's inter-corporate money market. Several NBFCs act as brokers for non-financial corporations (Indian corporations take deposits from the public). Several NBFCs have begun merchant-banking activities.

In addition to a maximum deposit rate and a minimum deposit term, the RBI has restricted the ratio of NBFC liabilities (including non-deposit borrowing) for hire purchase finance, and equipment leasing companies to about ten times net worth, with much lower ratios for the other NBFCs. Those NBFCs that comply with prudential norms and credit rating stipulations can accept deposits without any ceiling. The NBFCs are not subject to required reserves against deposits, but must hold ten percent of their deposits in "liquid assets" (i.e., eligible government securities). A recent expert report on the sector (the Shah Report) recommended that the RBI continues to apply these regulatory controls. The report also recommended that the RBI applies capital-adequacy standards, as well as asset-classification and income-recognition standards. However, the supervision of NBFCs, has been minimal, mainly relating to their deposit taking activity. A comprehensive off-site surveillance is expected to be shortly in place. A more systematic on site inspection is also being introduced. Many NBFCs managers believe that on-site inspection can accomplish only a limited control function, and that it is essential to rely also on rating agencies, auditors, and internal controls to help supervise the sector.

Some Indian commercial bankers feel that the NBFCs take some business from them. While this is undoubtedly true, it is also clear that the NBFCs still carry out a large volume of vital investment business that the commercial banks cannot do efficiently. It would therefore make sense for a bank to lend money to NBFCs at relatively low rates, enabling them to reach riskier borrowers from whom the NBFCs are demonstrably able to recover more efficiently. The NBFCs themselves are increasingly finding that they are facing intense competition from development finance institutions, which are lending increasingly for smaller capital projects than they previously did.

Development of the kinds of financing NBFCs carry out is limited by the lack of a market in debt instruments, besides the absence of a market in securitized private asset-based debt. The development of money-market mutual funds would be a helpful step, since such funds could hold securitized debt originated by NBFCs arising from asset financing. Development of an enabling regulatory and legal environment for such funds would help strengthen the NBFCs sector, and help it fulfill its potential not only in financing capital assets, but also to help developing financing for consumer durables.

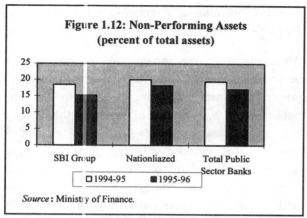

Figure 1.12: Non-Performing Assets
(percent of total assets)

□ 1994-95   ■ 1995-96

Source: Ministry of Finance.

production in 1996 led to the re-imposition of export ceilings on wheat and wheat products and, to contain price rises, public and eventually private wheat imports were temporarily allowed following the re-imposition of storage and credit controls. However, even this partial liberalization of exports exposes the shortcomings of the current food policy. The uneven liberalization of agriculture (across commodities and between domestic and external trade) has led to shifts in cropping patterns towards more commercial crops (hence less subject to trade restrictions) resulting in an excess demand for cereals. Because imports of cereals were restricted, external trade could not be used to smooth out price fluctuations. A recent study (S. Jha and P.V. Srinivasan, 1996) which explored the relative cost effectiveness of a variety of instruments--such as buffer stocks, canalized trade, variable levies--in stabilizing rice and wheat prices found that, of all possible options, current public sector buffer stocking operations are the costliest.

In deregulating--although partially--investment and domestic trade in agriculture, the government aims at encouraging private investment in agro-industry, modern storage facilities, and improving access to modern risk management instruments. In Table 1.4, the cells which remain shaded indicate areas where regulations persist. To date, the most far-reaching reforms have been in cotton and coffee. Cotton and coffee marketing are completely deregulated, except in Maharashtra where the state cotton monopoly procurement scheme remains imposing a fiscal burden of Rs. 5 billion in each of the last two years. In addition, investment in the production of fourteen important agro-industrial items (such as rice milling)

until now reserved to small scale industries has been deregulated. Together, these measures should encourage private sector investments in high-value agriculture and related marketing activities.

Public enterprise (PEs) reform has been one of the weakest elements in the reform process. While public enterprises are now more exposed to competition, their autonomy remains limited and has reduced the ability of their managers to introduce essential restructuring reforms such as large scale retrenchment, corporate reorganization, closure or selling of units-even those declared terminally sick--or joint ventures with private partners. In addition, central government equity remains high (over 90 percent in most cases) even in those enterprises operating in the tradable sector (Annex, Table 12). Thus, with a few exceptions, the financial performance of PEs has failed to improve. A Disinvestment Commission which was established in 1996 to examine options for reducing central government equity in central public enterprises submitted an approach paper in December 1996 articulating a strategy for reforming PEs. The strategy was discussed in public forums with Indian and foreign experts including those from major foreign consultancy firms dealing with privatization issues. On the basis of these consultations, the Commission issued two reports, in February and April 1997 outlining an approach to privatization and restructuring of public enterprises. Among the 40 central PEs being examined for full or partial privatization are such blue-chips as ONGC, SAIL, and IOC. In all, nine public enterprises have been recommended so far for full or partial privatization by the Disinvestment Commission. While these are encouraging steps, they are clearly not enough.

Economic Management Issues

Possible slow down in investment and growth

During 1996-97, a number of developments raised apprehension on the future course of the economy and on its capacity to sustain the rates of growth of the last three years. In particular, declines in the rates of growth of industrial production, of imports of capital goods (which declined by 7 percent), of corporate profits (5 percent), of lending commitments by specialized long-term financial institutions (30 percent), and of primary equity issues (17 percent) gave rise to concerns that *investment and growth* have declined.

The reasons were believed to be in a tepid stock market (Figure 1.13) which had led corporations to delay security issues (Annex, Table 13); high real interest rates which had depressed stock prices; and commercial banks' heightened aversion to risk (largely as a result of tighter enforcement of prudential regulations and the Indian Bank debacle), which had made it difficult to reach financial closure on investment projects, leading many firms to postpone investment decisions. Political uncertainty associated with the June 1996 inconclusive Parliamentary elections and the rapid change in governments with diverse political orientations, were additional factors.

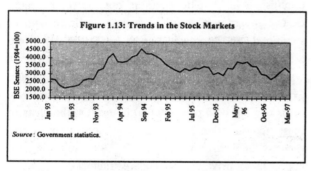

Figure 1.13: Trends in the Stock Markets

Source: Government statistics.

The authorities responded to this situation through a number of measures taken at different points in time. *First,* there was a relaxation of monetary policies which led to a decline in short-term real interest rates. In addition, in its April 1997 credit policy, the RBI reduced the cost of funds to the banks by lowering the ceiling on interest rate of deposits of more than 30 days and less than one year, and by deregulating interest rates on FCNR(B) deposits. Banks were also given more leeway in determining their risk exposure. *Second,* and as discussed above, a number of measures were introduced to encourage private investment--particularly FDI--with a special effort at improving the regulatory framework for private investment in infrastructure. *Third*, a pro-reform and confidence boosting budget was presented on February 28, 1997.

The 1997-98 budget: a creative but fiscally risky supply-side initiative

Amid concerns over sustainability of past growth performance, the *1997-98 Budget* sought to reactivate private investment and revive the stock market. The implicit logic is that a set of measures that sharply reduced taxation of profits combined with other measures that included allowing share buy-backs, announcing the reform of the company's act, and increasing the cap on ownership by foreign institutional investors in Indian companies from 24 percent of paid-up capital to 30 percent, would strengthen the stock market, encourage corporate investment and increase growth.

While continuing the process of structural reforms in several key areas, the budget introduced major tax (corporate and personal) and tariff cuts (Box 1.6), endorsed a key recommendation of the Tenth Finance Commission to improve the rules governing tax sharing between the central government and the states, (its implementation requires a Constitutional Amendment) and discontinued the central government automatic access to RBI financing. These tax measures, brought India's tax rates closer to those in East Asia, although the number of taxpayers remains relatively small.

The financial community reacted positively to the budget proposal. The proposed tax changes are expected to increase by 78 percent the disposable income of shareholders on a rupee of distributed profits. In spite of important disappointments, regarding the liberalization of insurance in particular, the budget confirmed the government commitment to reform. And by meeting its fiscal deficit target, the government boosted the confidence of the financial and business communities because this allayed fears of further monetary tightening and hence higher interest rates.

The previous lack of integration of dividend taxation between the corporate and personal tax system meant that dividends were taxed twice implying an effective tax burden on distributed corporate profits of 67.2 percent for the higher income taxpayers. The announced exemption of dividends under the individual income tax combined with the lowering of the corporate tax rate and the lower withholding rate will reduce the effective rate to 41.5 percent. As a result, the amount shareholders receive per rupee of earnings will rise by 78 percent. This measure, coupled with the elimination of restrictions on corporate share buybacks, is intended to boost share prices and revive the stock market. As a result, unless there are unforeseen supply-side shocks--such as an oil price hike or a drought--the government expects growth to remain at its current level. Combined with improvements in tax administration, the continuation of the growth momentum provides the basis for the

Table 1.4: Summary of Domestic and External Trade Reforms, 1993-94 to 1996-97						
Regulations	**Rice**	**Wheat**	**Sugar**	**Oilseeds**	**Cotton/ Textiles**	**Livestock**
At the Center's Level						
I. Marketing						
Movement controls		Lifted 1993	#	#	Repealed 1995	#
Storage controls			Stocking limits & turnover period increased 10/96	Lifted 2/97	Lifted 1995	#
Zoning	#	#		#	#	
Procurement levies (PDS)		#		#	#	
Small Scale Reservation	Rice milling repealed 2/97	#	#	Oilseed processing: increased investment ceiling 2/97	Apparel and Knitting: increased investment ceiling 2/97	Poultry feed & ice cream: repealed 2/97
Selective Credit Controls	Lifted 10/96	*Reintroduced 1/97*	Lifted 10/96	Lifted 10/96	Lifted 10/96	#
Licensing			Relaxed 12/96	Lifted 2/97	Lifted 2/97	
II. Pricing						
Price controls				Lifted 1994	#	#
Fixing processing margins	#	#	#	#	Ginning & Pressing Act repealed 2/97	#
Futures Banned					Ban lifted -cotton lint futures 2/97	
At States' Level						
Movement controls		#				#
Zoning	#	#		#	#	
Price controls	#	#		#	#	#
Fixing of processing margins	#	#	#	#	Ginning & Pressing Acts repealed 12/96	#
External Trade						
Exports	Liberalized 1994	*Export controls reintroduced 1996*	Liberalized subject to export quotas, 1997			Liberalized 1995
Imports			Liberalized 1994	Edible oil tariffs reduced to 20 % ,1996	(Except lint imports liberalized 1994)	
Note: Shaded areas indicate commodities where regulations still apply. # - not regulated						

forecast of tax revenues. Clearly, lower growth of nominal GDP would automatically reduce nominal revenues, with no corresponding automatic adjustment in expenditure. ***Thus, achieving the authorities' fiscal deficit target critically depends on the economy's growth performance and improved tax administration,*** the main downside risks of an otherwise credible budget forecast.

Fiscal adjustment in the 1997-98 budget

The 1997-98 Budget envisages a further fiscal adjustment but the target may be overoptimistic. The fiscal deficit target for 1997-98 has been set at 4.5 percent of GDP. The 0.5 percent of GDP fiscal correction over 1996-97 (Annex, Table 4) is expected to be achieved by a marginal increase in tax revenue as a share of GDP (through improvements in tax administration which would offset the significant tax cuts) and an increase in receipts from privatization while total expenditure in nominal terms is projected to remain at its 1996-97 level of 16 percent of GDP.

Fiscal vulnerabilities

A key question about the 1997-98 budget is whether it will be successful in stimulating private investment. While the budget has reduced the user cost of capital,

---

Box 1.6: 1997-98 Budget Main Tax Measures

The main reforms introduced in the budget consist of measures intended to revive the stock market and stimulate corporate investment. In the process, the budget also simplified the tax system and introduced measures to strengthen compliance. The main tax measures include:

Personal and Corporate Taxation

- The maximum marginal personal income tax rate has been reduced to 30 percent from 40 percent and the lowest rate to 10 percent from 15 percent
- The corporate tax rate for domestic companies has been reduced from 43 to 35 percent (48 percent for foreign companies).
- The Minimum Alternative Tax (MAT) on book profits has been reduced from 12.9 percent to 10.5 percent. Export profits will no longer be subject to it and payments under the MAT will be creditable for five years against assessments under the regular corporate income tax.
- The dividend taxation at the individual income tax level has been replaced by a 10 percent final withholding on corporate distributions.
- The interest tax on government bonds has been abolished
- The capital gains tax rate for NRIs has been reduced from 20 to 10 percent to achieve neutrality with capital gains rate applicable to FIIs.
- Administrative measures to improve reporting include: (i) a revamped presumptive taxation scheme (requiring individuals owning a car, a truck, a house, or having traveled abroad, to file tax returns); and (ii) a new Voluntary Disclosure Scheme or tax amnesty to report undeclared assets held abroad or in India to bring black or underground economy money into the tax net. The assets or income declared under the scheme would be taxed under the new highest marginal tax rate in return for immunity from prosecution or additional taxation.

Trade Taxation

- The peak tariff has been reduced from 50 percent to 40 percent and several tariffs below the maximum were reduced as well. The tariff rate on capital goods has been reduced from 25 to 20 percent but project-related capital goods imports which enjoyed a variety of concessional rates would face a uniform 20 percent tariff. The customs duty rate on capital goods imported under the Basic Export Promotion. Capital Good Scheme (EPGC) has been reduced from 15 percent to 10 percent. The 2 percent across the board import surcharge has been maintained.

Excises Measures

- The excise duty rate is further reduced, with the aim of establishing a four -rate structure within three years.
- The small dealers and manufacturers threshold for participation in the full MODVAT crediting system has been raised to simplify and lessen the excise tax burden on this sector.
- The service tax is widened to include *inter alia* goods transported by road, car rentals, and air travel agents.

and monetary policy has lowered interest rates, how will private investment respond is unclear. *Second*, the government expects an improvement in tax compliance to compensate for the cost of the proposed tax cuts. Administrative measures (such as tax amnesties and tax filing requirements for those living in urban areas, who meet certain criteria) have been proposed to enforce compliance, but their impact is difficult to assess and the budget contains little in the way of base-broadening measures. In the past, government tax cuts seem to have encouraged compliance. However, there is a risk that with rates much lower than in the past, tax cuts may result in revenue loss even with improvements in compliance. *Third*, a number of other developments might lead to further public sector fiscal deterioration. These are the accommodations of the salary increases recommended by the Fifth Pay Commission and their implications for the states and public enterprises wage bills; the implications of lack of adjustment in petroleum prices; pressures to increase other subsidies and transfers to the states, particularly if the government is unable to reduce the food subsidy to those states unable to improve targeting as it plans to

do through the forthcoming two-tier targeted PDS system (Box 1.7).

The Fifth Pay Commission (FPC) recommendations were presented in February 1997. As a result of an increase of 25-30 percent in average staff employment (pay and allowances), and partial payment of arrears for the period January 1996 to March 1997, the central government's salary bill is expected to increase in 1997-98 by Rs. 112 billion (0.8 percent of GDP). Inclusive of civilian staff, military personnel and railways staff, the salary bill will rise to 2.8 percent of GDP in 1997-98, after having declined from 2.7 to 2.2 percent of GDP over the past six years (and to an estimated 2.0 percent in 1997-98 without the FPC award). While Central Government expenditure on wages is relatively small, states' expenditure on wages is significantly higher at around 5 to 8 percent of state GDP. Significant wage increase by state governments (in the past, states have followed the center in wage adjustments) would considerably further erode their finances. In addition, salaries in public enterprises are based on pay levels in the civil service. While essential to restore the competitiveness of pay in the civil

---

Box 1.7: The Targeted Public Distribution System

GOI has announced its intention to introduce sweeping reforms in the Public Distribution System (PDS) in an effort to raise its cost-effectiveness in reaching the poor. According to recently issued guidelines, the Targeted PDS (TPDS) would offer two separate distribution channels: one aimed at households below the poverty line, and the other for the population above the poverty line.

Under the first channel targeted to the poor households, the central government would transfer to state governments wheat and rice at about half the issue price set for the PDS. The monthly ration under the TPDS would be set at 10 kg per poor household in the state. The number of poor households in a state would be the one determining by the recently approved Expert Group's methodology. This would effectively determine for each state a maximum entitlement based on the number of poor households in the state--a vast improvement in relation to the present system in which the amount of foodgrain that a state can draw from the PDS is left at the discretion of the state and thus leads to situations where states with a high incidence of poverty utilized PDS much less than states with a low incidence of poverty. The Central Government would leave to State governments the responsibility of designing and implementing targeting mechanisms for reaching the poor, and corresponding guidelines were recently issued by the Ministry of Food. State governments would need to be in a position to identify the poor, issue special cards, and deliver foodgrain to the intended beneficiaries. The central government would monitor the states' performance in identifying and delivering foodgrains to the beneficiaries, for which reporting requirements have been developed. These features of the TPDS will encourage the states to improve targeting or else, at least in theory, their access to the TPDS could be discontinued.

Under the second and non-targeted channel, which the guidelines indicate would be phased out gradually, the central government would transfer to state governments wheat and rice at an issue price which would remain close to the market price. Access to this non-targeted TPDS channel would be universal. It is proposed that--as an interim measure--the quantities to be allocated to each state be based on the average lifting of wheat and rice over the last ten years by the states.

service, in the absence of offsetting measures, a significant pay increase would also weaken the finances of public enterprises.

Also, an important contingent liability for the Central Government is the sizable deficit of the Oil Coordination Committee (OCC) Account--originally established as a self-financing buffer account to stabilize rather than subsidize domestic petroleum prices. Partly because of the subsidies, and partly due to rising costs of oil imports, the Oil Pool Account deficit in 1996-97 reached Rs. 98 billion. In the absence of price adjustment, this might imply a monthly accrual of Rs. 8 billion in subsidies, the rate at which the oil pool account has been accumulating losses since march 1997.

Another potential source of fiscal pressure for the center is expected from the central government proposed retargeting of the food subsidy to families below the poverty line with effect from June 1997 (Box 1.7). The cost of this new program has been budgeted at Rs. 77 billion in 1997-98 (0.5 percent of GDP) compared with Rs. 62 billion (0.4 percent of GDP) under the existing program. There is a major risk of cost overruns on account of this new PDS. The budget projection for the food subsidy implicitly assumes that not all states will be able to implement the new scheme in 1997-98. If more states than expected submit their lists of eligible beneficiaries, there will be an expenditure overrun. A second risk of expenditure overrun is if the government fails to reduce the food subsidy to states unable to improve targeting.

In summary, given these risks, in the course of the current fiscal year, additional resource mobilization measures (such as acceleration of privatization, reduction in central government subsidies or further expenditure cuts) may become necessary to ensure that the 1997-98 fiscal deficit target is met and inflationary expectations dampened. Analyses of the sustainability of India's fiscal stance indicate that a swift fiscal contraction is essential to stabilize interest payments on the large central government domestic debt (Annex, Tables 14 and 15); allow trade and financial liberalization to proceed with little macroeconomic risk; raise investors' confidence in the reform process; reduce the excessively large public debt stock to lower real interest rates, and free up financial resources for the rapid expansion of private investment. Reduction of consolidated fiscal imbalances requires lower central and state governments deficits, as well as a better financial performance by public enterprises. A target of around 4 percent of GDP (which is close to the target set at the beginning of the reform program) for the consolidated central and state governments deficit may be a realistic goal to be achieved in the next 3-4 years. Subsidy cuts could provide the resources needed to achieve this fiscal deficit target.

External account vulnerabilities

While the outlook for the external environment facing India over the next decade remains positive, there are some important downside risks. *First*, dependency on oil imports continues to rise at faster rates than GDP growth. In particular, petroleum subsidies have fueled consumption leading to an acceleration of oil imports (increasing the vulnerability of the balance of payments to unforeseen oil price shocks) as a result of the inability of the public sector oil companies to increase oil production. Domestic production is leveling off and, current trends persisting, India's oil imports will reach US$12 billion in the next three years from US$7.2 billion in 1995-96. Potential production is thought to be significantly higher than present levels but foreign investment in the upstream sector--critical to achieving major output supply--has not been forthcoming. *Second*, in the event that any of the fiscal pressures discussed above materializes, it could increase the current account deficit beyond the safely sustainable limit. *Third*, the maintenance of a competitive exchange rate is essential. Given the fiscal vulnerabilities, this task will become even more complex because recent liberalization measures are likely to encourage further capital inflows.

Chapter 2 | *CHANGING STATES' DEVELOPMENT POLICIES*

India is a union of 25 states, the largest 15 of which are nation-like--with populations between 20 million people (Haryana) and 160 million (Uttar Pradesh)--and account for over 90 percent of the country's population. The Constitution gives the states considerable autonomy to define their development policies. In particular, they are responsible (sometimes in conjunction with the central government) for ensuring the provision and regulation of education, health, power, agriculture, irrigation, water, road transport, and urban services. State and local governments--which are subordinated to the states--are responsible for 60 percent of all government spending, and a much higher proportion (90 percent) of public spending on health, education, and roads. They also have a major role regulating labor and agricultural markets. Per-capita income levels and indicators of human resource development vary considerably across states (Table 2.1). There is growing awareness that improvement in the states' economic management is essential for India to sustain high rates of economic growth.

State Issues: A Summing Up

India's pre-1991 development strategy and inter-governmental transfers have shaped the states' development policies

Before reforms started in 1991, India's states could not depend on private capital for their development. National policies excluded it from important sectors and, where permitted, central licensing authorities, not the enabling environment, determined the volume and composition of private investment. Consequently, a state's pace of development was determined by its ability to expand public investment in agriculture (extension services, agro-industry, storage), infrastructure (power, ports, roads, irrigation, transport

services, water), and manufacturing (most states own a large and diversified set of public enterprises producing everything from coal and cement to fertilizer and toys). For this, states relied mostly on resources transferred from the central government.

India's system of intergovernmental transfers has three basic resource transfer mechanisms. The *first* consists of transfers recommended by the Finance Commission, a body created by the Constitution which requires the President of India to appoint such Commission every five years. The Finance Commission provides recommendations to the central government for a five-year period on how it should share with the states its tax collections (personal income taxes, excluding income from agriculture which only the states can tax, and excises) and on the desired level of other forms of financial assistance to the states. There have been 10 Finance Commissions thus far, the last one completed its work in late 1994. Finance Commissions command considerable respect, and their recommendations have been generally adopted by the central government.

A major objective of successive Finance Commissions has been to achieve a better match between the responsibilities the Constitution assigns to the states, and the revenues they rely on (mostly sales tax, state excises, and other taxes on transactions and property) which vary considerably from state to state depending on their level of development, administrative capabilities, and strength of governance. Until the early 1990s, successive Finance Commissions recommended levels of financial support for each state on the basis of their per-capita income, and projected gap between current revenue and expenditure ("gap filling" approach). Fiscal performance or indicators of tax effort were not taken into account. The Ninth Finance Commission (which made recommendations for 1990-95) explored the use of indicators of fiscal

Table 2.1: India - State Profiles, 1995-96					
State	Population	Per-Capita Income [a] (US$)	Female Literacy (percent) [b]	Infant Mortality Rate [c] (per 1000 births)	Poverty Incidence (Headcount index)
					Rural	Urban
India	929	350	39.3	79	36.7	30.5
Andhra Pradesh	72.0	289	32.7	71	28.9	30.8
Bihar	95.4	146	22.9	73	63.5	39.7
Gujarat	44.8	411	48.6	67	35.4	30.7
Haryana	18.2	459	40.5	75	..	..
Karnataka	48.2	301	44.3	73	41.0	29.7
Kerala	31.0	279	86.2	17	31.1	23.1
Madhya Pradesh	72.5	229	28.9	104	45.4	39.8
Maharashtra	86.4	490	52.3	59	47.8	36.2
Orissa	34.4	191	34.7	115	40.3	40.8
Punjab	22.1	521	50.4	56	25.2d	11.4d
Rajasthan	48.4	238	20.4	90	47.5	29.4
Tamil Nadu	58.4	335	51.3	58	36.7	31.3
Uttar Pradesh	150.7	200	25.3	98	41.6	34.3
West Bengal	73.6	251	46.6	65	27.3	22.5

a. Per-Capita Income data is based on per-capita gross state domestic product at current rupees and converted to US$ by the average exchange rate.
b. 1991 census.
c. Data pertains to 1992.
d. Including Haryana.
Source: CSO; CMIE; Planning Commission; World Bank Report on Poverty in India.

capacity on which it based some of its recommendations for transfers, but this was applied to the 10 "Special Category States"--mostly financially weak states (e.g. Kashmir, Assam, Himachal Pradesh). In general, the Finance Commission awards have not penalized poor fiscal performance as they recommended central grants to balance the states' current accounts. This approach was radically changed with the Ninth and Tenth Finance Commissions which made their recommendations for financial support on the basis of normative current account deficits rather than the ones projected by the states.

The *second* is financial support recommended by the Planning Commission, a body that although not created by the Constitution, also enjoys considerable respect and is chaired by the Prime Minister. The Planning Commission was set up soon after Independence. Its mandate was, and still is, rooted in India's pursuit of a centrally planned development strategy. Its major responsibilities include formulating (based on bilateral consultations with the states), five-

year development plans for the central and state governments, and annual plans within the five-year framework, and propose corresponding financing plans. Resources for financing the states' development plans come from four sources. (a) Direct central government financial support for projects in the states' plans in the form of 30 percent grants and 70 percent loans (90 percent grant, 10 percent loan for "Special Category States") at interest rates (currently 12 percent) in line with the cost of borrowing for the central government, and maturities of 20 years. (b) "Market borrowings" which designate resources from captive sources of finance, that is placement of state-issued bonds with banks (as part of their SLRs), insurance companies and non-government pension and provident funds, which are mandated to invest in "designated securities". The central Government allocates between states the SLR securities while states compete for the other forms of borrowing. (c) "Centrally Sponsored Schemes" which are development programs conceived by the central government, which also finances them in percentages varying between 50 and 100 percent. (d) Official external development finance.

Third, each state is allowed to borrow from the central government annually 75 percent of the increase in saving deposits with the postal system in that state. States can also resort to the RBI for short-term borrowing, but they must balance their accounts every 15 days. They can only access financial markets if granted permission by the central government--which is seldom given because the central government has avoided providing financial support to the states outside the framework of the Finance and Planning Commissions. The Constitution requires States to seek the Center's consent for any borrowing if they are indebted to the Center or have an outstanding loan guaranteed by the Center (at present, all States are indebted to the Center). Also, the Constitution bars the states from borrowing in international financial markets.

However this hard budget constraint has been diluted by diverting to current expenditure resources destined to investments, building up arrears with public enterprises, and rolling over debts to financial intermediaries specialized in financing state governments (such as HUDCO). While this dilution is believed to have become serious in the case of highly indebted states, there are no reliable data to ascertain its significance. Also, even these sources of distress financing are being exhausted. Recently, the central public enterprises have been instructed by the central government to discontinue supplies to states in arrears. Thus, Coal India has implemented a "cash-and-carry" policy for supplies to the State Electricity Boards (SEBs) in arrears, and the National Thermal Power Corporation has, at times, cut power supplies. In addition, since 1995, up to 15 percent of the statutory central government transfers to a state can be retained to help clear the SEBs' arrears with central public enterprises.

India's system of transfers has a number of positive features. It provides a transparent rule-based framework which makes transfers predictable. By subjecting state borrowings to central government approval and precluding access to external finance, it has imposed a relatively hard budget constraint and

spared India from the moral hazards and macroeconomic crises witnessed in federated states of Latin America--many of which were triggered by state governments excessive borrowings with the implicit central government guarantee. And, over the years, successive Finance Commissions have attempted to reduce regional inequalities by prescribing higher per-capita levels of financial support to the poorest states.

Some aspects of the system of transfers have discouraged states' fiscal discipline

These positive features notwithstanding, intergovernmental transfers have discouraged fiscal discipline by the states in several ways. *First,* starting in the early 1970s and until very recently, the Finance and Planning Commissions recommended gradually but persistently increasing central government transfers to the states, from about 3 percent of GDP in 1970-71, to a peak of over 7 percent in the mid-1980s (Figure 2.1). In addition, the country's rapidly growing pool of financial savings and the large preemption of these savings by the government (for example, the SLR was 38.5 percent of commercial banks incremental deposits in 1990-91) provided ample resources for "market borrowings". Last but not least, successive Finance Commissions established a tradition of unconditional debt forgiveness, from which only the 10th Finance Commission departed--it was the first time that a Finance Commission made no significant recommendation for unconditional debt forgiveness. These developments built expectations that the states needed not be overly concerned with mobilizing resources since ever-expanding and politically more expedient financing would be forthcoming. As a result, throughout the 1970s and 1980s, the states expanded investments in physical infrastructure (power, roads, irrigation, ports, roads), and provision of social services, without establishing mechanisms for cost recovery and for maintaining these assets in the long run. Prices charged for power, water, irrigation and other services declined to levels equivalent to a small fraction--in some cases zero--of production costs and are at the origin of extremely large implicit and explicit subsidies which are estimated at 7 percent of GDP for "non-merit" goods.

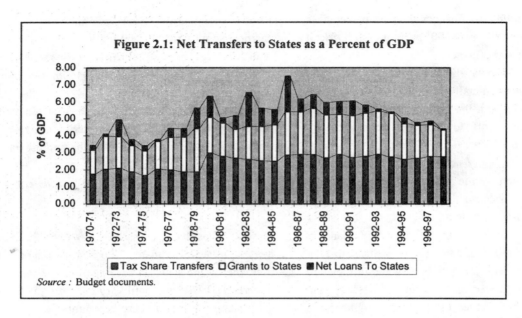

Figure 2.1: Net Transfers to States as a Percent of GDP

Source : Budget documents.

Second, until recently, successive Finance Commissions have based their recommendations for financial support on the states' projected gap between current revenue and current expenditure--thus penalizing states running current account surpluses and discouraging their efforts at resource mobilization.

Third, the Planning Commission authorizes for funding the operating as well as the capital costs of states' new programs for the first five years from their inception. This encourages the states to initiate new programs even when additional own revenue cannot be mobilized to finance them in the long run. The cumulative effect of this heavy subsidization of incremental programs has been to foster employment and expenditure growth while creating chronic shortages of funds for operations and maintenance.

Fourth, and more generally, since all borrowing (whether from the central government or "market borrowing") by the states is at the same terms--and all states pay the same interest rates regardless of their financial condition--this eliminates a potentially powerful incentive for states to improve their financial performance.

The states face three crises--fiscal, infrastructure, human resources development

By the second half of the 1980s, it became evident that the states were experiencing considerable fiscal difficulties. They had created a large infrastructure and expanded social services without establishing adequate tax or price mechanisms to recover their cost, finance their maintenance, or ensure their needed expansion. They had expanded public employment to the point that in most states wages and pensions absorb between 4-5 percent of the state GDP (Karnataka, Maharashtra, Gujarat), and 9-10 percent of state GDP is not infrequent (Rajasthan, AP, Orissa, Bihar, UP). They had contracted debt without establishing the financial base for its servicing--with some finding its servicing increasingly difficult. And they launched welfare programs that could not be sustained in the long-run. As a result, fiscal stress became evident. Already in the mid-1980s, spending on capital, education, health, and operations and maintenance started to decline while spending on interest payments continued to increase (Figure 2.2 and Table 2.2). The current account balance (after grants) also declined. And much of the emerging infrastructure crisis that India faces today is due to insufficient and declining resources for operations and maintenance. These trends were exacerbated by the stabilization and reform program started in 1991. Central government transfers ceased to grow, and eventually started to decline. With financial liberalization, interest rates increased and interest payments absorbed an increasingly large share of state resources. Gradually but persistently, most states found themselves increasingly unable to play their role in

India's development: that is, to provide key infrastructure services and develop the country's human resources.

Besides development-related reasons, weakening state finances have become a subject of concern to the central government because it is the states' largest creditor. About 60 percent of the states' debt is owed to the central government, and the remaining 40 percent is mostly held by central-government owned banks and insurance companies. Gross central government lending to the states has been at around 3 percent of GDP in recent years, and the states' loan repayments

Table 2.2 : State Government Finances, 1980-1997 (percent of GDP)										
	1980-81	1985-86	1989-90	1990-91	1991-92	1992-93	1993-94	1994-95	1995-96 R.E.	1996-97 B.E.
Revenue receipts	12.0	13.0	12.9	12.6	13.2	12.9	13.0	12.8	12.4	11.7
Tax revenue	7.7	8.4	8.6	8.4	8.6	8.6	8.5	8.4	8.5	8.4
State own taxes	4.9	5.6	5.7	5.6	5.8	5.7	5.7	5.8	5.8	5.7
State share in central taxes	2.8	2.9	2.9	2.7	2.8	2.9	2.7	2.6	2.7	2.8
Non-tax revenue	4.4	4.6	4.3	4.2	4.6	4.4	4.5	4.4	3.9	3.2
of which grants from centre	2.0	2.6	2.4	2.5	2.5	2.5	2.6	2.1	1.9	1.8
Revenue expenditure [A+B+C]	11.0	12.6	13.2	13.4	14.0	13.6	13.5	13.5	13.5	12.8
A. Developmental (1+2)	7.7	8.8	8.9	9.1	9.5	9.0	8.8	8.2	8.4	7.8
1. Social services	4.4	5.1	5.3	5.2	5.0	4.9	4.8	4.7	5.0	4.7
2. Economic services	3.4	3.7	3.7	3.9	4.4	4.1	3.9	3.5	3.4	3.1
B. Non-developmental	3.1	3.6	4.1	4.1	4.3	4.5	4.6	5.1	5.0	4.9
of which interest payments	1.1	1.4	1.7	1.7	1.8	2.0	2.0	2.1	2.1	2.2
To center	0.7	0.7	1.0	1.0	1.1	1.1	1.2	1.2	1.2	1.2
To others	0.4	0.6	0.7	0.8	0.7	0.9	0.9	1.0	0.9	1.0
C. Transfer to local bodies	0.2	0.2	0.1	0.1	0.2	0.2	0.1	0.1	0.1	0.2
Net current balance	1.1	0.4	-0.3	-0.8	-0.8	-0.7	-0.5	-0.6	-1.1	-1.2
Capital expenditure [A+B+C]	3.8	3.1	2.6	2.5	2.1	2.2	2.1	2.3	2.3	2.1
A. Developmental (1+2)	2.3	2.0	1.7	1.7	1.6	1.5	1.5	1.8	1.5	1.4
1. Social services	0.3	0.3	0.3	0.2	0.3	0.2	0.2	0.2	0.3	0.3
2. Economic services	2.0	1.8	1.4	1.4	1.3	1.2	1.3	1.5	1.3	1.1
B. Non-developmental	0.1	0.0	0.1	0.0	0.0	0.0	0.0	0.0	0.1	0.1
C. Loans and advances (net)	1.5	1.0	0.8	0.8	0.5	0.7	0.5	0.4	0.7	0.6
Gross fiscal deficit	2.8	2.7	2.9	3.3	2.9	3.0	2.6	2.9	3.4	3.3
Finance by instrument:										
Market loans	0.2	0.5	0.6	0.5	0.5	0.5	0.5	0.4	0.5	0.4
Loans from center (Net)	0.9	2.7	1.7	1.8	1.5	1.2	1.2	1.4	1.3	1.3
Small savings & Provident funds	0.3	0.4	0.5	0.6	0.5	0.5	0.5	0.5	0.4	0.4
Other	1.4	-1.0	0.1	0.5	0.4	0.7	0.3	0.5	1.2	1.2
Memo Items										
Primary Deficit	1.7	1.3	1.2	1.6	1.2	1.0	0.6	0.8	1.3	1.1
Total Debt Outstanding	17.6	20.5	20.6	20.6	20.5	20.2	19.8	19.3	19.4	19.3
of which: Owed to Centre	12.1	13.4	13.6	13.4	13.1	12.8	12.3	11.6	11.7	11.5

Note: BE = Budget estimates; RE = Revised estimates.
Source: Ministry of Finance, Union budget documents; Reserve Bank of India, RBI bulletins on state finances.

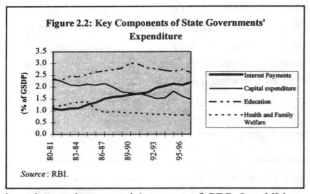

Figure 2.2: Key Components of State Governments' Expenditure

Source: RBI.

have hovered at around 1 percent of GDP. In addition, similarly large financial resources flow between state-owned public enterprises, particularly electricity generators and distributors, and central government public enterprises. As a result, there are multiple channels through which weaknesses in state finances can have an impact on the central government.

State Reforms: Priorities and Progress

The program of stabilization and reform underway since 1991 has radically changed the framework within which states' development policies are implemented. States now can attract private capital in such sectors as power, irrigation, ports, roads, and all areas of manufacturing--and it is their ability to attract private capital which now determines a state's growth performance. Development spending now needs to be more narrowly focused on the state's areas of comparative advantage, where it complements rather than substitutes for the private sector. This is a radical departure from the pre-1991 period, when the volume of public development spending was a key determinant of a state's growth performance (Box 2.1).

Attracting private capital requires states to provide an enabling and investor-friendly environment. That is, good quality and abundant infrastructure, an educated labor force, a business-friendly public administration, and moderate levels of taxation. Significant reforms are needed to bring this about in India's states. In particular, it requires: (i) policy, pricing, institutional, and regulatory reforms to translate private sector interest to invest in infrastructure into commercially viable ventures--and improvements in the states' capacity to manage commercially enforceable contracts; (ii) an environment conducive to efficient

public investment in areas where the public sector will remain important such as roads and urban services; (iii) public expenditure restructuring (such as privatization, freeze on employment, and reduction of consumption subsidies) to eliminate wasteful spending and make room for priority programs in public infrastructure, health and education; and (iv) tax reforms to provide stable sources of revenue at a low efficiency cost.

In many states, policy, pricing and institutional reforms of key sectors would bring about the needed fiscal restructuring. For example, power and irrigation sector reforms would generate large fiscal gains in virtually all of India's 25 states. In some states (Maharashtra, Karnataka, Gujarat), such reforms, alone, would be sufficient to restore fiscal sustainability. In others (AP, Rajasthan, Tamil Nadu, West Bengal, Haryana), putting the states' public finances on a sustainable path would require more comprehensive reforms of public expenditures, such as public enterprise reform, freeze on public employment, reduction in consumption subsidies and, for some of the states, a rationalization and retargeting of welfare programs (Box 2.2). And finally, in poor and highly indebted states (Figure 2.3) such as Orissa, Bihar, and UP, sectoral reforms and public expenditure restructuring may need to be complemented by debt refinancing.

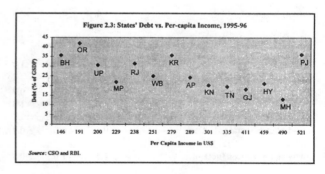

Figure 2.3: States' Debt vs. Per-capita Income, 1995-96

Source: CSO and RBI.

Reforming infrastructure policies

Several states have already started to implement such reforms. ***In power,*** recognizing that SEBs' creditworthiness must be restored to attract private independent power producers, some states (Orissa, Gujarat, UP, Rajasthan, Haryana) have recently adopted a new power sector policy that endorses: (i) creation of an independent regulatory agency, (ii) tariffs reflecting costs, (iii) competition among

---

Box 2.1: Reforms in Rajasthan

With a growth rate of 6 percent over the past 15 years, Rajasthan has emerged as one of India's fastest growing state. This is a significant achievement given initial natural and social resource endowments--three-fifths of the state is desert and, before its constitution in 1962, Rajasthan consisted of several principalities and chieftancies where wealth was concentrated and economic and social development limited. Over the last 15 years, growth was achieved through rapidly increasing public spending on power, irrigation, potable water, roads, manufacturing, tourism, health, and education. However, this development strategy has led the public sector to provide a wide range of goods and services (power, irrigation, water, manufacturing goods) at prices well below cost. This has created large claims on the budget and diverted resources away from essential spending on operations, maintenance and social sectors. Public infrastructure has deteriorated, while the development of the state's human resources continues to lag behind that of the country. In particular, at 20 percent, female literacy is India's lowest. Private investment has declined, from over 10 percent of the state GDP (GSDP) in the late 1980s to less than 8 percent in recent years. The state's fiscal deficit has increased from 3.5 percent of GSDP in 1990-93 to 5.5 percent in 1994-97. Interest payments have risen from 14 percent to 20 percent of total revenue. Salaries, pensions and interest absorb two-thirds of revenue.

Cognizant of the changed developmental context after 1991, and its unsustainable fiscal position, the Government of Rajasthan has decided to redefine its development strategy, focusing the role of the public sector on its areas of comparative advantage and providing an enabling environment for private capital. Consequently, the key objectives of the Ninth Five-Year Plan (1997-2002) include (a) exit strategies for the government from sectors such as power, where the private sector could be relied upon for needed investments; (b) strategies for improved pricing and management in other sectors, particularly water; and (c) accelerating progress towards universalization of primary education.

Regarding *power* sector reform, the state's Council of Ministers approved a draft of the Rajasthan Power Sector Reforms Bill in 1997, which aims at recasting the role of government away from ownership and commercial operations to policy formulation and regulation; eliminating of power subsidy with the exception of cross-subsidization of agriculture; and facilitating private investment in power generation and distribution. In a situation of excess demand and long waiting periods for rural power connections, an innovative method of tariff rationalization has been implemented, called the *"Nursery Scheme"*, where agricultural consumers can jump the queue by paying higher rates (Rs. 1.20 per Kwh compared with Rs. 0.50 charged for ordinary metered connections).

A draft *water* policy is under consideration, to ensure judicious and economic utilization of this scarce resource (Rajasthan accounts for 10 percent of India's area and for about 5 percent of population but only one percent of the country's water resources). The proposed policy includes rationalization of water rates to reflect its scarcity and to cover annual maintenance costs plus part of the fixed costs, as well as the promotion of users' participation in irrigation management.

Fiscal reforms implemented by GOR include ambitious and comprehensive reforms of sales taxes and sales tax administration, which may set a model for other Indian states to follow. They include the abolition of internal and external checkpoints, adoption of self-assessment for all dealers, reduction in the number of rates and modernization of administrative procedures. Other reforms being prepared or implemented include (a) review and restructuring of the entire public expenditure program including zero-base review of personnel and subsidies; (b) rationalization of the size of the civil service; (c) reducing the role of the government in public enterprises reform through institutional reforms, divestment, privatization or closure; and (d) strict annual ceilings on net borrowing by the state to reduce the fiscal deficit to below 3.5 percent of GSDP by 2001-02, from its current average level of 5.5 percent in 1994-97.

---

independent power producers, (iv) divestiture of shares in the power generating public companies, and (v) restructuring and privatization of the distribution functions of the SEBs (Box 2.3).

This approach was laid out in a Common Minimum National Action Plan for Power (CMNAP), issued by the Ministry of Power in December 1996, on the basis of agreements reached in two Chief Ministers'

meetings (Box 2.4). Steps have been taken to implement it. The objectives and content of the program have been inspired by the pioneering reforms in Orissa several years ago when the state started implementing a comprehensive power sector reform program that goes well beyond the CMNAP's recommendations (Box 2.3). Other states are interested in arresting the rapid deterioration of power supply in

Box 2.2: Establishing Fiscal Sustainability in Andhra Pradesh

Ample mineral resources, abundant water, and fertile land make of Andhra Pradesh (AP) one of India's richest states in terms of resources. In addition, at the time of Independence, AP had one of the country's largest area under irrigation. Its potential and good initial conditions notwithstanding, at 4.6 percent per year in the last 15 years, the state has grown at lower rates than the country's average, and considerably lower than India's six fastest growing states (5.7 percent)--and the divergence has been increasing in the recent past. At the heart of AP's performance is the state's inability to provide essential infrastructure and social services. Over the last several decades, implicit and explicit subsidies and rapidly growing public employment have absorbed an increasingly large share of the state's budget, and diverted resources away from essential investments in infrastructure, operations and maintenance, and social services. Total explicit and implicit subsidies now amount to 6 percent of GSDP. Power and food subsidies alone absorb two-thirds of total subsidies. About 90 percent of state's own revenue is spent on salaries. At the same time, education and health spending fell from 5 percent of GSDP in 1986-87 to 4 percent in 1995-96. Public investment and O&M declined from 6 percent of GSDP to 4 percent in the same period.

Since July 1996, the state government has taken important measures to improve public finances and sector policies. In particular, it has increased the cost of subsidized rice from Rs. 2 to Rs. 3.5 per kg, and reduced per-family allocations by 25 percent. It has also raised power tariffs by 20-60 percent to non-agricultural consumers, and by 10-25 times in the case of agricultural tariffs. Facing to strong opposition to these measures, the government later reduced these increases by about 40 percent. While this is a significant increase, the revised average tariffs for farmers still cover only 9 percent of production costs. Other measures included tax increases; the first steps towards the reform of the power sector along the lines established in the CMNAP, and significant increases in irrigation charges alongside with important institutional reforms, such as the creation of Water User Associations and the devolution of operation and maintenance to them. Additional measures being contemplated include containment of the wage bill, further reduction of food subsidies, partial relaxation of prohibition, privatization, further adjustments of water and power rates, and other revenue enhancement efforts. The key fiscal objective is to achieve fiscal sustainability through a change in the composition of public expenditure. That is, a significant reduction in rice subsidies and employment in the state government and a corresponding increase in expenditure in social and infrastructure sectors particularly in primary education and health, nutrition, irrigation, and road sectors. Fiscal reforms will be accompanied by significant changes in sector policies--restructuring of the power sector; improvement in service delivery of primary education, primary health, and nutrition; strengthening of O&M management in roads and irrigation sectors, and acceleration of users' participation in the management of public canal irrigation network. If successfully implemented the reform program would put AP on a path of faster economic growth and social development.

their respective areas (Box 2.5) and are considering implementing the program. At the same time, however, Punjab, Bihar and Kerala, have already backtracked from the CMNAP's objectives by offering free electricity for farmers.

In water, investment for rehabilitation and modernization, combined with volume-based pricing and institutional changes would provide the basis for efficient water use, cost recovery, and improved service delivery in canal irrigation. Rehabilitation and modernization of irrigation schemes would restore the reliability of water delivery without which farmers will be reluctant to pay higher water charges. It will also permit the introduction of volume-based pricing of water and improved water management practices as recommended by the 1992 Report of the Committee on Pricing of Irrigation Water. Institutional reforms, such

as the creation of Water Users' Associations, would provide the basis and necessary financial incentives for improved cost recovery as well as improved accountability in the delivery of water services to farmers. Tamil Nadu, AP, and Orissa recently initiated reforms that would lead to improved cost recovery, quality of service delivery to farmers, and systems turnover to water users. Karnataka, in its 1995 Agricultural Policy Resolution, proposed radically to transform institutional incentives in the irrigation sector, but has been slow in implementing reforms. In the case of urban water, where there is considerable private sector interest to invest, but only marginal efforts to develop the necessary policy and institutional framework, some reform-minded municipalities (Cochin, Tirippur, Devas) have nonetheless been successful at attracting private capital and expertise.

Box 2.3: State Power Reforms: A Beginning

At the state level, Orissa--which has led the reforms--has enacted an amendment to India's national electricity acts of 1910 and 1948: the Orissa Electricity Reform Act which became effective on April 1, 1996. Orissa subsequently established the ***Orissa Electricity Regulatory Commission***, India's first state-level regulatory commission in the power sector. The Commission announced its first tariff decision and issued its licenses to the transmission and distribution company (GRIDCO) in March 1997. The Commission's Tariff Order inter alia authorizes GRIDCO to adjust its tariffs effective from April 1, 1997. The Commission restructured residential and agricultural tariffs so as to contain cross-subsidization. *This Order is bound to influence similar tariff proceedings and orders of future regulatory commissions in other states in India..*

The Common Minimum National Action Plan for Power (Box 2.2), requires the Government to present to the Parliament in the course of 1997 a new bill (central act) to create inter alia the Central Electricity Regulatory Commission (CERC) and require the states to establish their own state electricity regulatory commissions (SERCs).

Without waiting for the new central act, a few states are preparing their power reform programs, including the creation of regulatory commissions along the lines of the Orissa Electricity Regulatory Commission. *Two states, Haryana, and Rajasthan*, have already submitted their reform legislations for central government clearance, ahead of formal submission to their respective State Assemblies.

At the center, under the proposed new central act, the new CERC would take some of the functions of the Central Electricity Regulatory Authority (CEA), in particular the setting of tariffs for central sector utilities (such as NTPC) and tariff issues currently handled by CEA (such as IPP tariff issues). The exact division of work between CERC and CEA remains to be worked out in detail. More importantly, unlike CEA today, CERC is expected to have the authority to notify the tariffs of central utilities, instead of MOP. This should help avoid, for example, the current long delays in setting tariffs for new NTPC and POWERGRID projects. The remaining CEA would become MOP's technical adviser..

At the state level, the impact of the proposed new central act is more difficult to foresee. If enacted, the new central act would facilitate state power reforms, by allowing reform-minded states to proceed with their reform legislation without central clearances. That state-center consultation and clearance process took some time in the case of the Orissa project, but may take much less in subsequent projects, particularly after the processing of some of the current cases (Haryana, Rajasthan and Uttar Pradesh) is completed. It is also possible, depending on the exact scope of the central law, that states might still have to seek central clearances on other aspects of their reform legislation. For example, the Orissa Electricity Reform Act goes beyond the currently expected scope of the central law. If another state wishes to enact a similar act, notwithstanding the possible enactment of the central act, it would still need further central clearances. Finally, some states might simply ignore the new act, just like most states today are ignoring some of the financial requirements of the Electricity (Supply) Act, 1948. Because of these considerations, it is of course possible, that the proposed central act in its final form will only enable and promote, but not require, the establishment of SERCs and related retail tariff adjustments.

Ahead of the proposed new central act, the Government promulgated an Ordinance in January 1997 to: (a) facilitate the establishment of transmission licensees; and (b) open power transmission to private investment. The Parliament did not immediately convert the Ordinance into an act as had been proposed by the Government and the Ordinance has therefore lapsed. However, it is expected that the matter be considered by the Parliament again in the forthcoming session. If approved, this new act would enable the implementation of private sector transmission projects.

Reforming the Public Work Departments (PWDs) will remove a major impediment to efficient *road* construction. To overcome the capacity constraints of PWDs, private professional engineering firms need to be contracted to investigate and design large costly sections of road suitable for construction by machine-intensive methods alone. Downsizing and retraining of in-house PWD engineering staff will be required, especially those involved in the construction of main roads. This new approach would be consistent with a smaller but very important role for state PWDs as planner, administrator, and maintainer of roads. The private sector would investigate and design roads, supervise construction and maintenance, and supply material and equipment. Such a division of responsibilities is common to developed countries and is generally efficient. There have been several initiatives to develop toll roads with private sector involvement and this is a further reason for the PWDs to focus on strengthening their planning and regulatory capacity. These reforms are urgently needed because as much as inadequate resources for maintenance, the state of decay of India's roads is also the result of the PWDs' operational approach.

Indian ports face acute capacity shortages and low productivity levels, largely as a result of past constraining institutional framework with government controls over the Port Trusts, control over traffic, and lack of inter-port competition. During the past year, the Central Government has initiated several measures to improve the institutional framework and attract private investment to ports. Maritime state governments have also initiated similar reforms to develop their ports and relieve major ports. Some states have already identified projects worth US$1 billion to develop their medium ports. However, despite the attractiveness of such investments to the private sector, they will be considered a complement to, but not a full substitute for, investments by the states or individual Port Trusts.

India's *cities and towns* are facing a crisis of serious proportions stemming from chronic underinvestment in urban areas and consequent shortages of key urban services. At the heart of the problem are the cities' weak fiscal base--eroded by state legislation imposing rent controls, limits on the amount of land an individual can hold, restrictions on land markets, and unrealistically low water charges. In some of the main cities, revenues are excessively dependent on inefficient taxes which need to be eliminated--such as octroi. Thus, any program of urban reform would need to include measures to: (a) improve urban areas' use of the existing resource base (such as a better cost recovery and enforcement of existing taxes); (b) strengthen the resource base and make it more efficient (such as lifting rent controls in the major cities, eliminating octroi, establishing efficient land markets with an effective system of land titling); and (c) establish a rule-based, efficient system of capital grants to replace the present system. Such measures would provide the basis for the restoration of the finances of the country's cities and towns--and thus restore their capacity to invest in critically needed infrastructure. Over time, they would help municipalities become creditworthy borrowers, able to access capital markets and mobilize financing for critically needed investments. Albeit on a small scale, there are already several promising initiatives underway (such as the Tamil Nadu Urban Fund)

Box 2.4: The December 1996 Common Minimum National Action Plan for Power

The Central Government will set up an independent Central Electricity Regulatory Commission (CERC), which will *inter alia* set the bulk tariffs for all Central generating and transmission utilities. The Central Government would make a comprehensive review of the role of the Central Electricity Authority (CEA). Techno-economic approval of competitively bid power projects will be simplified and CEA shall not be concerned with capital cost, tariff and other commercial aspects of the project. However, CEA appraisal will continue for planning and other related matters. The Central Government will develop a national policy on hydro power development.

The role of the Foreign Investment Promotion Board will be minimized by putting as many projects on the automatic clearance route as feasible.

Each State/Union Territory shall set up an independent State Electricity Regulatory Commission (SERC). These SERCs will, initially, fix tariffs only with possible cross-subsidization between categories of consumers. No sector shall, however, pay less than 50 per cent of the average cost of supply (cost of generation, transmission and distribution). Tariffs for agricultural sector will not be less than paise 50/kWh, to be brought to 50 per cent of the average cost in not more than three years. States will have to provide for the financial implications of deviations from tariffs recommended by a SERC. To enable setting up of CERC and SERCs, the Central Government will amend Indian Electricity Act, 1910, and Electricity (Supply) Act, 1948 and amend accordingly the relevant Acts and Rules to allow private participation in transmission. State governments will allow maximum possible autonomy to the State Electricity Boards (SEBs) and agree to a gradual program of private sector participation in the distribution of electricity. Finally, States will encourage cogeneration/captive power plants. To facilitate the "wheeling" of power or through the grid, States shall formulate clear and transparent policies for purchase of power and "wheeling" charges which provide fair returns to the Cogeneration/Captive power plant owners.

which, by providing access to capital markets, have created incentives for municipalities to improve their financial management.

Restructuring states' public expenditures

The key challenge facing the states today is to improve cost recovery by eliminating explicit and implicit subsidies, and reduce unproductive expenditures. Drastic measures need to be taken to increase cost recovery for publicly supplied goods and services where there are no externalities or "merit" considerations involved. On the employment front, recruitment needs to be controlled in order to reduce the wage bill, especially in light of the likely implementation of the Fifth Pay Commission recommendations. Welfare programs need to be consolidated into a limited number of well-defined and targeted schemes. States may also need to resist implementing centrally-sponsored schemes--which they view as additional source of revenue--without examining their financial implications and their relevance to state priorities. In order to limit the interest burden, a more careful selection of projects based on their rate of return needs to be established. Public enterprises need to be subjected to a hard budget constraint by discontinuing the practice of converting debt to equity. Privatization of enterprises engaged in activities that could be provided more efficiently by the private sector, could provide considerable efficiency and fiscal gains.

Such measures would enable the states to mobilize resources for critical spending on rural infrastructure and human resources thus arresting recent declines. State subsidies account for 7 percent of GDP, almost twice India's total spending on health and education. Expenditures on health and education are not only a small share of total state GDP but this share has been declining (Figure 2.2). There is room to enhance efficiency of service delivery, cost effectiveness, and allocations of expenditure. But spending needs to increase as well. To achieve universal enrollment and higher quality education by 2007, for instance, states such as Andhra Pradesh, Uttar Pradesh, Bihar, Rajasthan, Madhya Pradesh, and West Bengal would have to increase their real outlays for primary education at a rate of 13 percent per year (World Bank,

---

Box 2.5: Haryana Sees the Benefits of Reform

Over the last 5 years, the total net transfers from the state to HSEB was conservatively estimated at Rs. 20.5 billion (US$680 million), equivalent to the cost of constructing a 500-MW plant. Also, it was estimated that if Haryana were to reform its power sector, the net present value of the economic benefits of the reform would amount to some Rs. 72 billion (about US$2 billion).

Since then, Haryana has decided to restructure and substantially privatize its power sector. The government's ultimate objective is to withdraw from the power sector as an operator and regulator of utilities and to have competing, commercially operated utilities functioning in an appropriately-regulated power market. Haryana's power sector reform program involves: (i) the unbundling and structural separation of generation, transmission, and distribution into separate services to be provided by separate companies; (ii) the incorporation of the new companies under the Companies Act; (iii) privatization of the entire distribution system; (iv) private sector participation in generation and transmission utilities; (v) competitive bidding for new generation; (vi) the development of an autonomous power sector regulatory agency; (vii) supply and end-use efficiency improvements and enhanced environmental protection; and (viii) reforming of electricity tariffs at the bulk power, transmission, and retail levels. The Haryana Electricity Reform Act, which the Government expects to propose to the next session of the State Assembly (July-August 1997), will provide the legal basis for the implementation of these reforms.

The World Bank is assisting Haryana in preparing this reform program and has started to process an operation to finance part of the large investment program that Haryana will need to implement to rehabilitate and expand its transmission and distribution systems. Such financial support will be in the order of US$350-400 million. Other bilateral institutions are also expected to contribute.

1997). A similar dilemma confronts the states with the lowest levels of health care and--to varying degrees-- all of India, where per capita government spending of US$2-3 a year is too low to meet the 50-year-old promise of insuring universal access to care in Primary Health Centers (for preventive and basic services). Increasing public expenditures for health by roughly half needs to be kept as a goal, but in the fiscally straitened circumstances of many states, it may be more realistic in the short term to aim for a phased reorientation of outlays so that three fourths of them go to the primary and secondary sectors with priority given to the provision of medicines and essential supplies.

Strengthening resource mobilization

On the revenue front, besides increased cost recovery, reforms need to focus on improving the efficiency of taxation, and ensuring tax harmonization across states. Major states need to take the lead in ensuring that states collectively adhere to the recommendations of the December 1995 Committee of State Finance Ministers to eliminate industrial incentives and harmonize their sales tax policies. The acceleration of states' sales tax reform could help the establishment of a VAT. The tax base could be broadened further by taxing agricultural income which the states--to whom the constitution delegates this taxation--chose not to tax.

Improving the design of inter-governmental transfers

Recognizing negative incentive effects implicit in its transfer mechanism, the Tenth Finance Commission (TFC) has recommended a number of innovative and bold measures to enhance states' fiscal discipline. In particular, the TFC's recommendation (which the central government has accepted but which requires a constitutional amendment for its implementation) to shift the base for revenue sharing from a high share of two taxes (personal income tax and excises) to a lower share of total tax revenue (the proposed ratio is 71:29 between the center and the states), would provide states with a stable source of revenue while improving incentives for enhanced tax collection by the center. The TFC's second recommendation that central debt forgiveness be tied to states' own initiatives to retire their debt also would strengthen fiscal discipline at the state level. Finally, the phasing out by the year 2000 of grants to states on the basis of the gapfill approach would remove incentives for states to run current account deficits and encourage fiscal correction. However, less progress has been made regarding the financing of state plans. Efforts are needed to ensure that borrowed resources are utilized only for such investment expenditures that yield a return adequate to meet the cost of borrowing, which should reflect a state's creditworthiness. The latter would provide strong incentives to improve their fiscal management.

Chapter 3 | *SUSTAINING RAPID GROWTH*

India's overarching development objective during its Ninth Plan period (1997-02) is "accelerated growth with equity", that is achieving and sustaining 7-8 percent annual rates of growth, compared to about 5 percent during the 1980s, and about 6 percent during the Eighth Plan period (1992-97), and ensuring that this growth benefits the poor. A broad consensus has emerged across India's political spectrum for this objective and for continuing the liberalization of the economy. At what speed this will be done remains however an unresolved--yet critical--issue because it will determine the country's growth performance.

Policy Priorities

The rapid growth of the last few years has shown how much India stands to gain from *deregulation* and *fiscal adjustment*. It has also shown that the economy is facing capacity constraints, most notably in *infrastructure*. High *interest rates* are an indication of stress on domestic resources which has been at the origin of pressures put on the authorities to accelerate, perhaps prematurely, the opening of the capital account--a development that in all circumstances would need to be carefully synchronized with India's progress in reducing fiscal imbalances, in restoring the health of its banking system, in opening its trade account, and in diversifying its exports. Resources are also being strained in *agriculture*. Over the last few decades, India's agriculture has grown dependent on extremely large subsidies (on power, water, fertilizer, to name just the main ones) which may initially have contributed to the spread of technological advances, but which now put an unsustainably large burden on central and state government budgets, and also are at the origin of microeconomic distortions and misuse of resources (of which overexploitation of groundwater resources and poor energy conservation practices are

two important examples) which reduce productivity growth. These and other priority areas for reform are discussed below.

The centrality of fiscal adjustment. As in the past several years, reducing India's consolidated public sector deficit remains of central importance for the achievement of the country's development goals. While gains have been made in reducing the central government deficit, those have been offset by the large cost (0.8 percent of GDP in 1996-97) of subsidizing oil products. As a result, the consolidated public sector deficit has remained at the relatively high level of 9 percent of GDP for the past few years. Yet, it is only with a more rapid and more significant decline in fiscal imbalances that the high real interest rates that have prevailed in the recent past will decline. A target of 4 percent of GDP for the consolidated central and state governments deficit (from 6.8 percent of GDP at present) may be a realistic goal to achieve in the next 3-4 years while privatization of public enterprises would enable the government to retire public debt and reduce interest costs. The benefits of a more rapid correction of fiscal imbalances go well beyond just lower interest rates and higher investment. Lower fiscal deficits and interest rates would provide the favorable conditions for an acceleration of banking reform, would help improve the health of the financial system, would provide more flexibility to the RBI in the conduct of monetary policy, would reduce pressure for opening the capital account ahead of the structural reforms needed to make it a success, and would make it easier to manage the balance of payments, surges in capital inflows, and possible external shocks. International experience shows that a strong fiscal position has a central role in managing effectively the capital and current accounts of the balance of payments.

Also, as highlighted in the May 1997 government paper on subsidies, central and state government deficits are linked to significant microeconomic distortions whose cost they bear. Again in this case, the benefits of fiscal corrections go beyond improvements in the macroeconomic framework--because they are tantamount to correcting severe price distortions and misguided sector policies which are hampering development. Power is one well known case where the correction of price distortions would not only reduce state governments fiscal imbalances (by close to 2 percent of GDP), but would also lead to a more efficient use of resources, and provide the basis for private capital in power and the much needed capacity expansion. Similarly, correction of oil price distortions through elimination of administrative controls would not only reduce the consolidated public sector deficit but also reduce the overuse of subsidized fuels such as diesel and kerosene, and eliminate an important deterrent to private sector entry in oil exploration and refining. The deregulation of oil prices may need to be accompanied with some temporary explicit budget subsidy to cushion the impact of price increases on low-income groups, but it would enable the government to make explicit the cost of current oil price policies, and remove uncertainties related to the policy regime. Similar situations exist in a number of other sectors such as irrigation and urban water supply where the fiscal cost is just a fraction of the costs that distortions put on the economy--by encouraging the misuse of resources and deterring private investment.

In addition to the macro-and micro-economic dimensions of fiscal adjustment, a third, and at least as important one, is that of expenditure composition, particularly at the level of the states. In most states, unproductive expenditure to finance the cost of subsidies, an excessively large labor force, and government activities which are not of a development nature, all absorb a large share of state governments budgets. To a large extent, the deterioration of India's infrastructure, and the difficulties the country is experiencing to mobilize resources to accelerate the development of its human resources are the result of states' pricing and sectoral policies and the associated implied subsidies--and it is also with the states that lies their resolution. Recent declines in central government

financial support to the states have provided some--but as yet insufficient--impetus to the states to start taking corrective actions.

Addressing the challenge of infrastructure. Much has been said and written on India's extraordinarily large infrastructure problems. The recently completed report of an Expert Group on infrastructure provides a sobering review of India's tremendous infrastructure problems and makes three recommendations to address them. The *first* is *fiscal reforms* to strengthen state and local governments capacity to mobilize resources to invest in infrastructure. This is particularly important for infrastructure of a public nature where benefits are best captured through taxation. The *second* is *regulatory and pricing reforms* to translate India's immense infrastructure needs into viable commercial ventures, capable of attracting private capital. The *third* is *financial sector reforms* to enable the large pool of India's financial savings to flow to high returns infrastructure investments.

Progress has been achieved at the level of the central government in the recent past on issues related to *fiscal and regulatory reform.* At the level of the states, however, while there have been initiatives of reform in some of the most progressive states, these have not been commensurate with the severity of the situation and circumscribed to a few states. In the *financial sector,* the last four years have seen a transformation of the banking system and capital markets. Yet, a large segment of the financial system-- insurance companies and pension funds--remains under government ownership and control. Unless the financial resources mobilized by contractual saving institutions are made available to the entire economy, India will not be able to develop long-term debt markets on the scale needed to contribute to the financing of India's large infrastructure needs. It would be important to deregulate the sector, end the state monopoly on insurance, and open insurance to private sector capital and expertise as has been recommended by the 1995 government appointed Malhotra Committee.

Banking reforms. It is also becoming evident that the public banks need more operational autonomy-- within a strengthened RBI supervisory framework--and a change in the incentives framework to respond to the growing competition from new private banks and NBFCs. Further banking and financial deregulation (reducing government equity in the capital of public banks and further reductions in the SLR) would reduce the influence of government on commercial banks' basic business decisions (such as on hiring, on pay scales, branch expansion or closure). It would also eliminate the current restrictions to entry and thus permit more vigorous competition from private banks. The RBI is gradually strengthening its oversight capabilities, and this provides the basis for a further deregulation of the banking system. At the same time, to ensure adequate provision of credit to agriculture, it would be essential to bring rural credit reform to its logical conclusion. A coherent strategy for increasing flows to agriculture and other rural economic activities must address issues of access to financial services by the rural population in general, as well as the financial sustainability of the rural financial institutions themselves. Further measures are needed to encourage and facilitate an orderly re-orientation of India's rural financial system from the supply-led approach of concessional, targeted agriculture credit, to the systematic development of demand-oriented rural financial markets.

Deregulating agriculture. Deregulation would enable agriculture to achieve potentially large efficiency gains (estimated at several percentage points of GDP) and provide a basis for the removal of subsidies. The 1997-98 Budget contains the first steps of a promising beginning of reforms at the level of the central government, which could provide impetus--although it has not thus far--for similar reforms at the level of the states. Deregulation of agro-industry is also crucial. Important segments of the agro-industrial sector are still regulated by industrial licenses or scale limitations which impose large costs on an industry characterized by economies of scale. Similarly, the development of the storage industry has been hampered by a complex system of controls--which may be responsible for the significant losses of grain production every year because of the poor quality and high cost of storage. Because the incomes of the poor are so closely associated to the fortunes of the agricultural sector, a liberalization of agriculture would

not only have positive growth effects, it would also help increase the incomes of the poor.

Completing the liberalization of the trade and investment regimes remains an important policy objective. Since reforms started in 1991, India's import-weighted tariff has been reduced from 87 percent to around 20 percent at present. The 1997-98 budget indicates that the process will continue, until India reaches the tariff levels of its East Asian neighbors--that is around 10-15 percent at present. There are also indications that the government intends to eliminate restrictions on consumer goods in a phased manner. Implementation of this agenda would improve considerably the competitiveness of India's manufacturing, as would a further deregulation of the investment regime. The radical liberalization of the last six years notwithstanding, important regulations continue to restrict investment in small scale industries and agro-industries. There is ample evidence, including the recent Abid Hussain Report and other studies in India and elsewhere to show that small scale industries benefit more from adequate access to infrastructure, finance, and imported inputs, than protection from competition. The economic costs of size limitation in agro-industry and manufacturing are significant, particularly because these industries are usually export-oriented and labor-intensive. While some liberalization measures were taken recently, the remaining constraints are severe. As trade liberalization proceeds, small industry domestic producers will be at a disadvantage compared with foreign competitors whose costs bear the gains of large-scale productions systems.

Managing the capital account. Historically, India had a highly restrictive capital account regime. Foreign direct investment (FDI) was strictly limited; external commercial borrowing was tightly controlled; and capital outflows were prohibited. Substantial inflows from non-resident Indians (NRIs) were, however, channeled through the banking system. After 1991, the FDI regime was substantially liberalized. FIIs were allowed to purchase equity directly in India (also debt since last year), while Indian corporates were allowed to issue GDRs abroad. Since then, restrictions on access and use of GDR funds have been further relaxed while the range of FII investments in capital markets has been broaden (Figure 3.1). Other types of capital flows have remained controlled but conditions have been gradually relaxed. Short-term capital flows are generally limited to trade-related flows or inflows from NRIs, although small size borrowing up to three years is now permitted subject to RBI approval. Foreign holdings of Treasury bills remain prohibited, but holdings of longer-term government securities are permitted. The capital account is now sufficiently open to induce significant response of capital movements to the macroeconomic situation. The pace of NRI inflows, FII investments, GDR issues, and the leads and lags in trade finance are all sensitive to expectations on exchange rate and interest rate movements. However, the authorities still have scope, which they have used effectively in the past, to encourage or discourage capital inflows while arbitrage between domestic and international markets remains imperfect in the presence of remaining restrictions. Following a procedure established at the time of the Stand-By with the IMF in 1991-92, an indicative ceiling for commercial borrowing is set annually (US$3.5 billion during the Stand-By, raised to US$7.5 million in 1996-97 and US$8 billion in 1997-98) and discretionary authority is used to orient borrowing to priority areas such as infrastructure, and to limit short term borrowing.

While full capital account liberalization remains a desirable longer-term goal, a cautious approach remains appropriate until fiscal consolidation has been achieved, the instruments and markets for indirect monetary control are more fully developed, the commercial banking system is strengthened, trade liberalization is complete and exports sufficiently diversified. Otherwise, there would be a danger of

prompting volatile financial conditions and sharp cross-border surges in short-term funds that would be difficult to manage and could put serious stress on the domestic banking system. Consistent with this objective, the pace of liberalization of restrictions on debt-related capital and short-term capital would need to be gradual, tailored to the pace of fiscal consolidation, progress in strengthening the domestic financial system, and export performance.

External Prospects and Financing

Overview. India's stabilization and reform program has been implemented in the midst of favorable external circumstances. International real interest rates have been relatively low, terms of trade stable, and India's export markets grew at relatively high rates. External conditions are expected to remain favorable in the foreseeable future (Annex, Table 16). The export growth rate is expected to stabilize at around 11 percent a year on average over the period 1997-2006 (Annex, Table 17) mostly on account of the phased increase in the growth rates of quotas under the Agreement on Textiles and Clothing, before their elimination in 2005. (See the 1996 CEM for a comprehensive discussion of India's export prospects by commodity group and Annex, Table 18). Obviously, reaching this export growth would require addressing the problems of export finance and poor infrastructure, roads and port handling in particular.

Under the expected favorable external conditions, a satisfactory resolution of the policy issues discussed above would create the basis for India to sustain, and possibly exceed, its recent growth performance and the Ninth Plan growth targets. It is difficult to anticipate, however, whether the necessary reforms will be implemented at a sufficiently rapid pace. Contrary to the initial phase of reform when initiatives by a few ministries (Finance, Commerce and Industry) and the RBI were sufficient to transform India's policy regime, the reforms that are necessary in this phase require determined action by a much wider range of central ministries (of which Telecommunication, Power, Petroleum, Surface Transport, Agriculture, Food Supplies are a few examples) and the states--with whom lie the initiative for the most critical reforms.

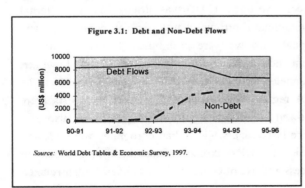

Figure 3.1: Debt and Non-Debt Flows

Source: World Debt Tables & Economic Survey, 1997.

Therefore, underlying the projections in Table 9 (Annex) is the assumption that the reforms will be implemented at a somehow slower pace than what would be required to sustain growth in the 7-9 percent range, and that growth will be in the 6-6.5 percent range. In this scenario, the current account deficit is projected to remain at a comfortable level, below 2 percent of GDP, during the forecast period. India's external debt of US$94 billion would decline as a share of GDP from the present 27 percent to 22 percent by the end of the decade, and 17 percent by the year 2006. As a share of current account receipts, the debt service ratio is expected to decline from around 24 percent in 1996-97 to 13 percent by the end of the decade and 11 percent by 2006. At the same time, profits and other remittances flows on account of non-debt capital inflows would increase.

Private and official capital flows. In 1996, private net capital flows to all developing countries grew by 32 percent reaching a record level of US$244 billion. A broader range of investors and lenders participated in the private financing of developing countries needs; maturities shortened and yield premia narrowed for most developing countries. The long-term outlook for sustained net inflows of private capital to developing countries remains favorable. Such factors as moderate world real interest rates, continued liberalization in developing countries (which will continue to reduce the perceived risk and raise the expected rate of return from investing in emerging markets), portfolio diversification in industrial countries are likely to support further significant growth in private flows over the coming decade and India stands to attract a significant share of these private flows with the shift to private financing especially of infrastructure investment. As the new investor base of institutional investors and pension funds expands, more of the private capital flows are likely to take the form of portfolio--especially equity-flows. While the large inflows of portfolio capital to India has been part of the broader flow to emerging markets in the first half of the 1990s in general, there are clearly country-specific factors at play. These include the existence of well-known corporate names with established track records in India; rule-based and reasonably well developed stock markets; familiar accounting and legal systems;

and the potential for growth in a large domestic market.

India will continue to need to rely on official development assistance, notwithstanding the growing role of private inflows. Besides India's low level of per capita GDP (US$350), official development assistance is also critically necessary for India to meet its enormous needs for infrastructure and human resource development. As indicated in the ***Poverty Assessment Report***, distributed to members of India Development Forum (IDF), India's poverty remains widespread and the lives of many of India's more than 300 million poor are burdened by poor health, illiteracy, and social inequalities. Prospects for improving their standards of living depend on India's ability to promote growth and invest in human resources development. While the private sector shows strong interest in investing in a number of infrastructure areas, particularly power and telecommunications, an important role remains for public sector investment in some key areas--such as roads, rural infrastructure and social services--which would need to be substantially increased. Such investments are crucial for sustaining rapid growth and ensuring that the poor participate in the growth process. The Bank therefore recommends that the members of the IDF should aim for official development assistance that directly supports priority public investments in physical infrastructure and human capital development. This investment would also help crowd-in the necessary complementary private investment particularly in physical infrastructure. In addition to the financial flows, official development assistance is also crucial to build institutional capacity particularly at the level of the state and local governments. Therefore, as had last year's CEM, this report makes a case for India's continued access to long-term assistance, including a substantial concessional component. In view of its still current high debt burden, India would need to continue to prudently manage its external debt. With an expected modest current account deficit of 2 percent of GDP over the next few years and the necessary build-up of reserves, India would still require total gross financing of close to US$14 billion in 1997-98, and an average of about US$17 billion in each of the following four years. Bilateral and multilateral participants at last year's India Development Forum pledged about US$6.7 billion in official assistance to India's development efforts as a recognition of India's strong commitment to reform and need to accelerate growth and reduce poverty and a similar amount is expected for this year. Debt and non-debt commercial sources are expected to account for the country's remaining financing needs.

ANNEX

Table 1: Growth performance, 1981-97
(percentage)

	1981-90	1990-91	1991-92	1992-93	1993-94	1994-95	1995-96[a]	1996-97[b]
GDP at Factor Cost	5.5	5.4	0.8	5.3	6.0	7.2	7.1	6.8
Agriculture	3.4	3.8	-2.3	6.1	3.6	4.6	-0.1	3.7
Industry	6.9	7.2	-1.3	4.2	6.8	9.4	11.6	8.7
Mining & Quarrying	7.4	10.7	3.7	1.1	2.0	8.1	7.0	1.7
Manufacturing	7.2	6.1	-3.7	4.2	8.5	10.2	13.6	10.6
Electricity, Gas, & Water	8.9	6.5	9.6	8.4	7.1	8.6	9.1	4.2
Construction	4.4	11.6	2.2	3.4	1.3	6.9	5.3	4.6
Services	6.6	5.2	4.9	5.5	7.3	7.5	8.8	7.4

a. Quick estimates.

b. Advance estimates.

Source: CSO, National Accounts Statistics, 1996; Quick and Advance Estimates.

Table 2: Index of industrial production, 1981-97
(annual percent increase)

	Weight	1981-91	1990-91	1991-92	1992-93	1993-94	1994-95	1995-96	1996-97
Overall Index	100.0	7.8	8.2	0.6	2.3	6.0	9.4	11.7	6.7
Basic Goods	39.4	7.5	3.8	6.2	2.6	9.4	5.5	8.7	7.0
Capital Goods	16.4	11.5	17.4	-12.8	-0.1	-4.1	24.8	17.8	8.5
Intermediates	20.5	6.2	6.1	-0.7	5.3	11.7	3.7	10.2	7.1
Consumer Goods	23.6	6.7	10.4	-1.8	1.9	4.0	8.7	12.5	3.9
Durables	2.6	13.0	14.8	-12.5	-0.7	16.1	10.2	37.1	4.3
Non-Durables	21.0	5.7	9.4	1.2	2.5	1.3	8.4	6.4	3.8

Source: CSO and Economic Survey, 1997.

Table 3: Domestic demand, 1981-96
(percent of GDP at market prices)

	1981-91		1990-91		1991-92		1992-93		1993-94		1994-95		1995-96	
Total Consumption Expenditure	78.3	(4.8)	73.6	(3.7)	73.7	(1.4)	72.9	(3.9)	72.7	(4.5)	70.3	(4.0)	69.3	(5.9)
Government final consumption	11.1	(7.2)	11.5	(3.3)	11.3	(-0.5)	11.1	(3.3)	11.1	(6.1)	10.5	(1.8)	10.6	(5.1)
Private final consumption	67.2	(4.5)	62.1	(3.8)	62.4	(1.8)	61.7	(4.0)	61.6	(4.2)	59.7	(4.4)	58.7	(6.0)
Gross Capital Formation	23.2	(5.9)	25.2	(12.2)	22.7	(-11.0)	24.0	(12.3)	21.3	(-5.8)	24.0	(19.8)	26.2	(17.9)
Gross Fixed Capital Formation	21.1	(6.8)	23.2	(9.9)	22.1	(-4.0)	22.5	(6.9)	21.5	(3.4)	22.4	(14.8)	24.6	(18.3)
Household Sector	7.2	(9.3)	9.9	(9.1)	6.9	(-35.2)	8.0	(26.5)	6.2	(-23.8)	6.9	(28.3)	9.7	(64.3)
Change in Stocks	2.1		2.1		0.6		1.5		-0.2		1.6		1.6	
Domestic Demand	101.5	(5.1)	98.8	(5.7)	96.4	(-1.5)	96.9	(5.7)	94.2	(2.1)	94.3	(7.5)	95.6	(8.8)
Memo Items:														
Gross Domestic Savings	20.5		23.6		22.8		21.2		23.1		24.9		25.6	
Public Savings	2.7		1.0		1.9		1.5		0.5		1.8		1.9	
Household Financial	7.6		8.7		10.1		8.4		10.8		11.5		8.8	
Private Corporate Sector	2.1		2.8		3.2		2.8		3.5		3.9		4.1	

Note: Real growth rate in parentheses.

a. Average of 1981-82 through 1991-92.

Source: Central Statistical Organization, National Accounts Statistics 1996 and Quick Estimates 1997.

Table 4: Central government finances, 1990-98
(percent of GDP)

	90-91	91-92	92-93	93-94	94-95	95-96	96-97 BE	96-97 RE	97-98 BE
A. Revenue	10.3	10.7	10.5	9.3	9.6	10.0	10.5	10.4	10.5
Tax revenue	8.0	8.1	7.7	6.6	7.1	7.5	7.8	7.7	7.8
Corporation tax	1.0	1.3	1.3	1.2	1.4	1.5	1.6	1.5	1.5
Income tax	1.0	1.1	1.1	1.1	1.3	1.4	1.4	1.5	1.5
Excise duties	4.6	4.6	4.4	3.9	3.9	3.7	3.8	3.7	3.6
Customs	3.9	3.6	3.4	2.7	2.8	3.3	3.6	3.5	3.6
Other	0.3	0.4	0.5	0.3	0.2	0.3	0.3	0.3	0.4
Less: States' share	2.7	2.8	2.9	2.8	2.6	2.7	2.8	2.8	2.8
Non-tax Revenue	2.2	2.6	2.8	2.7	2.5	2.6	2.7	2.7	2.7
(Interest receipts)	1.6	1.8	1.8	1.9	1.7	1.7	1.7	1.7	1.7
B. Revenue expenditure[a]	13.7	13.3	13.1	13.4	12.8	12.7	13.0	12.6	12.6
Interest payments	4.0	4.3	4.4	4.5	4.6	4.6	4.8	4.6	4.7
Subsidies	2.3	2.0	1.7	1.6	1.4	1.2	1.3	1.3	1.3
Food	0.5	0.5	0.4	0.7	0.5	0.5	0.5	0.5	0.5
Fertilizer	0.8	0.8	0.9	0.6	0.6	0.6	0.7	0.6	0.6
Others	1.0	0.7	0.4	0.3	0.2	0.1	0.2	0.2	0.1
Defense	2.0	1.9	1.7	1.9	1.7	1.7	1.5	1.7	1.8
Grants to states	2.5	2.5	2.5	2.6	2.1	1.9	1.9	1.9	1.6
Wages and salaries[b]	0.7	0.7	0.7	0.6	0.6	0.6	0.9	0.6	0.8
Other	2.2	2.0	2.1	2.1	2.4	2.7	2.6	2.5	2.4
C. Capital expenditure	2.3	1.9	1.9	1.6	1.6	1.2	1.1	1.1	1.2
Defense	0.9	0.8	0.8	0.8	0.7	0.7	0.6	0.7	0.6
D. Gross Loans	3.7	2.9	2.4	2.5	2.5	2.3	2.3	2.4	2.2
to states and UTs	2.5	2.0	1.7	1.7	2.0	2.3	1.9	1.9	1.8
to PEs[c]	0.7	0.6	0.4	0.6	0.5	0.4	0.4	0.3	0.3
Others	0.5	0.3	0.2	0.2	0.0	0.1	0.1	0.1	0.1
E. Recovery of loans	1.1	1.0	0.9	0.8	0.7	0.6	0.6	0.6	0.6
F. Net lending (D-E)	2.6	1.9	1.4	1.8	1.8	1.7	1.8	1.7	1.6
G. Disinvestment in Pes	0.0	0.5	0.3	0.0	0.6	0.1	0.4	0.0	0.3
Fiscal Deficit (A-B-C-F+G)	8.3	5.9	5.7	7.4	6.1	5.5	5.0	5.0	4.5
Financed by:									
Reserve Bank of India (net)	3.1	1.0	0.5	0.2	0.2	1.8	0.5	n.a	1.1
Marketable Securities (net)	0.9	1.9	2.3	3.6	1.2	1.3	n.a	n.a	n.a
Other Domestic Borrowing (net)	3.8	2.2	2.1	3.0	4.1	2.2	n.a	n.a	n.a
External Borrowing (net)	0.6	0.9	0.8	0.6	0.5	0.2	0.2	0.2	0.2
Memo Items:									
Total Expenditure (B+C+D)	19.7	18.1	17.3	17.5	16.9	16.2	16.4	16.0	16.0
Total Expenditure (B+C+F)	18.6	17.1	16.5	16.8	16.2	15.6	15.9	15.4	15.4
Total Revenue (A+G)	10.3	11.2	10.8	9.3	10.1	10.2	10.9	10.4	10.9
Central Transfers to states[d]	5.0	4.5	4.2	4.4	4.1	3.7	3.7	3.8	3.4
Primary Deficit[e]	4.3	1.6	1.3	2.9	1.4	0.9	0.2	0.4	-0.2
Non-interest spending[f]	15.6	13.8	12.9	13.0	12.2	11.7	11.6	11.4	11.3

Note: BE= budget estimates; RE=revised estimates.

a. Revenue expenditure is the budget terminology for current expenditure.

b. Excludes wages and salaries of defense personnel (armed troops).

c. Revised Estimates unless otherwise mentioned.

d. Includes grants from centre and gross loans from centre.

e. Fiscal deficit minus interest payments.

f. B+C+D-interest.

Source: Government of India, Budget documents.

Table 5: Selected monetary indicators, 1990-97

(Rupees billion)

Money Aggregate	1991-92		1992-93		1993-94		1994-95		1995-96		1996-97p	
Sources of Reserve Money	995	*(100)*	1108	*(100)*	1387	*(100)*	1693	*(100)*	1945	*(100)*	2000	*(100)*
Net RBI credit to Government	940	*(44)*	984	*(39)*	993	*(3)*	1015	*(7)*	1213	*(79)*	1235	*(38)*
Net foreign exchange assets (RBI)	188	*(93)*	226	*(34)*	514	*(103)*	747	*(76)*	741	*(-2)*	949	*(377)*
Other assets (net)	-133	*(-37)*	-103	*(27)*	-121	*(-6)*	-69	*(17)*	-10	*(24)*	-184	*(-315)*
Sources of Broad Money	3170	*(100)*	3668	*(100)*	4344	*(100)*	5314	*(100)*	6040	*(100)*	6980	*(100)*
Net bank credit to Government	1583	*(35)*	1762	*(36)*	2039	*(41)*	2224	*(19)*	2574	*(58)*	2845	*(22)*
Credit to commercial sector	1880	*(32)*	2201	*(65)*	2378	*(26)*	2897	*(54)*	3409	*(70)*	3737	*(36)*
Net foreign exchange assets	212	*(21)*	244	*(6)*	526	*(42)*	759	*(24)*	772	*(-1)*	966	*(21)*
Other assets (net)	-504	*(12)*	-540	*(-7)*	-599	*(-9)*	-566	*(3)*	-715	*(-21)*	-568	*(16)*
Memo Items:												
M3/ Base Money		3.2		3.3		3.1		3.1		3.1		3.5
M3/ GDP		57.4		58.2		59.4		61.9		61.3		62.0
Growth rates												
Reserve money		13.4		11.3		25.2		22.1		14.9		2.8
M3		19.3		15.7		18.4		22.3		13.7		15.6
Nominal GDP (factor cost)		15.7		14.1		16.0		17.3		14.8		14.3

P: Provisional.

Note: The flow as a percentage of the change in base money or the change in broad money stock is in parentheses. Increases in foreign assets following a devaluation are offset by declines in other assets.

Source: RBI.

Table 6: Key interest rates, 1990-97

	Call Money Rate[a] (Mumbai)	Treasury Bills[b]		Prime Lending Rate[c]	Maximum[d] Deposit Rate	Certificates of Deposit[f]	Inflation[g]
		364-day	91-day				
1994-95							
June	6.7	10.0	8.8	15.0	10.0	7.5 - 12.0	11.8
September	15.3	9.4	9.1	15.0	10.0	7.5 - 12.0	8.9
December	9.7	9.8	10.3	14.0	10.0	8.0 - 12.0	11.2
March	13.7	11.9	12.0	15.0	11.0	10.0 - 15.0	10.6
1995-96							
June	14.4	12.6	12.6	15.5	12.0	11.0 - 14.5	9.2
September	12.1	12.9	12.7	15.5	12.0	10.0 - 14.8	8.9
December	16.8	13.0	13.0	16.5	12.0[d]	12.0 - 22.9	6.4
March	28.8	13.1	13.0	16.5	12.0[d]	12.0 - 23.0	5.1
1996-97							
June	10.9	13.0	12.4	16.5	12.0[d]	11.0 - 19.3	4.4
September	8.4	12.6	10.2	16.0	12.0[d]	9.0 - 15.3	6.7
December	8.1	10.3	8.2	15.5	11.0[e]	8.5 - 16.0	6.7
March	4.4	10.1	7.9	14.5	11.0[e]	7.0 - 15.8	7.6

Note: Unless otherwise specified, interest rates/yields are those prevailing at the end of the month.

a. Call money rate of major commercial banks, average for the month.

b. Implicit yield at cut-off price (for the last auction in the month). 364-day Treasury Bills were introduced in April 1992, and are sold through periodic auctions. No fresh 182-day Treasury Bills were issued after April 16, 1992. Since January 1993, 91-day Treasury Bills are being periodically auctioned. Earlier they were sold on tap at 4.6 percent.

c. Since October 18, 1994, lending rates of scheduled commercial banks were freed for credit limits of over Rs. 200,000; at 13.5 percent per annum for credit limits over Rs 25,000 and upto Rs 200,000; and at 12 percent per annum for credit limits upto and inclusive of Rs 25,000. The rates shown from this period indicates Prime Lending Rate (Prime Lending Rate of the State Bank of India).

d. Refers to rate on term deposit. Up to April 1992 rates were fixed for different maturities. Since April 1992 only a maximum deposit rate is specified. Beginning October 1, 1995, the maximum rate of 12 percent refers only to deposits of less than two years. The rate was freed for deposits above two years.

e. Banks were given freedom to fix their own interest rates on domestic term depostits with a maturity of over one year effective July 1996. Accordingly interest rates on upto one year deposits was prescribed at not exceeding 11 percent per annum.

f. Effective interest rate (range) of CDs of all maturities, issued during the last fortnight of the month.

g. Wholesale price index, annual increase, point-to-point.

Source: RBI Monthly Bulletin, various issues; Report on Currency and Finance; Centre for Monitoring Indian Economy (CMIE), Monthly Review of the Indian Economy.

Table 7: Real exchange rate of India's main trading partners and competitors 1981-96

	Export Share	1981	1989	1990	1991	1992	1993	1994	1995	1996
India										
in US$		0.93	1.05	1.00	1.26	1.17	1.28	1.17	1.21	1.17
in SDR		0.76	0.98	1.00	1.27	1.13	1.24	1.20	1.28	1.18
REER a/		0.56	0.91	1.00	1.28	1.30	1.29	1.28	1.41	1.30[c]
India's Main Market										
USA	17.2	1.20	1.05	1.00	1.02	1.01	1.00	0.97	0.95	0.92
Japan	13.5	1.47	1.10	1.00	0.98	0.97	0.88	0.82	0.83	0.92
Germany	12.8	1.69	1.18	1.00	1.03	1.03	1.12	1.01	0.91	1.01
United Kingdom	10.8	1.56	1.29	1.00	1.02	1.16	1.16	1.07	1.04	0.95
Belgium b/	8.3	1.75	1.23	1.00	1.02	1.00	1.07	0.95	0.86	0.90
France b/	6.6	1.75	1.21	1.00	1.03	1.01	1.08	0.98	0.88	0.92
Italy	4.6	1.88	1.24	1.00	1.04	1.19	1.32	1.23	1.14	1.06
Netherlands	3.3	1.64	1.18	1.00	1.01	1.00	1.08	0.99	0.90	0.95
India's Main Competitors										
Indonesia		0.81	1.11	1.00	1.06	1.06	1.06	1.00	0.95	0.81
Malaysia b/		1.03	1.03	1.00	0.97	0.87	0.84	0.80	0.76	0.74
Philippines b/		0.99	0.93	1.00	0.84	0.74	0.75	0.61	0.59	0.57
Thailand		1.16	1.10	1.00	0.99	1.00	0.98	0.92	0.85	0.77[c]
Korea		1.12	1.01	1.00	1.04	1.06	1.07	1.01	0.95	1.00
Singapore		1.06	1.15	1.00	1.08	1.10	1.10	1.00	0.96	0.72
Hong Kong, China b/		1.39	1.11	1.00	0.91	0.82	0.76	0.69	0.64	0.60

Notes: 1. Increase = depreciation.

2. Data pertains to averages of December.

3. Index of country's nominal exchange rate vis-a-vis the US$ divided by this country's wholesale price index or, if not available, the consumer price index.

a. Real effective exchange rate, based on the IMF's information Notice System (INS) methodology. Trade Weights are based on trade flows overaged over 1990-92.

b. Uses CPI.

c. Data pertains to January 1997.

d. Data pertains to November 1996.

Source: IMF, International Financial Statistics; World Bank Staff Estimates.

Table 8: Foreign direct and portfolio investment
(US$ million)

	1990-91	1991-92	1992-93	1993-94	1994-95	1995-96	1996-97[p]
Direct Investment							
Foreign Direct Investment	165	150	341	620	1314	1929	2359
Portfolio Investment	0	8	92	3493	3581	2214	2775
Foreign Institutional Investment	0	0	1	1665	1503	2009	1855
Euro-issues/ GDR	0	0	86	1463	1839	149	900
Others [a]	0	8	5	365	239	56	20
Total Direct and Portfolio Investment	**165**	**158**	**433**	**4113**	**4895**	**4143**	**5134**
Memo items:							
Foreign Currency Convertible Bonds (FCCB) [b]	0	0	0	914	34	125	400
Floating Rate Notes (FRN)	0	0	0	0	167	n.a.	n.a.

n.a.: Not available.

P: Provisional.

a. Includes NRI portfolio investments, offshore funds, and others.

b. FCCBs is treated as commercial borrowing before conversion into equity.

Source: Reserve Bank of India; Ministry of Finance, Economic Survey, 1996-97.

Table 9: Balance of payments, 1991-97
(US$ billion)

| | Actuals | | | | | | ---Projected--- | | |
	90-91	91-92	92-93	93-94	94-95	95-96	96-97	97-98	98-99
Total exports of GNFS	23.0	23.3	23.6	27.9	32.8	40.2	43.9	49.5	55.7
Merchandise (FOB)	18.5	18.3	18.9	22.7	26.9	32.4	33.9	38.5	43.7
Non-factor services	4.6	5.0	4.7	5.3	5.9	7.7	10.1	11.0	12.0
Total imports of GNFS	31.5	24.9	26.8	29.8	38.2	48.8	53.1	60.3	67.3
Merchandise (CIF)	27.9	21.1	23.2	25.1	31.8	41.7	44.8	51.1	57.6
Non-factor services	3.6	3.8	3.6	4.7	6.3	7.1	8.3	9.2	9.8
Resource balance	-8.5	-1.6	-3.2	-1.9	-5.4	-8.6	-9.1	-10.8	-11.6
Net factor income	-3.8	-3.9	-3.7	-3.8	-3.6	-4.2	-4.4	-4.5	-5.0
Factor receipts	1.1	0.8	0.7	0.3	1.3	1.0	0.9	1.2	1.2
Factor payments	4.9	4.7	4.4	4.0	4.9	5.2	5.3	5.7	6.2
Interest (scheduled)[a]	4.8	4.6	4.1	4.2	4.3	4.6	4.1	4.0	3.9
of which interest payments on NRI	1.3	1.0	0.9	0.9	1.0	1.5	1.4	1.6	1.7
Other factor payments[b]	0.1	0.1	0.3	-0.2	0.6	0.6	1.2	1.7	2.3
Net private current transfers	2.1	3.8	2.8	3.8	6.2	7.0	9.8	10.0	10.1
Current receipts	2.1	3.8	2.8	3.6	6.2	7.0	9.8	10.0	10.2
of which workers remittances	1.9	3.4	2.5	3.1	5.0	5.3	7.8	8.0	8.1
Current payments	0.0	0.0	0.0	-0.2	0.0	0.0	0.0	0.0	0.0
Current account balance	-10.2	-1.7	-4.2	-1.8	-2.8	-5.8	-3.8	-5.3	-6.5
Official capital grants	0.5	0.5	0.4	0.4	0.5	0.4	0.4	0.3	0.3
Foreign investments	0.2	0.2	0.6	4.2	4.9	4.1	5.1	6.0	7.0
Direct foreign investments	0.2	0.2	0.3	0.6	1.3	1.9	2.4	3.0	3.5
Portfolio investments	0.0	0.0	0.2	3.6	3.6	2.2	2.8	3.0	3.5
Net long-term borrowing	3.9	4.3	3.9	4.2	2.0	-0.1	2.5	1.3	1.9
Disbursements (net of NRI)	5.1	6.9	5.1	7.1	6.0	5.7	6.6	6.1	7.1
Repayments (scheduled)[c]	2.7	2.9	3.3	4.0	4.8	6.8	7.8	5.8	5.7
Other long-term inflows (net)[c]	1.5	0.3	2.1	1.1	0.8	0.9	3.7	1.0	0.5
Other capital flows	1.3	-0.9	-3.0	0.4	1.5	-1.7	1.7	-0.9	-0.9
Net short-term capital	1.0	-1.5	-0.7	-2.7	0.6	-0.7	n.a.	n.a.	n.a.
Capital flows n.e.i.[d]	-1.2	-1.2	-0.9	-1.1	-1.1	-1.0	-0.8	-0.9	-0.9
Errors and omissions	0.5	0.5	0.4	0.4	0.5	-0.7	2.5	0.0	0.0
Changes in net international reserves[e]	2.8	-2.6	0.3	-8.5	-6.9	3.7	-5.9	-1.4	-1.9
IMF (net)	1.0	0.8	1.3	0.2	-1.2	-1.7	-1.0	-0.7	-0.4
Change in Gross Reserves	1.8	-3.4	-1.0	-8.7	-5.7	5.4	-4.9	-0.7	-1.4
Memo items:									
Current Account Balance / GDP	-3.4	-0.7	-1.7	-0.7	-0.9	-1.8	-1.1	-1.4	-1.6
Gross Foreign Exchange Reserves	2.3	5.7	6.7	15.5	21.2	17.4	22.4	23.1	24.5
in months of imports (goods)	1.0	3.3	3.5	7.4	8.0	5.0	6.0	5.4	5.1
External Debt (percent of GDP)	28.1	34.0	37.0	36.4	33.4	28.6	26.8	26.3	24.6
Debt Service (percent of total current receipts)	31.3	28.5	28.6	26.3	25.5	27.2	23.6	17.2	15.0

a. World Bank Debt Reporting System.

b. Includes interest on military debt to the FSU and returns on foreign investments.

c. Net flows in NRI deposit schemes, except the non-repatriable NR(NR)D Scheme.

d. Servicing of the Russia debt.

e. (-) = indicates increase in assets.

Source: Government of India; RBI; Ministry of Commerce; World Bank Staff estimates.

Table 10: Sectorwise import tariffs
(import weighted averages)

	1990/91	1992/93	1993/94	1994/95	1995/96	1996/97	1997/98
Whole Economy	87.0	64.0	47.0	33.0	25.2	22.4	20.3
Agricultural Products	81.1	50.4	42.3	16.7	10.0	11.1	10.3
Consumer Goods	152.8	130.7	86.3	47.8	36.1	33.2	25.0
Intermediate Goods	77.1	55.4	42.4	30.6	21.9	19.1	17.6
Capital Goods	97.1	74.4	49.7	37.4	29.1	29.3	24.0
Mining	60.3	34.2	34.3	30.2	29.9	23.6	23.3
Manufacturing	92.3	70.4	50.2	33.9	24.5	22.1	19.7

Source: World Bank Staff Estimates.

Table 11: Performance of the Indian public sector banks, 1995-96

	Net Profit Rs. billion	Return on Assets[a]	Equity on Assets[b]	Operating Expenses[c]	Deposits[d]	Inv. in Gov. Securities[e]	NPAs Ratio[f]
SBI Group	7.9	0.4	0.5	3.0	65.8	20.2	15.3
Nationalized Banks	-11.6	-0.3	3.9	2.8	77.8	21.2	18.2
Total Public Sector Banks	-3.7	-0.1	2.7	2.8	73.4	20.9	17.1
State Bank of India	8.3	0.6	0.3	3.0	64.1	20.3	16.0
Bank of India	2.8	0.8	1.6	2.5	77.2	17.6	14.5
Canara Bank	2.5	0.8	1.5	2.6	78.8	16.7	11.1
Bank of Baroda	2.0	0.5	1.5	2.3	75.5	16.4	16.2
Oriental Bank of Commerce	1.7	1.6	1.7	2.0	78.1	21.4	5.7
Corporation Bank	1.1	1.4	1.5	2.1	78.7	19.0	9.7
Union Bank of India	0.8	0.4	1.6	2.6	82.5	20.1	9.9
State Bank of Patiala	0.5	0.6	0.3	2.4	72.0	17.8	11.5
Dena Bank	0.5	0.6	1.7	2.9	74.7	23.1	13.4
State Bank of Hyderbad	0.5	0.6	0.2	2.9	71.8	19.3	15.6
State Bank of Bikaner & Jaipur	0.3	0.4	0.5	3.3	67.0	18.6	12.5
State Bank of Mysore	0.3	0.5	0.7	3.6	78.9	22.0	14.5
State Bank of Travancore	0.3	0.4	0.5	2.8	76.3	20.0	11.7
Syndicate Bank	0.2	0.1	7.9	3.3	78.3	27.4	21.0
Bank of Maharashtra	0.1	0.2	9.2	3.6	73.1	27.2	21.9
State Bank of Indore	0.1	0.4	0.5	3.3	71.9	21.1	14.2
Andhra Bank	0.1	0.1	5.7	3.1	80.4	25.4	11.6
Allahabad Bank	0.1	0.0	6.0	2.9	78.6	19.5	24.0
Indian Overseas Bank	0.0	0.0	7.1	2.6	77.4	23.6	20.4
Central Bank of India	-0.7	-0.3	5.4	3.3	81.5	23.4	20.9
Punjab National Bank	-1.0	-0.3	1.1	3.1	82.6	22.9	18.7
Punjab & Sind Bank	-1.3	-1.8	7.4	2.9	78.3	22.0	22.6
State Bank of Saurashtra	-2.3	-4.4	6.0	2.7	59.7	22.9	10.6
United Bank of India	-2.3	-2.1	12.4	2.9	79.6	32.1	38.0
UCO Bank	-2.4	-1.5	10.2	3.1	70.1	24.4	24.5
Vijaya Bank	-2.5	-3.4	3.4	3.2	80.0	28.7	20.4
Indian Bank	-13.4	-6.9	3.4	2.6	69.0	18.3	34.2

a. Net Profit over total assets.

b. Net Profit over capital.

c. Operating Expenses over total assets.

d. Deposits over total liabilities.

e. Investments in Government Securities over total assets.

f. Non-performing advances as percentage of total advances.

Source: Indian Banks' Association, Performance Highlights of Banks, 1995-96.

Table 12: Year-wise/PSU-wise details of shares disinvested since 1991-92

S.No.	Name of the PSE	Percent of Central Govt. Holding					
		1991	1992	1993	1994	1995	1996
1	Andrew Yule	71.3	62.8	62.8	62.8	62.8	62.8
2	Bharat Earthmovers Ltd.	100.0	80.0	80.0	80.0	60.1	60.1*
3	Bharat Electronics Ltd.	100.0	80.0	80.0	80.0	75.9	75.9
4	Bharat Heavy Electricals Ltd.	100.0	80.0	79.5	79.5	67.7	67.7
5	Bharat Petroleum Corpn. Ltd.	100.0	80.0	70.0	69.6	66.2	66.2
6	Bongaigaon Refineries & Petro. Ltd.	100.0	80.0	74.6	74.6	74.5	74.5
7	CMC Ltd.	100.0	83.3	83.3	83.3	83.3	83.3
8	Cochin Refineries Ltd.	61.2	55.0	55.0	55.0	55.1	55.0
9	Dredging Corpn. Ltd.	100.0	98.6	98.6	98.6	98.6	98.6
10	Fert. & Chem. (Travancore) Ltd.	100.0	97.5	97.4	97.4	97.4	97.4
11	HMT Ltd.	100.0	95.1	90.3	90.3	90.3	90.3
12	Hindustan Cables Ltd.	100.0	96.4	98.0	98.0	98.0	96.0
13	Hindustan Copper Ltd.	100.0	100.0	98.9	98.9	98.9	98.9
14	Hindustan Organic Chemicals Ltd.	100.0	80.0	80.0	80.0	56.9	56.9*
15	Hindustan Petroleum Corpn. Ltd.	100.0	80.0	70.0	69.7	60.3	51.0*
16	Hindustan Photofilms Mfg. Co. Ltd.	100.0	87.5	87.5	87.5	87.5	87.5
17	Hindustan Zinc Ltd.	100.0	80.0	75.9	75.9	75.9	75.1
18	Indian Petrochemicals Corpn. Ltd.	100.0	80.0	81.0	62.4	62.4	61.4
19	Indian Railway Const. Co.Ltd.	100.0	99.7	99.7	99.7	99.7	99.7
20	Indian Telephone Industries Ltd.	99.7	79.7	77.8	77.7	77.0	77.0
21	Madras Refineries Ltd.	84.6	67.7	67.7	51.8	51.8	51.8
22	Mahanagar Telephone Nigam Ltd.	100.0	80.0	80.0	80.0	67.2	65.7#
23	Minerals & Metals Trading Corpn.	100.0	99.3	99.3	99.3	99.3	99.3
24	National Aluminium Co. Ltd.	100.0	97.3	87.2	87.2	87.2	87.2
25	National Fertilizers Ltd.	100.0	97.7	97.7	97.7	97.7	97.7
26	National Minerals Dev. Corpn Ltd.	100.0	100.0	98.9	98.4	98.4	98.4
27	Neyveli Lignite Corporation	100.0	95.4	93.9	94.2	94.2	93.3
28	Reshtriya Chemicals & Fertilizers	100.0	94.4	92.5	92.5	92.5	92.5
29	Shipping corpn. of India	100.0	81.5	81.5	81.5	80.1	80.1
30	State Trading Corpn.	100.0	92.0	91.0	91.0	91.0	91.0
31	Steel Authority of India Ltd.	100.0	95.0	89.5	89.5	89.0	88.9#
32	Videsh Sanchar Nigam Ltd.	100.0	85.0	85.0	85.0	85.0	82.0
33	Container Corporation of India	100.0	100.0	100.0	100.0	80.0	76.9#
34	Indian Oil Corporation	99.9	99.9	99.9	99.9	96.1	91.0
35	Oil & Natural Gas Corporation	100.0	100.0	100.0	100.0	98.0	96.1
36	Engineers India Ltd.	100.0	100.0	100.0	100.0	94.0	94.0
37	Gas Authority of India Ltd.	100.0	100.0	100.0	100.0	96.6	96.6
38	Indian Tourism & Dev. Corp.	100.0	100.0	100.0	100.0	90.0	90.0
39	Kudermukh Iron & Ore Company Ltd.	100.0	100.0	100.0	100.0	99.0	99.0
40	Industrial Dev. Bank of India	100.0	100.0	100.0	100.0	100.0	72.1

figures are provisional, as the shares sold in Oct. 1995 are yet to be transferred in favour of successful Bidders.
* These companies had floated public issues. Percentage of Govt. holding after proposed public issue is not known.
Source: Economic Survey, 1997.

Table 13: Details of mobilisation in the primary market

	1994-95		1995-96		1996-97	
	No of Issues	Amount (Rs. bill)	No of Issues	Amount (Rs. bill.)	No of Issues	Amount (Rs. bill.)
Non-government Public Limited Companies	1678	264.2	1677	161.7	856	105.6
Government Companies (Equities +Bonds)	7	8.9	2	10.0	3	6.6
Public Sector undertakings (PSU bonds)	10	30.7	9	22.9	10	33.9
Banking/financial Institutions	2	4.3	6	34.7	6	43.5
Total	1697	308.0	1694	229.3	875	189.6
Memo Item						
Euro/FCCB Issues	31	67.4	5	13.0	16	55.9

Note: Date are provisional. In case of PSU Bonds the cumulative data are based on the details as and when made available to RBI by PSUs.
Source: RBI.

Table 14: Evolution of the public debt stock, 1990-96
(percent of GDP at end of period)

	91-92	92-93	93-94	94-95	95-96	96-97p
I. Domestic debt						
General Government[a]	58.0	57.8	60.1	57.6	62.0	59.9
Center [b]	51.1	50.7	52.9	50.5	54.7	52.6
States [c]	6.9	7.1	7.2	7.1	7.3	7.4
II. External debt [d]						
General Government	18.7	20.3	20.8	19.8	17.0	--
RBI (net) [e]	1.0	1.3	-1.4	-5.1	-4.5	-4.1
Non-financial Public Enterprises	5.5	5.7	5.7	5.0	4.1	--
III. Total debt (I + II)						
General Government	76.8	78.0	80.9	77.4	79.0	--
Center	69.8	71.0	73.7	70.3	71.7	--
States	6.9	7.1	7.2	7.1	7.3	--
Memo items:						
General government debt held by RBI (net)	15.6	14.1	12.5	10.7	11.3	9.8
Center	15.3	13.8	12.2	10.5	11.0	9.6
States	0.3	0.3	0.3	0.3	0.2	0.2

P. Projections.

--: Not available.

a. Includes debt held by RBI..

b. Excludes State's holding of Center debt.

c. Excluding States' debt to Center.

d. Based on World Bank Estimates evaluated at exchange rates prevailing in the relevant year.

e. RBI external debt minus foreign currency assets.

Source: RBI report on Currency and Finance; Budget Documents, and World Bank Debt Reporting System.

Table 15: Interest rates and payments on public debt
(percent per annum)

	1991-92	1992-93	1993-94	1994-95	1995-96	1996-97[a]
Central Government:						
1. Implicit Interest Rate on:						
Market Borrowings	10.4	10.4	11.3	11.9	12.0	12.1
Small Savings	9.9	9.4	12.2	13.4	13.2	11.9
External Debt	4.1	3.2	3.1	2.9	2.9	3.2
2. Interest Rate on New Issues of Dated Securities[b c]	11.5	12.5	13.1	12.0	13.8	--
3. Memo item: RBI Subscription of Dated Securities	48.2	22.1	4.3	1.6	17.5	--
General Government:						
Interest payments (percent of GDP)	5.1	5.3	5.4	5.6	5.6	5.8
Interest payments (percent of total tax revenue)	30.2	32.5	35.7	36.8	36.9	38.4
Non-financial Public Sector:						
Interest payments (percent of GDP)	6.1	6.4	6.5	6.5	6.5	6.6
Inflation rate (WPI)	13.7	10.1	8.4	10.9	7.7	7.5

a. Projected.

b. For 1990-91 - 1991-92, average of maximum and minimum rate on new placements. For the remaining years, weighted average of cutoff yields at auction, excluding funding operations.

c. For 1996-97 April -Feb .

Source: Economic Survey; RBI; and staff estimates.

Table 16: External environment for India
(annual average percentage change)

	1974-80	1981-90	1991-96	1997-06
World GDP				
OECD	2.5	2.9	1.7	2.7
LMICs excl. E.Eur & FSU	4.7	2.7	2.1	5.3
World Trade	4.9	4.7	6.4	6.4
GDP growth of trading partners	4.4	3.6	1.4	3.5
Export Market Import gr. a	--	--	6.7	6.1
Terms of Trade				
LMICs excl. E.Eur & FSU	7.1	-3.0	-0.9	0.0
India	-5.6	-1.6	2.9	0.2
Interest rates				
Nominal US$Libor	9.5	10.0	5.0	6.1
Real US$Libor	0.2	5.0	1.9	3.1
Key Commodity Prices, in real terms				
Oil	29.4	-7.7	-4.3	-2.8
Rice	-6.0	-7.2	1.2	-1.3
Wheat	-7.6	-5.6	4.6	-3.9
Tea	-0.3	-2.0	-5.6	-0.8
Fertilizers	3.4	-4.8	0.3	-0.7
Cotton	-5.0	-4.4	-2.9	-0.6

--: Not available.

Note: Regional projections are taken from GEP Update, August 1996. Commodity prices are from Commodity Quarterly, February 1997. Commodity specifications used are: oil-crude oil, average, spot; rice - Thai 5 %; wheat - US, HRW; Tea - auctions, average; Fertilizer - Potassium Chloride; Cotton - Cotlook A index.
a. Import growth of major trading partner weighted by India's exports to them.
Source: International Economics Department, February 1997.

Table 17: Sources and growth of India's foreign exchange earnings

	Period simple average (US$ billion)					Shares of current account revenue, %					Real average growth rate, p.a.%			
	85-90	91-95	95	96	97-06	85-90	91-95	95	96	97-06	85-90	91-95	96	97-06
Million of current US$														
Merchandise export	13.3	23.9	32.8	34.9	71.2	66.6	67.1	67.6	67.0	75.5	9.5	15.8	8.2	10.6
Non-factor services	3.8	6.1	7.2	7.6	12.8	18.9	17.1	14.8	14.6	13.6	2.5	6.3	2.8	6.1
Travel	1.3	2.3	2.9	3.1	--	6.5	6.4	6.0	5.9	--	7.4	6.9	3.8	--
Transport	0.8	1.5	2.0	2.1	--	4.0	4.4	4.1	4.1	--	9.3	17.4	2.9	--
Other services	1.7	2.0	2.3	2.4	--	8.4	5.6	4.7	4.6	--	-2.7	-0.7	1.3	--
Factor income	0.5	0.8	1.0	1.1	1.0	2.3	2.3	2.1	2.1	1.0	-8.7	4.1	6.8	-5.4
Private transfers	2.4	4.8	7.5	8.5	9.3	12.2	13.5	15.5	16.3	9.9	-4.7	15.3	10.0	-1.3
Current account revenue	19.9	35.6	48.5	52.1	94.2	100	100	100	100	100	5.8	14.0	6.2	9.0
Import of goods & NFS	24.1	33.6	47.7	49.8	95.1						9.3	17.7	4.5	8.9
As a ratio of GDP in percent														
Current account balance	-2.2	-1.0	-1.7	-1.5										
Official transfers	0.2	0.1	0.1	0.1										
Foreign direct investment	0.0	0.3	0.6	0.7										
Portfolio equity flow	0.0	0.7	0.7	1.0										
Net long-term borrowing	1.9	1.1	0.7	1.4										
Private loans	1.1	0.4	0.2	0.3										

--: Not available.
Source: Staff estimates based on Apr-Dec 1996 trade data.

Table 18: Performance of key export sectors
(in US$, percent)

	Average growth				Share in total exports	
	1974-84	1985-95	1996	1997-05	1994-96	2005
Agriculture and all	4.4	8.5	38.0	6.5	18.6	10.8
Textiles and garments	8.6	17.3	12.0	18.9	30.4	47.1
Gems and jewelry	6.0	16.8	-9.4	14.0	17.6	18.7
Chemicals	16.2	27.3	15.0	12.8	6.9	6.7
Engineering goods (excl. auto parts)	1.5	13.9	3.7	12.6	7.1	6.8
Auto parts	-6.5	21.7	1.0	19.2	1.7	2.7
Leathers, total	8.0	7.5	-6.2	2.7	2.7	1.1
Others	14.4	7.6	1.0	6.3	15.9	9.0
Total	8.1	13.1	6.4	13.2	100	100

Source: Staff estimates based on Apr-Dec 1996 trade data.

STATISTICAL
APPENDIX

CONTENTS

IV. Public Finance

V. Money and Credit

VI. Agriculture, Industry, Transport, Energy and Prices

Table A1.1 (a)
National Accounts Summary
(Rs. billion at current prices)

	1986-87	1987-88	1988-89	1989-90	1990-91	1991-92	1992-93	1993-94	1994-95	1995-96
GDPfc	2600.30	2948.51	3527.06	4086.62	4778.14	5527.68	6307.72	7318.91	8583.40	9857.87
Agriculture	824.13	923.79	1140.73	1270.51	1480.01	1727.71	1930.45	2236.02	2580.86	2747.52
Industry	737.46	838.29	1000.73	1196.93	1400.25	1540.74	1784.47	2043.49	2456.88	2963.10
Mining	67.96	70.85	92.08	103.08	117.85	128.03	145.89	168.65	181.87	196.69
Manufacturing	461.66	528.65	628.63	770.76	891.60	963.05	1110.44	1277.85	1560.15	1938.00
Construction	152.17	176.11	206.77	235.86	286.16	322.46	367.00	408.29	484.33	565.88
Electricity	55.67	62.68	73.25	87.23	104.64	127.20	161.14	188.70	230.53	262.53
Services	1038.71	1186.43	1385.60	1619.18	1897.88	2259.23	2592.80	3039.40	3545.66	4147.25
Net Indirect Taxes	329.19	383.50	430.76	481.59	577.20	640.31	751.46	778.75	953.40	1127.89
GDPmp	2929.49	3332.01	3957.82	4568.21	5355.34	6167.99	7059.18	8097.66	9536.80	10985.76
Resource Gap (M-X)	80.87	85.93	124.93	112.19	151.79	39.01	93.81	58.07	168.11	288.01
Imports (g+nfs)	255.25	296.23	388.59	465.46	565.11	610.00	776.69	934.85	1197.87	1632.54
Exports (g+nfs)	174.37	210.31	263.66	353.28	413.32	570.99	682.88	876.78	1029.76	1344.54
Total Expenditure	3010.36	3417.94	4082.75	4680.40	5507.13	6207.00	7152.99	8155.73	9704.91	11273.77
Consumption	2331.37	2669.12	3118.64	3578.45	4155.57	4806.32	5456.43	6401.00	7416.39	8391.96
General Gov't	346.25	408.43	473.31	542.03	617.79	694.59	785.96	899.31	1003.61	1164.57
Private	1985.12	2260.69	2645.33	3036.42	3537.78	4111.73	4670.47	5501.69	6412.78	7227.39
Investment	678.99	748.82	964.11	1101.95	1351.56	1400.68	1696.56	1754.73	2288.52	2881.81
Fixed Investment	620.52	721.94	856.69	1027.75	1240.04	1365.03	1588.57	1749.96	2140.38	2702.63
Change in Stocks	58.47	26.88	107.42	74.20	111.52	35.65	107.99	4.77	148.14	179.18
Domestic Savings	598.12	662.89	839.18	989.76	1199.77	1361.67	1602.75	1696.66	2120.41	2593.80
Net Factor Income	-26.16	-32.06	-38.10	-53.85	-68.37	-96.20	-107.32	-118.42	-113.68	-139.10
Current Transfers	29.75	34.99	38.42	38.01	37.14	92.75	80.29	120.00	194.67	234.23
National Savings	601.72	665.83	839.50	973.92	1168.53	1358.22	1575.71	1698.24	2201.40	2688.94
Foreign Savings	77.27	82.99	124.61	128.03	183.03	42.46	120.85	56.49	87.12	192.87
GDP per capita (Rs.)	3799.60	4228.44	4916.55	5557.43	6383.00	7205.60	8095.39	9118.99	10549.56	11941.04
Per capita private consumption	2574.74	2868.89	3286.12	3693.94	4216.66	4803.42	5356.04	6195.60	7093.78	7855.86
Average Exchange Rates:										
Rupees per US $	12.79	12.97	14.48	16.66	17.95	24.52	28.95	31.37	31.40	33.46
Rupees per SDR[a]	15.45	17.12	19.26	21.37	24.85	33.43	37.14	43.89	45.79	50.48
Memo Items:										
Priv. Consumption (CSO)	1999.98	2240.61	2589.93	2900.72	3323.64	3851.50	4353.17	4989.27	5698.00	6452.51
Population (mill)	771.00	788.00	805.00	822.00	839.00	856.00	872.00	888.00	904.00	920.00

Note: Exports, Imports, Foreign Savings, Net Factor Income and Capital Transfers numbers are used from the BOP.

a. Arrived at by crossing U.S. Dollar/ SDR rate with the RBI reference rate. *Source:* Economic Survey.

Source: CSO, National Accounts Statistics 1996 and CSO Quick Estimates.

Table A1.1 (b)
National Accounts Summary
(Rs. billion at 1980-81 prices)

	1986-87	1987-88	1988-89	1989-90	1990-91	1991-92	1992-93	1993-94	1994-95	1995-96
GDPfc	1632.71	1703.22	1884.61	2014.53	2122.53	2139.83	2252.68	2388.64	2560.95	2742.09
Agriculture	532.81	534.79	622.14	632.63	656.53	641.18	680.09	704.64	737.23	736.28
Industry	463.82	493.67	538.66	593.98	637.00	628.67	655.03	699.43	765.34	853.90
Mining	29.78	30.80	35.42	38.01	42.07	43.62	44.12	45.01	48.67	52.10
Manufacturing	324.45	348.18	378.65	422.85	448.63	432.00	450.05	488.23	538.02	611.19
Construction	75.37	77.77	83.79	88.07	98.33	100.47	103.86	105.17	112.40	118.36
Electricity	34.22	36.92	40.80	45.05	47.97	52.58	57.00	61.02	66.25	72.25
Services	636.08	674.76	723.81	787.92	829.00	869.98	917.56	984.57	1058.38	1151.91
Net Indirect Taxes	219.79	237.63	248.84	259.14	279.85	272.72	290.92	277.89	307.35	336.45
GDPmp	1852.50	1940.85	2133.45	2273.67	2402.38	2412.55	2543.60	2666.53	2868.30	3078.54
Terms of Trade Effect	24.62	14.79	23.60	22.89	9.16	14.39	12.39	22.97	15.57	-29.24
Gross Domestic Income	1877.12	1955.64	2157.05	2296.56	2411.54	2426.94	2555.99	2689.50	2883.87	3049.30
Resource Gap (M-X)	86.68	70.63	95.32	76.34	70.66	27.28	39.83	38.70	56.11	30.11
Imports (g+nfs)	195.86	192.51	223.07	221.76	228.95	201.64	227.21	253.19	288.91	336.41
Capacity to import	133.80	136.67	151.36	168.31	167.45	188.75	199.76	237.47	248.36	277.06
[Exports (g+nfs)]	109.18	121.88	127.76	145.42	158.29	174.36	187.38	214.50	232.79	306.30
Total Expenditure	1963.80	2026.27	2252.37	2372.90	2482.20	2454.22	2595.81	2728.20	2939.98	3079.41
Consumption	1562.09	1608.41	1756.60	1866.06	1913.35	1947.89	2026.87	2174.37	2260.89	2278.95
General Gov't	208.49	226.60	238.68	252.15	260.59	259.12	267.79	284.96	290.01	304.94
Private	1353.60	1381.81	1517.92	1613.91	1652.76	1688.77	1759.08	1889.41	1970.88	1974.01
Investment	401.71	417.86	495.77	506.84	568.85	506.33	568.94	553.83	679.09	800.46
Fixed Investment	359.97	399.55	427.70	464.83	510.91	490.46	524.61	553.82	627.72	742.55
Change in Stocks	41.74	18.31	68.07	42.01	57.94	15.87	44.33	0.01	51.37	57.91
Domestic Savings	315.03	347.23	400.45	430.50	498.19	479.05	529.11	515.13	622.98	770.35
Net Factor Income	-20.07	-20.83	-21.87	-25.66	-27.70	-31.80	-31.40	-32.07	-27.42	-28.66
Current Transfers	22.83	22.74	22.06	18.11	15.05	30.66	23.49	32.50	46.95	48.27
National Savings	292.20	324.49	378.40	412.39	483.15	448.39	505.63	482.63	576.03	722.08
Foreign Savings	83.92	68.73	95.13	83.89	83.32	28.42	47.74	38.27	36.58	10.50
GDP per capita (Rs.)	2402.72	2463.01	2650.25	2766.02	2863.38	2818.40	2916.97	3002.85	3172.90	3346.24
Per capita private consumption	1755.65	1753.57	1885.61	1963.40	1969.92	1972.86	2017.30	2127.72	2180.17	2145.66
Rupee Deflators (1980-81=100):										
GDPmp	158.14	171.68	185.51	200.92	222.92	255.66	277.53	303.68	332.49	356.85
Imports(g+nfs)	130.32	153.88	174.20	209.90	246.83	302.52	341.85	369.22	414.62	485.28
Exports(g+nfs)	159.71	172.56	206.38	242.94	261.11	327.49	364.44	408.77	442.35	438.96
Total Expenditure	153.29	168.68	181.26	197.24	221.86	252.91	275.56	298.94	330.10	366.10
Govt. Consumption	166.08	180.24	198.30	214.96	237.07	268.06	293.50	315.59	346.06	381.90
Priv. Consumption	146.65	163.60	174.27	188.14	214.05	243.47	265.51	291.19	325.38	366.13
Fixed Investment	172.38	180.69	200.30	221.10	242.71	278.32	302.81	315.98	340.98	363.97
Total Investment	169.02	179.20	194.47	217.42	237.60	276.63	298.20	316.84	337.00	360.02

Note: Exports, Imports, Foreign Savings, Net Factor Income and Capital Transfers numbers are used from the BOP.

Source: CSO, National Accounts Statistics 1996 and CSO Quick Estimates.

Table A1.2 (a)
Gross Domestic Product at Factor Cost - By Industry of Origin
(Rs. billion at current prices)

	1986-87	1987-88	1988-89	1989-90	1990-91	1991-92	1992-93	1993-94	1994-95	1995-96
Agricultural Sector	824.13	923.79	1140.73	1270.51	1480.01	1727.71	1930.45	2236.02	2580.86	2747.52
Agriculture	744.05	835.15	1041.03	1154.47	1351.62	1592.99	1779.10	2062.19	2374.91	2525.44
Forestry & Logging	57.58	61.78	68.28	78.23	82.81	83.90	88.54	98.36	102.61	107.04
Fishing	22.50	26.86	31.42	37.81	45.58	50.82	62.81	75.47	103.34	115.04
Industry Sector	737.46	838.29	1000.73	1196.93	1400.25	1540.74	1784.47	2043.49	2456.88	2963.10
Mining & Quarrying	67.96	70.85	92.08	103.08	117.85	128.03	145.89	168.65	181.87	196.69
Manufacturing	461.66	528.65	628.63	770.76	891.60	963.05	1110.44	1277.85	1560.15	1938.00
Registered	282.54	322.07	390.50	483.69	555.53	608.43	688.93	813.38	982.17	1210.39
Unregistered	179.12	206.58	238.13	287.07	336.07	354.62	421.51	464.47	577.98	727.61
Electricity,Gas &Water	55.67	62.68	73.25	87.23	104.64	127.20	161.14	188.70	230.53	262.53
Construction	152.17	176.11	206.77	235.86	286.16	322.46	367.00	408.29	484.33	565.88
Services Sector	1038.71	1186.43	1385.60	1619.18	1897.88	2259.23	2592.80	3039.40	3545.66	4147.25
Transport, Storage & Com.	165.37	199.38	238.72	277.31	339.13	410.04	488.92	560.76	660.42	763.59
Railways	37.65	43.56	47.51	55.75	64.33	73.42	84.46	96.48	112.03	123.06
Other Transport	105.10	124.68	152.29	177.85	223.11	275.22	328.39	370.40	430.08	501.54
Storage	2.80	3.17	3.34	3.88	4.45	4.77	5.23	5.75	6.67	7.66
Communication	19.82	27.97	35.58	39.83	47.24	56.63	70.84	88.13	111.64	131.33
Trade, Hotels etc.	345.51	384.33	452.22	529.10	618.83	708.07	827.69	982.46	1166.03	1404.59
Banking & Insurance	96.64	111.43	134.13	171.31	210.96	295.15	312.32	421.76	500.19	574.65
Real Estate etc.	126.45	136.13	148.43	164.46	178.06	195.41	214.07	235.75	262.78	286.25
Public Admin & Defence	149.33	179.48	208.58	241.33	271.09	314.41	362.50	399.55	447.30	524.26
Other Services	155.41	175.68	203.52	235.67	279.81	336.15	387.30	439.12	508.94	593.91
GDP at Factor Cost	2600.30	2948.51	3527.06	4086.62	4778.14	5527.68	6307.72	7318.91	8583.40	9857.87

Source: CSO, National Accounts Statistics 1996 and CSO Quick Estimates.

Table A1.2 (b)

Gross Domestic Product at Factor Cost - By Industry of Origin

(Rs. billion at 1980-81 prices)

	1986-87	1987-88	1988-89	1989-90	1990-91	1991-92	1992-93	1993-94	1994-95	1995-96
Agricultural Sector	532.81	534.79	622.14	632.63	656.53	641.18	680.09	704.64	737.23	736.28
Agriculture	489.95	492.58	579.40	585.68	609.91	593.98	633.27	657.13	687.06	685.17
Forestry & Logging	30.90	29.86	29.40	31.95	31.05	30.83	29.50	28.81	28.65	28.49
Fishing	11.96	12.35	13.34	15.00	15.57	16.37	17.32	18.70	21.52	22.62
Industry Sector	463.82	493.67	538.66	593.98	637.00	628.67	655.03	699.43	765.34	853.90
Mining & Quarrying	29.78	30.80	35.42	38.01	42.07	43.62	44.12	45.01	48.67	52.10
Manufacturing	324.45	348.18	378.65	422.85	448.63	432.00	450.05	488.23	538.02	611.19
Registered	195.21	209.02	231.26	263.36	276.57	270.24	278.74	311.12	341.72	387.05
Unregistered	129.24	139.16	147.39	159.49	172.06	161.76	171.31	177.11	196.30	224.14
Electricity,Gas &Water	34.22	36.92	40.80	45.05	47.97	52.58	57.00	61.02	66.25	72.25
Construction	75.37	77.77	83.79	88.07	98.33	100.47	103.86	105.17	112.40	118.36
Services Sector	636.08	674.76	723.81	787.92	829.00	869.98	917.56	984.57	1058.38	1151.91
Transport, Storage & Com.	84.83	92.27	98.04	106.63	111.64	117.85	123.98	130.57	141.48	155.73
Railways	15.14	15.76	15.60	16.23	16.77	17.78	17.58	17.46	17.69	19.06
Other Transport	56.51	62.61	67.92	75.01	78.53	82.75	87.35	92.09	99.67	108.44
Storage	1.70	1.69	1.64	1.70	1.77	1.75	1.80	1.88	1.90	1.92
Communication	11.48	12.21	12.88	13.69	14.57	15.57	17.25	19.14	22.22	26.31
Trade, Hotels etc.	208.52	218.01	233.85	252.31	265.80	268.27	286.50	310.57	343.73	393.99
Banking & Insurance	66.92	73.99	86.23	102.69	111.69	131.07	138.61	161.11	176.31	183.46
Real Estate etc.	92.24	94.72	97.93	101.34	105.31	108.65	112.23	116.00	120.50	125.20
Public Admin & Defence	88.07	97.04	103.42	112.14	113.28	115.70	121.70	124.83	127.10	135.10
Other Services	95.50	98.73	104.34	112.81	121.28	128.44	134.54	141.49	149.26	158.43
GDP at Factor Cost	1632.71	1703.22	1884.61	2014.53	2122.53	2139.83	2252.68	2388.64	2560.95	2742.09

Source: CSO, National Accounts Statistics 1996 and CSO Quick Estimates.

Table A1.2 (c)
Implicit Price Deflators for GDP at Factor Cost
(1980-81=100)

	1986-87	1987-88	1988-89	1989-90	1990-91	1991-92	1992-93	1993-94	1994-95	1995-96
Agricultural Sector	154.68	172.74	183.36	200.83	225.43	269.46	283.85	317.33	350.08	373.16
Agriculture	151.86	169.55	179.67	197.12	221.61	268.19	280.94	313.82	345.66	368.59
Forestry & Logging	186.34	206.90	232.24	244.85	266.70	272.14	300.14	341.41	358.15	375.71
Fishing	188.13	217.49	235.53	252.07	292.74	310.45	362.64	403.58	480.20	508.58
Industry Sector	159.00	169.81	185.78	201.51	219.82	245.08	272.43	292.17	321.02	347.01
Mining & Quarrying	228.21	230.03	259.97	271.19	280.13	293.51	330.67	374.69	373.68	377.52
Manufacturing	142.29	151.83	166.02	182.28	198.74	222.93	246.74	261.73	289.98	317.09
Registered	144.74	154.09	168.86	183.66	200.86	225.14	247.16	261.44	287.42	312.72
Unregistered	138.59	148.45	161.56	179.99	195.32	219.23	246.05	262.25	294.44	324.62
Electricity,Gas &Water	162.68	169.77	179.53	193.63	218.14	241.92	282.70	309.24	347.97	363.36
Construction	201.90	226.45	246.77	267.81	291.02	320.95	353.36	388.22	430.90	478.10
Services Sector	163.30	175.83	191.43	205.50	228.94	259.69	282.58	308.70	335.01	360.03
Transport, Storage & Com.	194.94	216.08	243.49	260.07	303.77	347.93	394.35	429.47	466.79	490.33
Railways	248.68	276.40	304.55	343.50	383.60	412.94	480.43	552.58	633.30	645.65
Other Transport	185.98	199.14	224.22	237.10	284.11	332.59	375.95	402.22	431.50	462.50
Storage	164.71	187.57	203.66	228.24	251.41	272.57	290.56	305.85	351.05	398.96
Communication	172.65	229.07	276.24	290.94	324.23	363.71	410.67	460.45	502.43	499.16
Trade, Hotels etc.	165.70	176.29	193.38	209.70	232.82	263.94	288.90	316.34	339.23	356.50
Banking & Insurance	144.41	150.60	155.55	166.82	188.88	225.19	225.32	261.78	283.70	313.23
Real Estate etc.	137.09	143.72	151.57	162.29	169.08	179.85	190.74	203.23	218.07	228.63
Public Admin & Defence	169.56	184.95	201.68	215.20	239.31	271.75	297.86	320.08	351.93	388.05
Other Services	162.73	177.94	195.05	208.91	230.71	261.72	287.87	310.35	340.98	374.87
GDP at Factor Cost	159.26	173.11	187.15	202.86	225.12	258.32	280.01	306.40	335.16	359.50

Source: Derived from Tables 1.2(a) and 1.2(b).

Table A1.3
Gross Savings and Investment
(Rs. billion)

	1986-87	1987-88	1988-89	1989-90	1990-91	1991-92	1992-93	1993-94	1994-95	1995-96
					(At current prices)					
GROSS NATIONAL SAVINGS	601.72	665.83	839.50	973.92	1168.53	1358.22	1575.71	1698.24	2201.40	2688.94
Households	469.58	535.70	675.30	783.19	964.77	1044.44	1269.65	1363.07	1653.49	2024.51
Private corporate sector	52.12	57.90	83.19	116.50	149.40	194.90	198.41	290.19	375.51	453.36
Public sector	80.02	72.23	81.01	74.23	54.36	118.88	107.65	44.98	172.40	211.07
Foreign Savings	77.27	82.99	124.61	128.03	183.03	42.46	120.85	56.49	87.12	192.87
GROSS DOMESTIC INVESTMENT	678.99	748.82	964.11	1101.95	1351.56	1400.68	1696.56	1754.73	2288.52	2881.81
Change in stocks	58.47	26.88	107.42	74.20	111.52	35.65	107.99	4.77	148.14	179.18
GROSS FIXED CAPITAL FORMATION	620.52	721.94	856.69	1027.75	1240.04	1365.03	1588.57	1749.96	2140.38	2702.63
By Type of Asset:										
Construction	305.73	347.87	414.45	478.92	583.63	669.32	756.26	813.26	951.29	1109.45
Machinery & Equipment	314.79	374.07	442.24	548.83	656.41	695.71	832.31	936.70	1189.09	1593.18
By Sector:										
Public sector	332.54	345.71	398.66	438.62	501.76	587.37	601.17	674.71	845.21	917.03
Private sector	287.98	376.23	458.03	589.13	738.28	777.66	987.40	1075.25	1295.17	1785.60
GDPmp at current prices	2929.49	3332.01	3957.82	4568.21	5355.34	6167.99	7059.18	8097.66	9536.80	10985.76
					(At 1980-81 prices)					
GROSS DOMESTIC INVESTMENT	401.71	417.86	495.77	506.84	568.85	506.33	568.94	553.83	679.09	800.46
Change in Stocks	41.74	18.31	68.07	42.01	57.94	15.87	44.33	0.01	51.37	57.91
GROSS FIXED CAPITAL FORMATION	359.97	399.55	427.70	464.83	510.91	490.46	524.61	553.82	627.72	742.55
By Type of Asset:										
Construction	145.90	150.45	164.23	170.69	187.57	191.91	197.49	194.65	209.35	218.96
Machinery & Equipment	214.07	249.10	263.47	294.14	323.34	298.55	327.12	359.17	418.37	523.59
By Sector:										
Public sector	192.31	186.60	195.39	196.51	206.01	210.12	195.08	208.57	244.53	240.93
Private sector	167.66	212.95	232.31	268.32	304.90	280.34	329.53	345.25	383.19	501.62

Note: Exports, Imports, Foreign Savings, Net Factor Income and Capital Transfers numbers are used from the BOP.

Source: CSO, National Accounts Statistics 1996 and CSO Quick Estimates.

Table A1.4
Disposable Income and Its Uses
(Rs. billion at current prices)

	1986-87	1987-88	1988-89	1989-90	1990-91	1991-92	1992-93	1993-94	1994-95	1995-96
GDPmp	2929.49	3332.01	3957.82	4568.21	5355.34	6167.99	7059.18	8097.66	9536.80	10985.76
Net Factor Income from abroad	-26.16	-32.06	-38.10	-53.85	-68.37	-96.20	-107.32	-118.42	-113.68	-139.10
Other current transfers	29.75	34.99	38.42	38.01	37.14	92.75	80.29	120.00	194.67	234.23
Disposable income	2933.09	3334.94	3958.14	4552.36	5324.10	6164.54	7032.15	8099.24	9617.79	11080.90
Private disposable income	2506.82	2854.28	3403.82	3936.10	4651.95	5351.07	6138.54	7154.95	8441.78	9705.26
Public disposable income	426.27	480.66	554.32	616.26	672.15	813.47	893.61	944.29	1176.01	1375.64
Gross National Savings	601.72	665.83	839.50	973.92	1168.53	1358.22	1575.71	1698.24	2201.40	2688.94
Private savings	521.70	593.60	758.49	899.69	1114.17	1239.34	1468.06	1653.26	2029.00	2477.87
Public savings	80.02	72.23	81.01	74.23	54.36	118.88	107.65	44.98	172.40	211.07
Final Consumption	2331.37	2669.12	3118.64	3578.45	4155.57	4806.32	5456.43	6401.00	7416.39	8391.96
Private Consumption	1985.12	2260.69	2645.33	3036.42	3537.78	4111.73	4670.47	5501.69	6412.78	7227.39
Public Consumption	346.25	408.43	473.31	542.03	617.79	694.59	785.96	899.31	1003.61	1164.57

Note: Exports, Imports, Foreign Savings, Net Factor Income and Capital Transfers numbers are used from the BOP.
Source: CSO, National Accounts Statistics 1996 and CSO Quick Estimates.

Table A1.5 (a)
Gross Domestic Investment by Industry of Origin
(Rs. billion at current prices)

	1986-87	1987-88	1988-89	1989-90	1990-91	1991-92	1992-93	1993-94	1994-95	1995-96
Agricultural Sector	77.34	91.81	99.84	111.12	128.53	147.76	181.13	187.43	227.66	274.04
Agriculture	70.45	83.89	90.63	100.25	115.92	133.90	166.14	170.09	207.37	249.37
Forestry & Logging	2.36	2.56	2.95	3.81	4.56	4.43	4.51	4.82	4.94	6.29
Fishing	4.53	5.36	6.26	7.06	8.05	9.43	10.48	12.52	15.35	18.38
Industry Sector	265.57	329.22	470.77	454.02	543.38	572.81	765.51	721.56	1043.11	1240.60
Mining & Quarrying	44.59	42.17	47.89	63.04	66.26	63.36	65.85	65.36	151.82	115.97
Manufacturing	115.41	170.86	298.59	248.62	310.95	303.02	484.38	408.80	606.94	797.48
Registered	69.34	118.71	238.14	171.46	223.83	223.07	377.81	298.63	456.90	600.39
Unregistered	46.07	52.15	60.45	77.16	87.12	79.95	106.57	110.17	150.04	197.09
Electricity,Gas &Water	95.13	103.78	112.95	123.44	144.06	188.95	189.84	221.74	251.38	285.65
Construction	10.44	12.41	11.34	18.92	22.11	17.48	25.44	25.66	32.97	41.50
Services Sector	317.73	274.14	315.01	405.84	511.11	562.91	593.72	744.46	870.15	990.47
Transport, Storage & Com.	78.76	80.58	106.44	128.22	143.33	161.56	196.99	240.57	257.04	306.68
Railways	22.88	21.52	26.37	26.43	30.78	33.17	49.19	55.81	49.91	50.99
Other Transport	44.58	43.98	57.93	73.64	83.25	95.81	97.32	126.29	134.66	161.91
Storage	0.74	0.78	0.76	0.88	0.69	0.46	0.49	0.97	0.92	0.89
Communication	10.56	14.30	21.38	27.27	28.61	32.12	49.99	57.50	71.55	92.89
Trade, Hotels etc.	78.18	17.09	2.96	55.99	87.92	75.07	30.08	81.68	112.93	77.94
Banking & Insurance	8.67	14.76	21.06	23.60	30.86	49.79	47.28	68.76	97.60	127.39
Real Estate etc.	80.92	90.09	101.56	118.06	147.35	168.24	194.09	216.53	243.01	281.42
Public Admin & Defence	55.01	55.08	62.24	55.78	75.13	82.27	95.17	106.32	121.29	152.09
Other Services	16.19	16.54	20.75	24.19	26.52	25.98	30.11	30.60	38.28	44.95
Gross Domestic Investment	660.64	695.17	885.62	970.98	1183.02	1283.48	1540.36	1653.45	2140.92	2505.11
Memo Items										
Gross Domestic Investment [a]	611.56	764.56	969.72	1146.49	1481.95	1441.13	1695.49	1914.98	2478.04	3007.60
Errors & Omissions	-67.43	15.74	5.61	44.54	130.39	40.45	-1.07	160.25	189.52	125.79
Gross Domestic Investment (unadjusted) [b]	678.99	748.82	964.11	1101.95	1351.56	1400.68	1696.56	1754.73	2288.52	2881.81

a. Refers to CSO's savings-based estimate of investment.
b. Refers to Gross Capital Formation unadjusted for errors and omissions, which is CSO's direct estimate of investment based on physical flows.

Source: CSO, National Accounts Statistics 1996 and CSO Quick Estimates.

Table A1.5 (b)
Gross Domestic Investment by Industry of Origin
(Rs. billion at 1980-81 prices)

	1986-87	1987-88	1988-89	1989-90	1990-91	1991-92	1992-93	1993-94	1994-95	1995-96
Agricultural Sector	43.55	47.78	47.33	47.91	50.76	52.12	58.73	55.74	62.44	69.27
Agriculture	40.11	44.14	43.46	43.53	45.94	47.29	53.72	50.38	56.78	63.01
Forestry & Logging	1.24	1.24	1.26	1.51	1.68	1.40	1.26	1.25	1.15	1.32
Fishing	2.20	2.40	2.61	2.87	3.14	3.43	3.75	4.11	4.51	4.94
Industry Sector	158.56	192.19	258.80	220.23	242.27	218.46	276.73	240.69	327.12	360.88
Mining & Quarrying	27.22	24.33	25.47	29.92	28.44	23.80	22.23	19.83	47.55	34.36
Manufacturing	67.40	101.59	170.07	122.64	141.93	118.20	180.70	139.28	194.71	236.87
Registered	41.50	74.44	141.00	88.26	106.35	91.05	145.77	105.85	151.40	184.35
Unregistered	25.90	27.15	29.07	34.38	35.58	27.15	34.93	33.43	43.31	52.52
Electricity,Gas &Water	57.31	58.55	56.57	57.72	61.51	69.32	64.32	72.24	74.09	76.99
Construction	6.63	7.72	6.69	9.95	10.39	7.14	9.48	9.34	10.77	12.66
Services Sector	181.94	136.82	141.48	174.49	205.83	196.60	185.85	226.02	245.55	252.96
Transport, Storage & Com.	48.43	45.70	53.82	58.75	60.43	59.93	67.39	79.89	79.17	88.18
Railways	12.40	10.04	11.11	9.82	10.55	9.97	14.36	15.71	12.14	11.67
Other Transport	29.57	27.43	31.94	36.50	37.88	38.64	36.81	46.28	46.07	51.61
Storage	0.37	0.34	0.30	0.35	0.27	0.13	0.13	0.29	0.25	0.22
Communication	6.09	7.89	10.47	12.08	11.73	11.19	16.09	17.61	20.71	24.68
Trade, Hotels etc.	54.08	9.99	-0.50	28.73	43.23	31.39	9.18	28.66	37.57	23.22
Banking & Insurance	5.23	8.77	11.31	11.42	13.71	19.44	16.93	23.60	30.51	36.63
Real Estate etc.	35.91	36.57	38.57	42.25	49.74	50.01	54.07	55.34	57.08	59.26
Public Admin & Defence	29.83	27.44	28.70	23.12	28.39	27.11	28.96	29.63	30.86	34.55
Other Services	8.46	8.35	9.58	10.22	10.33	8.72	9.32	8.90	10.36	11.12
Gross Domestic Investment	384.05	376.79	447.61	442.63	498.86	467.18	521.31	522.45	635.11	683.11
Memo Items										
Gross Domestic Investment [a]	362.59	426.57	498.57	526.98	622.57	520.86	568.59	604.55	734.67	835.02
Errors & Omissions	-39.12	8.71	2.80	20.14	53.72	14.53	-0.11	68.92	55.58	34.56
Gross Domestic Investment (unadjusted) [b]	401.71	417.86	495.77	506.84	568.85	506.33	568.94	553.83	679.09	800.46

a. Refers to CSO's savings-based estimate of investment.
b. Refers to Gross Capital Formation unadjusted for errors and omissions, which is CSO's direct estimate of investment based on physical flows.

Source: CSO, National Accounts Statistics 1996 and CSO Quick Estimates.

Table A1.5 (c)
Investment Deflators by Industry of Use
(1980-81=100)

	1986-87	1987-88	1988-89	1989-90	1990-91	1991-92	1992-93	1993-94	1994-95	1995-96
Agricultural Sector	177.59	192.15	210.94	231.93	253.21	283.50	308.41	336.26	364.61	395.61
Agriculture	175.64	190.05	208.54	230.30	252.33	283.15	309.27	337.61	365.22	395.76
Forestry & Logging	190.32	206.45	234.13	252.32	271.43	316.43	357.94	385.60	429.57	476.52
Fishing	205.91	223.33	239.85	245.99	256.37	274.93	279.47	304.62	340.35	372.06
Industry Sector	167.49	171.30	181.90	206.16	224.29	262.20	276.63	299.79	318.88	343.77
Mining & Quarrying	163.81	173.33	188.03	210.70	232.98	266.22	296.22	329.60	319.28	337.51
Manufacturing	171.23	168.19	175.57	202.72	219.09	256.36	268.06	293.51	311.71	336.67
Registered	167.08	159.47	168.89	194.27	210.47	245.00	259.18	282.13	301.78	325.68
Unregistered	177.88	192.08	207.95	224.43	244.86	294.48	305.10	329.55	346.43	375.27
Electricity,Gas &Water	165.99	177.25	199.66	213.86	234.21	272.58	295.15	306.95	339.29	371.02
Construction	157.47	160.75	169.51	190.15	212.80	244.82	268.35	274.73	306.13	327.80
Services Sector	174.63	200.37	222.65	232.59	248.32	286.32	319.46	329.38	354.37	391.55
Transport, Storage & Com.	162.63	176.32	197.77	218.25	237.18	269.58	292.31	301.13	324.67	347.79
Railways	184.52	214.34	237.35	269.14	291.75	332.70	342.55	355.25	411.12	436.93
Other Transport	150.76	160.34	181.37	201.75	219.77	247.96	264.38	272.88	292.29	313.72
Storage	200.00	229.41	253.33	251.43	255.56	353.85	376.92	334.48	368.00	404.55
Communication	173.40	181.24	204.20	225.75	243.90	287.04	310.69	326.52	345.49	376.38
Trade, Hotels etc.	144.56	171.07	-592.00	194.88	203.38	239.15	327.67	285.00	300.59	335.66
Banking & Insurance	165.77	168.30	186.21	206.65	225.09	256.12	279.27	291.36	319.90	347.78
Real Estate etc.	225.34	246.35	263.31	279.43	296.24	336.41	358.96	391.27	425.74	474.89
Public Admin & Defence	184.41	200.73	216.86	241.26	264.64	303.47	328.63	358.83	393.03	440.20
Other Services	191.37	198.08	216.60	236.69	256.73	297.94	323.07	343.82	369.50	404.23
Gross Domestic Investment	172.02	184.50	197.86	219.37	237.14	274.73	295.48	316.48	337.09	366.72
Memo Items										
Gross Domestic Investment [a]	168.66	179.23	194.50	217.56	238.04	276.68	298.19	316.76	337.30	
Gross Domestic Investment (unadjusted) [b]	169.02	179.20	194.47	217.42	237.60	276.63	298.20	316.84	337.00	360.02

a. Refers to CSO's savings-based estimate of investment.
b. Refers to Gross Capital Formation unadjusted for errors and omissions, which is CSO's direct estimate of investment based on physical flows.

Source: CSO, National Accounts Statistics 1996 and CSO Quick Estimates.

Table A1.6 (a)
Gross Domestic Investment in Public Sector
(Rs. billion at current prices)

	1986-87	1987-88	1988-89	1989-90	1990-91	1991-92	1992-93	1993-94	1994-95
Agricultural Sector	28.95	33.03	34.42	33.54	36.28	36.53	41.75	49.26	60.87
Agriculture	26.67	30.57	31.62	29.89	31.93	32.30	37.49	44.67	56.20
Forestry & Logging	2.23	2.42	2.78	3.62	4.33	4.20	4.25	4.56	4.66
Fishing	0.05	0.04	0.02	0.03	0.02	0.03	0.01	0.03	0.01
Industry Sector	188.05	192.84	204.32	235.48	277.65	324.88	309.66	296.84	416.33
Mining & Quarrying	42.09	40.96	47.59	62.46	65.04	61.92	63.76	63.36	147.98
Manufacturing	55.87	50.73	51.72	54.66	71.45	85.08	82.98	49.13	67.22
Electricity,Gas &Water	89.57	98.81	105.62	117.55	137.69	174.10	158.41	178.85	195.52
Construction	0.52	2.34	-0.61	0.81	3.47	3.78	4.51	5.50	5.61
Services Sector	124.42	104.72	154.91	186.64	207.58	203.96	276.22	348.16	359.89
Transport, Storage & Com.	50.78	46.40	61.50	75.92	79.58	92.16	123.71	159.62	158.54
Railways	22.88	21.52	26.37	26.43	30.78	33.17	49.19	55.81	49.91
Other Transport	16.78	10.12	13.48	21.86	19.73	26.67	24.36	45.68	36.50
Storage	0.56	0.46	0.27	0.36	0.46	0.20	0.17	0.63	0.58
Communication	10.56	14.30	21.38	27.27	28.61	32.12	49.99	57.50	71.55
Trade, Hotels etc.	-2.06	-22.61	-2.98	17.48	14.54	-16.67	12.74	35.89	22.71
Banking & Insurance	4.92	9.49	14.82	16.99	17.98	23.59	18.04	19.73	25.24
Real Estate etc.	6.51	6.70	7.57	7.32	6.16	8.66	10.19	10.78	12.05
Public Admin & Defence	55.01	55.08	62.24	55.78	75.13	82.27	95.17	106.32	121.29
Other Services	9.26	9.66	11.76	13.15	14.19	13.95	16.37	15.82	20.06
Gross Domestic Investment	341.42	330.59	393.65	455.66	521.51	565.37	627.63	694.26	837.09

Source : CSO, National Accounts Statistics 1996 and CSO Quick Estimates.

Table A1.6 (b)
Gross Domestic Investment in Public Sector
(Rs. billion at 1980-81 prices)

	1986-87	1987-88	1988-89	1989-90	1990-91	1991-92	1992-93	1993-94	1994-95
Agricultural Sector	15.44	15.76	14.82	13.01	13.15	11.35	11.79	12.72	14.38
Agriculture	14.25	14.58	13.62	11.56	11.54	10.02	10.61	11.53	13.29
Forestry & Logging	1.16	1.16	1.19	1.43	1.60	1.32	1.18	1.18	1.08
Fishing	0.03	0.02	0.01	0.02	0.01	0.01	0.00	0.01	0.01
Industry Sector	114.65	110.85	105.94	111.41	120.36	121.28	106.29	95.26	126.70
Mining & Quarrying	25.67	23.59	24.76	29.63	27.85	23.21	21.40	19.30	46.45
Manufacturing	34.68	30.36	28.61	26.50	32.49	33.32	30.60	16.65	21.71
Electricity,Gas &Water	53.85	55.59	52.65	54.81	58.56	63.38	52.79	57.61	56.94
Construction	0.45	1.31	-0.08	0.47	1.46	1.37	1.50	1.70	1.60
Services Sector	69.02	50.73	72.20	81.99	82.41	67.84	87.75	106.97	99.83
Transport, Storage & Com.	29.77	24.34	28.90	32.75	31.15	31.63	39.38	49.87	45.10
Railways	12.40	10.04	11.11	9.82	10.55	9.97	14.36	15.71	12.14
Other Transport	10.99	6.21	7.22	10.70	8.68	10.42	8.89	16.35	12.09
Storage	0.29	0.20	0.10	0.15	0.19	0.05	0.04	0.20	0.16
Communication	6.09	7.89	10.47	12.08	11.73	11.19	16.09	17.61	20.71
Trade, Hotels etc.	-1.65	-14.53	-1.94	9.56	7.19	-7.44	4.98	13.15	7.49
Banking & Insurance	3.02	5.71	8.05	8.26	8.03	9.27	6.55	6.94	8.03
Real Estate etc.	2.99	2.82	2.98	2.69	2.12	2.64	2.87	2.82	2.90
Public Admin & Defence	29.83	27.44	28.70	23.12	28.39	27.11	28.96	29.63	30.86
Other Services	5.06	4.95	5.51	5.61	5.53	4.63	5.01	4.56	5.45
Gross Domestic Investment	199.11	177.34	192.96	206.41	215.92	200.47	205.83	214.95	240.91

Source: CSO, National Accounts Statistics 1996 and CSO Quick Estimates.

Table A2.1
Balance of Payments
(US$ million at current prices)

	1986-87	1987-88	1988-89	1989-90	1990-91	1991-92	1992-93	1993-94	1994-95	1995-96
Exports of Goods and Non-Factor Services	13637	16217	18213	21201	23028	23288	23585	27947	32796	40181
Merchandise (fob)	10420	12646	14257	16955	18477	18266	18869	22683	26857	32433
Non-factor Services	3217	3571	3956	4246	4551	5022	4716	5264	5939	7748
Imports of Goods and Non-Factor Services	19962	22843	26843	27934	31485	24879	26825	29798	38150	48788
Merchandise (cif)	17740	19816	23618	24411	27914	21064	23237	25069	31840	41721
Non-factor Services	2222	3027	3225	3523	3571	3815	3588	4729	6310	7067
Trade Balance	-7320	-7170	-9361	-7456	-9437	-2798	-4368	-2386	-4983	-9288
Nonfactor Services Balance	995	544	731	723	980	1207	1128	535	-371	681
Resource Balance	-6325	-6626	-8630	-6733	-8457	-1591	-3240	-1851	-5354	-8607
Net Factor Income	-2046	-2472	-2632	-3232	-3810	-3924	-3707	-3775	-3621	-4157
Factor Service Receipts	501	446	397	936	1123	758	733	272	1264	1024
Factor Service Payments [a]	2547	2918	3029	4168	4933	4682	4440	4047	4885	5181
Net Current Transfers	2327	2698	2654	2281	2069	3783	2773	3825	6200	7000
Transfer Receipts	2339	2724	2670	2297	2083	3798	2784	3617	6220	7020
Transfer Payments	12	26	16	16	14	15	11	-208	20	20
Current Account Balance	-6043	-6400	-8607	-7684	-10198	-1732	-4174	-1801	-2775	-5764
Foreign Investment	208	181	287	350	165	158	587	4235	4895	4143
Direct Foreign Investment	208	181	287	350	165	150	341	586	1314	1929
Portfolio Investment	0	0	0	0	0	8	246	3649	3581	2214
Official Grant Aid	403	410	406	500	462	460	363	368	472	416
Net Medium & Long-Term Capital	4305	5406	8381	5351	3928	4313	3886	4219	1971	-91
Gross Disbursements (excl. NRI deposits)	4771	5309	8002	5022	5062	6926	5073	7150	5982	5744
Principal Repayments	2291	1894	1949	1966	2670	2903	3307	4027	4828	6780
Other LT Inflows (NRI)	1825	1992	2328	2295	1536	290	2120	1097	818	945
Capital Flows NEI	21	-847	-3016	-654	1307	-878	-3045	419	1476	-1654
Net Short-Term Capital	588	727	685	1143	1043	-1474	-730	-2714	638	785
Others [b]	-102	-731	141	167	-1193	-1240	-878	-1053	-1060	-963
Capital flows n.e.i. [c]	403	410	406	500	462	460	363	368	472	416
Overall Balance	719	743	-222	158	-2799	2611	-263	8538	6858	-2005
Net IMF Credit	-648	-1082	-1210	-1008	1028	773	1290	189	-1174	-1719
Change in Reserves (Excl. Gold) (- = increase)	-72	338	1432	850	1771	-3384	-1027	-8727	-5684	3724
Memorandum Items:										
End of Year Gross Reserves (Excl. Gold)	6729	6391	4959	4109	2338	5722	6749	15476	21160	17436
Reserves in Months of Imports	4.6	3.9	2.5	2.0	1.0	3.3	3.5	7.4	8.0	5.0
Current Account Balance / GDP	-2.6%	-2.5%	-3.1%	-2.8%	-3.4%	-0.7%	-1.7%	-0.7%	-0.9%	-1.8%
Debt Service Ratio [d]	32.0%	29.4%	28.0%	28.8%	31.3%	28.5%	28.6%	26.3%	25.5%	27.2%

Note: Debt related information is taken from the World Bank Debt Reporting System.

a. Includes interest on military debt to FSU and returns on foreign investments.
b. Corresponds to bilateral balance or servicing of the Russia debt from 1990-91 onwards.
c. Residual item including reserve valuation changes, rupee trade imbalance, etc.
d. As proportion of gross current receipts (GNFS exports + factor receipts + current transfer receipts).

Source: Government of India; Reserve Bank of India; Ministry of Commerce; Ministry of Finance, Economic Survey, various issues;
World Bank Staff estimates.

Table A2.2 (a)
Merchandise Exports
(US$ million at current prices)

	1986-87	1987-88	1988-89	1989-90	1990-91	1991-92	1992-93	1993-94	1994-95	1995-96
Primary Exports	3280	3288	3255	3852	4355	4189	3935	5002	5242	7300
Fish	422	411	435	412	535	589	602	813	1126	1011
Rice	154	261	229	256	257	308	337	410	384	1361
Cashews	257	243	191	221	249	276	259	334	397	368
Coffee	232	202	203	208	140	135	130	174	335	451
Tea	451	463	421	550	596	494	337	338	311	350
Spices	218	260	190	170	133	161	136	181	195	235
Iron Ore	428	427	465	557	584	585	381	438	413	518
Other Primary	1118	1020	1122	1478	1859	1641	1753	2313	2080	3006
Manufactured Exports	6458	8798	10696	12715	13783	13774	14607	17231	21088	24483
Chemicals	456	618	890	1287	1176	1591	1378	1813	2434	2953
Leather Manufactures	721	964	1051	1170	1449	1276	1278	1300	1611	1722
Textiles	995	1407	1312	1598	2266	2164	2153	2536	3297	3829
Garments	1041	1403	1452	1936	2235	2211	2394	2586	3282	3677
Gems & Jewellery	1622	2015	3034	3178	2923	2753	3072	3995	4500	5273
Engineering Goods	886	1141	1558	1967	2157	2246	2458	3023	3486	3618
Petroleum Products	321	500	349	418	522	417	476	398	439	454
Other Manufactures [a]	416	750	1050	1161	1053	1115	1398	1581	2039	2957
TOTAL EXPORTS (Commerce) [b]	9738	12086	13951	16568	18137	17963	18542	22233	26330	31783
Statistical Discrepancy	682	560	306	387	340	303	327	450	527	650
TOTAL EXPORTS (B.O.P.)	10420	12646	14257	16955	18477	18266	18869	22683	26857	32433

a. Including unclassified exports.
b. Net of crude petroleum exports.

Source: Ministry of Commerce (D.G.C.I.S); Reserve Bank of India; Ministry of Finance, Economic Survey, various issues;
World Bank Staff estimates.

Table A2.2 (b)
Merchandise Exports
(US$ million at 1980-81 prices)

	1986-87	1987-88	1988-89	1989-90	1990-91	1991-92	1992-93	1993-94	1994-95	1995-96
Primary Exports	3182	3097	3218	3983	4496	4365	4527	5714	5273	8166
Fish	357	354	386	424	480	570	570	679	778	766
Rice	97	152	137	165	197	265	227	300	348	2153
Cashews	236	228	202	266	305	288	344	404	440	540
Coffee	231	317	291	437	339	343	445	447	453	560
Tea	418	479	450	487	463	503	390	361	353	373
Spices	138	114	122	115	110	115	104	174	136	148
Iron Ore	468	461	541	578	530	490	344	431	428	530
Other Primary	1237	993	1089	1512	2073	1791	2104	2918	2337	3095
Manufactured Exports	6696	8411	9180	10414	11299	12673	14137	15905	18406	22531
Chemicals	463	542	847	1182	1584	2156	1333	1724	2268	2801
Leather Manufactures	770	899	957	961	979	956	1070	1151	1412	1527
Textiles	756	1074	915	1122	1329	1872	2512	2266	2868	3266
Garments	917	1142	1136	1485	1640	1758	1822	1806	2176	2514
Gems & Jewellery	1419	1602	2081	1908	1573	1645	2081	2639	2982	3625
Engineering Goods	978	1390	1728	2220	2470	2513	3228	3878	4455	7019
Petroleum Products	645	985	694	784	917	980	1241	1346	1086	1091
Other Manufactures [a]	749	778	823	752	808	793	850	1095	1158	688
TOTAL EXPORTS (Commerce) [b]	9878	11508	12398	14397	15795	17039	18664	21619	23679	30696
Statistical Discrepancy	691	533	272	337	296	288	329	438	474	627
TOTAL EXPORTS (B.O.P.)	10569	12041	12670	14734	16091	17326	18993	22057	24153	31324

a. Including unclassified exports.

b. Net of crude petroleum exports.

Source: Ministry of Commerce (D.G.C.I.S); Reserve Bank of India; Ministry of Finance, Economic Survey, various issues;
        World Bank Staff estimates.

Table A2.2 (c)
Export Unit Value Indices
(US$ terms: 1980-81 = 100)

	1986-87	1987-88	1988-89	1989-90	1990-91	1991-92	1992-93	1993-94	1994-95	1995-96
Primary Exports	103.1	106.1	101.2	96.7	96.8	96.0	86.9	87.5	99.4	89.4
Fish	118.1	116.1	112.7	97.2	111.5	103.2	105.6	119.9	144.8	132.0
Rice	159.1	172.2	167.5	155.6	130.5	116.4	148.7	136.8	110.4	63.2
Cashews	108.6	106.3	94.6	82.9	81.7	95.6	75.1	82.8	90.2	68.2
Coffee	100.4	63.7	69.8	47.7	41.4	39.5	29.2	39.0	74.1	80.5
Tea	108.0	96.8	93.4	113.0	128.9	98.2	86.6	93.5	88.0	93.8
Spices	158.3	228.1	155.3	147.3	121.4	139.3	130.4	104.0	142.9	159.1
Iron Ore	91.4	92.7	85.9	96.4	110.2	119.5	110.9	101.5	96.6	97.8
Other Primary	90.4	102.7	103.0	97.7	89.7	91.6	83.3	79.3	89.0	97.1
Manufactured Exports	96.5	104.6	116.5	122.1	122.0	108.7	103.3	108.3	114.6	108.7
Chemicals	98.5	114.0	105.1	108.9	74.3	73.8	103.4	105.2	107.3	105.5
Leather Manufactures	93.6	107.3	109.8	121.7	147.9	133.4	119.4	112.9	114.0	112.8
Textiles	131.5	131.1	143.4	142.4	170.6	115.6	85.7	111.9	114.9	117.3
Garments	113.6	122.9	127.8	130.4	136.3	125.8	131.4	143.1	150.8	146.3
Gems & Jewellery	114.3	125.8	145.8	166.6	185.9	167.4	147.6	151.4	150.9	145.5
Engineering Goods	90.6	82.1	90.2	88.6	87.4	89.4	76.2	78.0	78.3	51.5
Petroleum Products	49.8	50.8	50.3	53.4	57.0	42.5	38.4	29.5	40.5	41.6
Other Manufactures [a]	55.6	96.4	127.5	154.3	130.4	140.6	164.5	144.4	176.1	429.6
TOTAL EXPORTS (Commerce) [b]	98.6	105.0	112.5	115.1	114.8	105.4	99.3	102.8	111.2	103.5
Statistical Discrepancy	98.6	105.0	112.5	115.1	114.8	105.4	99.3	102.8	111.2	103.5
TOTAL EXPORTS (B.O.P.)	98.6	105.0	112.5	115.1	114.8	105.4	99.3	102.8	111.2	103.5

a. Including unclassified exports.
b. Net of crude petroleum exports.

Source: Ministry of Commerce (D.G.C.I.S); Reserve Bank of India; Ministry of Finance, Economic Survey, various issues;
World Bank Staff estimates.

Table A2.3 (a)
Merchandise Imports
(US$ million at current prices)

	1986-87	1987-88	1988-89	1989-90	1990-91	1991-92	1992-93	1993-94	1994-95	1995-96
Food	1068	1292	1203	714	690	426	702	550	1464	1243
Foodgrains	37	25	437	227	102	71	334	93	29	24
Edible Oils	479	709	503	127	182	101	58	53	199	652
Others	552	557	263	361	407	254	311	404	1236	567
Other Consumer Goods	594	600	700	800	851	637	782	680	790	1026
P.O.L	2187	3148	2938	3766	6005	5318	5887	5651	5681	7547
Crude Petroleum [a]	1672	2395	1891	2455	3409	3189	3691	3407	3285	3442
Petroleum Products	515	753	1047	1311	2596	2128	2196	2244	2396	4105
Capital Goods [b]	5074	5063	4805	5300	5834	4256	3743	5311	5567	6577
Intermediate: PRIMARY	2474	2997	3800	4488	4653	3821	4554	4533	4296	5405
Fertilizer Raw Material	218	243	301	329	348	311	279	194	288	287
Gems	1170	1538	1984	2546	2082	1968	2443	2634	1630	2083
Other	1087	1217	1515	1613	2222	1543	1832	1705	2378	3034
Intermediate: MANUFACTURES	4314	4056	6051	6151	6031	5058	6219	6575	10855	14556
Fertilizer Manufactures	387	132	341	737	636	649	699	632	764	1321
Iron & Steel	1134	982	1341	1383	1177	803	779	795	1082	1373
Non-Ferrous Metals	324	444	544	752	614	342	395	479	718	907
Others	2469	2497	3826	3279	3605	3264	4346	4670	8292	10953
TOTAL IMPORTS (Commerce) [a]	15712	17156	19497	21219	24065	19516	21888	23301	28654	36354
Statistical Discrepancy	2028	2660	4121	3192	3849	1548	1349	1768	3186	5367
TOTAL IMPORTS [a]	17740	19816	23618	24411	27914	21064	23237	25069	31840	41721

a. Net of crude oil exports.
b. 1987-88 onwards Capital Goods includes Project Goods.

Source: Ministry of Commerce (D.G.C.I.S); Reserve Bank of India; Ministry of Finance, Economic Survey, various issues; World Bank Staff estimates.

Table A2.3 (b)
Merchandise Imports
(US$ million at 1980-81 prices)

	1986-87	1987-88	1988-89	1989-90	1990-91	1991-92	1992-93	1993-94	1994-95	1995-96
Food	1527	1710	1968	865	807	446	1015	616	1368	1004
Foodgrains	56	35	1021	310	126	77	662	165	33	27
Edible Oils	770	980	539	160	259	111	51	56	171	485
Others	701	695	409	395	422	258	302	394	1164	493
Other Consumer Goods	567	513	555	643	647	475	559	487	546	655
P.O.L	5053	5944	6734	7272	8287	9409	11395	12156	11679	13487
Crude Petroleum [a]	4041	4630	4651	5089	5405	6264	7660	8145	7825	9036
Petroleum Products	1012	1314	2083	2183	2882	3145	3735	4012	3854	4451
Capital Goods [b]	4703	4203	3702	4142	4312	3081	2598	3697	3741	4080
Intermediate: PRIMARY	3038	2419	2841	3363	3314	2660	3076	3102	2826	3297
Fertilizer Raw Material	197	161	178	157	174	152	147	121	169	164
Gems	1127	1262	1511	1965	1521	1408	1676	1812	1082	1278
Other	1714	996	1151	1242	1619	1101	1253	1170	1575	1855
Intermediate: MANUFACTURES	4644	3529	4728	5057	4803	3969	4846	5025	7332	9236
Fertilizer Manufactures	813	320	472	876	808	835	1117	989	770	1302
Iron & Steel	1110	874	1275	1162	936	626	581	595	782	917
Non-Ferrous Metals	481	540	553	775	599	327	362	440	637	743
Others	2240	1795	2428	2244	2460	2181	2785	3001	5144	6274
TOTAL IMPORTS (Commerce) [a]	19531	18318	20528	21342	22171	20040	23488	25084	27492	31759
Statistical Discrepancy	2521	2840	4339	3210	3546	1590	1448	1904	3057	4689
TOTAL IMPORTS [a]	22052	21158	24867	24552	25717	21629	24935	26987	30549	36448

a. Net of crude oil exports.
b. 1987-88 onwards Capital Goods includes Project Goods.

Source: Ministry of Commerce (D.G.C.I.S); Reserve Bank of India; Ministry of Finance, Economic Survey, various issues;
World Bank Staff estimates.

Table A2.3 (c)
Import Unit Value Indices
(US$ Terms: 1980-81 = 100)

	1986-87	1987-88	1988-89	1989-90	1990-91	1991-92	1992-93	1993-94	1994-95	1995-96
Food	70.0	75.5	61.1	82.6	85.5	95.5	69.2	89.3	107.1	123.8
Foodgrains	66.1	72.0	42.8	73.1	80.3	91.9	50.4	56.0	89.3	88.7
Edible Oils	62.2	72.4	93.4	79.3	70.2	90.9	114.0	94.5	116.5	134.7
Others	78.8	80.2	64.5	91.4	96.5	98.6	102.8	102.5	106.2	115.0
Other Consumer Goods	104.8	117.1	126.1	124.5	131.5	134.3	140.0	139.6	144.7	156.7
P.O.L	43.3	53.0	43.6	51.8	72.5	56.5	51.7	46.5	48.6	56.0
Crude Petroleum	41.4	51.7	40.7	48.2	63.1	50.9	48.2	41.8	42.0	38.1
Petroleum Products	50.9	57.3	50.3	60.1	90.1	67.7	58.8	55.9	62.2	92.2
Capital Goods	107.9	120.5	129.8	128.0	135.3	138.1	144.1	143.7	148.8	161.2
Intermediate: PRIMARY	81.5	123.9	133.8	133.4	140.4	143.6	148.1	146.1	152.0	164.0
Fertilizer Raw Material	110.5	150.7	168.7	209.6	199.8	204.7	190.1	160.8	170.6	175.4
Gems	103.8	121.9	131.3	129.6	136.9	139.8	145.8	145.4	150.6	163.1
Other	63.4	122.2	131.6	129.9	137.3	140.2	146.2	145.8	151.0	163.5
Intermediate: MANUFACTURES	92.9	114.9	128.0	121.6	125.6	127.4	128.3	130.8	148.0	157.6
Fertilizer Manufactures	47.6	41.3	72.3	84.2	78.6	77.7	62.5	63.9	99.2	101.5
Iron & Steel	102.1	112.3	105.2	119.0	125.8	128.4	133.9	133.5	138.3	149.8
Non-Ferrous Metals	67.5	82.3	98.3	97.0	102.5	104.6	109.1	108.8	112.7	122.1
Others	110.2	139.1	157.6	146.1	146.5	149.6	156.0	155.6	161.2	174.6
TOTAL IMPORTS (Commerce)	80.4	93.7	95.0	99.4	108.5	97.4	93.2	92.9	104.2	114.5
Statistical Discrepancy	80.4	93.7	95.0	99.4	108.5	97.4	93.2	92.9	104.2	114.5
TOTAL IMPORTS	80.4	93.7	95.0	99.4	108.5	97.4	93.2	92.9	104.2	114.5

Source: Ministry of Commerce (D.G.C.I.S); Reserve Bank of India; Ministry of Finance, <u>Economic Survey</u>, various issues;
World Bank Staff estimates.

Table A2.4
Invisibles on Current Account
(US$ million)

	1986-87	1987-88	1988-89	1989-90	1990-91	1991-92	1992-93	1993-94	1994-95	1995-96
GROSS RECEIPTS	6057	6741	7023	7479	7757	9578	8233	9153	13423	15792
Non-Factor Services	3217	3571	3956	4246	4551	5022	4716	5264	5939	7748
of which:										
Transport	538	680	898	907	983	939	982	1433	1654	1950
Travel	1256	1431	1419	1433	1456	1977	2098	2222	2325	2900
Others	1423	1460	1639	1906	2112	2106	1636	1609	1960	2898
Factor Income	501	446	397	936	1123	758	733	272	1264	1024
Current Transfers [a]	2339	2724	2670	2297	2083	3798	2784	3617	6220	7020
GROSS PAYMENTS	4781	5971	6270	7707	8518	8512	8039	8568	11215	12268
Non-Factor Services	2222	3027	3225	3523	3571	3815	3588	4729	6310	7067
of which:										
Transport [b]	585	870	1027	1115	1093	1289	1485	1765	2200	2700
Travel	290	376	405	403	392	465	385	497	900	1400
Others	1347	1781	1793	2005	2086	2061	1718	2467	3210	2967
Factor Income	2547	2918	3029	4168	4933	4682	4440	4047	4885	5181
Current Transfers	12	26	16	16	14	15	11	-208	20	20
NET RECEIPTS	1277	770	753	-228	-761	1066	194	585	2208	3524
Non-Factor Services	995	544	731	723	980	1207	1128	535	-371	681
of which:										
Transport	-47	-190	-129	-208	-110	-350	-503	-332	-546	-750
Travel	966	1055	1014	1030	1064	1512	1713	1725	1425	1500
Others	76	-321	-154	-99	26	45	-82	-858	-1250	-69
Factor Income	-2046	-2472	-2632	-3232	-3810	-3924	-3707	-3775	-3621	-4157
Current Transfers	2327	2698	2654	2281	2069	3783	2773	3825	6200	7000

a. Excluding foreign grants, and including the Bhopal settlement in 1988-89.
b. Excluding freight included in c.i.f value of merchandise imports.

Note: Debt related information is taken from the World Bank Debt Reporting System.

Source: Ministry of Commerce (D.G.C.I.S); Reserve Bank of India; Ministry of Finance, Economic Survey, various issues;
World Bank Staff estimates.

Table A2.5
Decomposition of Recent Export Growth
(US$ million at current prices - annual averages)

	1984-85 to 89-90	1990-91 to 95-96	Increase	Contribution to Growth (%)
<u>Manufactured Exports</u>	8295	17494	9199	84.5
Consumption goods	5349	10630	5281	48.5
Leather	851	1439	588	5.4
Gems (gross)	2020	3753	1733	15.9
Garments	1255	2731	1476	13.6
Textiles	1224	2708	1484	13.6
Investment goods [a]	1189	2832	1642	15.1
Intermediate goods	1757	4033	2276	20.9
Chemicals	677	1891	1214	11.2
Petroleum Prod.	370	451	81	0.7
Others [b]	709	1691	981	9.0
<u>Primary Exports</u>	3322	5004	1682	15.5
Fish	389	779	390	3.6
Rice	200	510	309	2.8
Cashews	208	314	106	1.0
Coffee	207	228	21	0.2
Tea	507	404	-103	-0.9
Spices	206	173	-33	-0.3
Iron Ore	456	487	31	0.3
Other Primary	1148	2109	960	8.8
TOTAL EXPORTS (Customs) [c]	11617	22498	10881	100.0
Discrepancy	635	433	-202	
TOTAL EXPORTS (BOP) [c]	12252	22931	10679	
Memo:				
Gems (Net) [d]	519	1613	1094	

a. Refers to engineering goods.

b. Including unclassified exports.

c. Total exports, f.o.b., net of crude oil.

d. Exports less imports of gems and jewellery.

Source: Ministry of Commerce, (D.G.C.I.S.); Reserve Bank of India.

Table A3.1(a)
External Debt Summary: Debt Outstanding and Disbursed
(US$ million at current prices)

	1984-85	1985-86	1986-87	1987-88	1988-89	1989-90	1990-91	1991-92	1992-93	1993-94	1994-95	1995-96
A. Public & Publicly Guar. LT	24344	30273	37154	44354	50223	64939	71208	73450	77776	83532	86499	79725
1. Official Creditors	19226	22719	26376	30369	31191	43609	48353	49420	52973	55858	61885	57083
a. Multilateral	10462	12400	14268	16588	18061	19664	21768	23964	26130	27826	31475	29986
aa. of which IBRD	1688	2396	3475	4661	5590	6615	7685	8459	9067	9870	11120	9849
ab. of which IDA	8545	9750	10529	11615	12019	12521	13312	14203	15339	15978	17666	17499
b. Bilateral	8764	10319	12108	13781	13130	23945	26584	25457	26844	28032	30410	27097
2. Private Creditors	5118	7554	10779	13985	19032	21330	22855	24029	24803	27674	24613	22641
a. Commercial Banks	3915	5567	7679	10508	12938	14727	16145	16018	16954	18586	14439	13526
b. Suppliers Credits	465	629	805	715	632	539	434	431	644	878	1367	1205
c. Bonds (including IDB)	259	646	1087	1287	1846	2479	2707	4168	4088	3903	3853	3279
d. Other Private	479	712	1207	1475	3616	3586	3569	3412	3116	4307	4954	4632
B. Private Non-Guaranteed LT	1341	1497	1388	1652	1473	1551	1488	1545	1205	1770	6427	6618
C. Total LT DOD (A+B)	25685	31770	38542	46007	51696	66490	72696	74995	78981	85302	92925	86343
D. Use of IMF Credit	4456	4832	4768	4023	2573	1566	2623	3451	4798	5041	4312	2374
E. Short-Term Debt	3672	4358	4946	5673	6358	7501	8544	7070	6340	3626	4264	5049
F. Total External Debt (C+D+E)	33813	40960	48257	55702	60627	75557	83862	85516	90120	93968	101501	93766
Memo items:												
Total NRI Deposits	3265	4915	6595	8616	10482	12368	13953	13263	14523	14498	14661	13894
Military Debt to FSU	..	..	..	..	..	9972	11645	9222	9661	9160	8763	7488

.. Not available.

Source: World Bank, DRS data.

Table A3.1(b)
External Debt Summary: Disbursements
(US$ million at current prices)

	1984-85	1985-86	1986-87	1987-88	1988-89	1989-90	1990-91	1991-92	1992-93	1993-94	1994-95	1995-96
A. Public & Publicly Guar. LT	3825	4507	6271	6953	10155	7077	6384	6907	6940	7187	5933	5510
1. Official Creditors	1836	2080	2255	3624	3635	3559	3570	4367	4170	3661	3304	2932
a. Multilateral	1144	1404	1314	2269	2625	2105	2211	2757	2424	2084	2221	1894
aa. IBRD	291	329	641	1295	1716	1445	1219	1231	852	1216	741	589
ab. IDA	823	1047	656	917	755	566	762	953	1186	669	966	729
b. Bilateral	691	676	942	1355	1010	1453	1360	1610	1746	1577	1083	1038
2. Private Creditors	1989	2427	4016	3329	6520	3519	2814	2540	2769	3526	2628	2578
a. Commercial banks	1240	1727	2934	2969	3361	2623	1983	509	2129	1504	845	1258
b. Suppliers Credits	405	193	283	5	16	3	8	78	293	319	613	35
c. Bonds (including IDB)	232	320	339	116	679	705	427	1619	0	0	0	0
d. Other Private	113	187	460	239	2463	187	396	335	348	1702	1171	1286
B. Private Non-Guaranteed LT	450	503	325	348	175	240	214	309	254	1060	867	1179
C. Total LT Disbursements (A+B)	4275	5010	6596	7301	10330	7317	6598	7216	7193	8247	6800	6689
D. IMF	201	0	0	0	0	0	1754	1233	1624	323	0	0
E. Net Short-Term Capital	334	686	588	727	685	1143	1043	-1474	-730	-2714	638	785
F. Total Disbursements (C+D+E)	4476	5010	6596	7301	10330	7317	8352	8449	8817	8570	6800	6689

Source: World Bank, DRS data.

Table A3.1(c)
External Debt Summary: Principal Repayments
(US$ million at current prices)

	1984-85	1985-86	1986-87	1987-88	1988-89	1989-90	1990-91	1991-92	1992-93	1993-94	1994-95	1995-96
A. Public & Publicly Guar. LT	789	946	1811	1605	1670	1644	2351	2630	3001	3532	4705	6624
1. Official Creditors	550	656	851	1120	991	1117	1226	1466	1610	1892	2412	3799
a. Multilateral	132	162	242	508	397	467	609	703	838	1000	1103	1515
aa. of which IBRD	88	104	174	430	303	352	472	527	634	758	827	943
ab. of which IDA	41	53	61	69	81	98	114	141	155	174	194	226
b. Bilateral	418	494	609	612	594	651	618	763	772	892	1309	2283
2. Private Creditors	240	290	960	485	679	527	1125	1164	1391	1641	2294	2826
a. Commercial Banks	178	200	773	284	367	223	269	320	469	650	992	1680
b. Suppliers Credits	32	45	120	98	96	98	113	82	100	124	188	127
d. Bonds (including IDB)	0	0	0	6	14	27	280	239	206	338	381	310
e. Other Private	29	44	67	97	202	178	464	523	617	530	732	708
B. Private Non-Guaranteed LT	305	363	480	290	280	322	318	273	306	495	123	156
C. Total LT Repayments (A+B)	1094	1308	2291	1894	1949	1966	2670	2903	3307	4027	4828	6780
D. IMF Repayments	134	264	648	1082	1210	1008	726	460	334	134	1174	1719
E. Total LT Repayments (C+D)	1228	1573	2938	2976	3160	2974	3395	3363	3641	4161	6003	8499

Source: World Bank, DRS data.

Table A3.1(d)
External Debt Summary: Net Flows
(US$ million at current prices)

	1984-85	1985-86	1986-87	1987-88	1988-89	1989-90	1990-91	1991-92	1992-93	1993-94	1994-95	1995-96
A. Public & Publicly Guar. LT	3036	3561	4460	5348	8485	5433	4033	4277	3938	3654	1228	-1114
1. Official Creditors	1286	1424	1404	2503	2644	2441	2344	2901	2560	1770	893	-867
a. Multilateral	1012	1242	1072	1761	2228	1639	1602	2054	1587	1084	1118	378
aa. of which IBRD	203	224	467	865	1414	1094	747	703	219	458	-86	-354
ab. of which IDA	782	994	595	848	675	468	648	812	1030	495	773	503
b. Bilateral	274	182	332	743	416	803	742	847	974	685	-225	-1245
2. Private Creditors	1749	2137	3056	2844	5841	2992	1689	1376	1378	1885	335	-247
a. Commercial Banks	1062	1527	2161	2685	2995	2400	1715	188	1660	855	-148	-423
b. Suppliers Credits	372	148	163	-93	-80	-96	-105	-5	193	195	425	-92
c. Bonds (including IDB)	232	320	339	110	665	678	147	1380	-206	-338	-381	-310
d. Other Private	83	142	393	143	2261	9	-67	-188	-269	1173	439	577
B. Private Non-Guaranteed LT	145	140	-155	59	-104	-82	-104	36	-53	565	744	1023
C. Total LT Repayments (A+B)	3181	3701	4305	5406	8381	5351	3928	4313	3886	4219	1971	-91
D. Net IMF Credit	67	-264	-648	-1082	-1210	-1008	1028	773	1290	189	-1174	-1719
E. Net Short Debt Flows	334	686	588	727	685	1143	1043	-1474	-730	-2714	638	785
F. Total Net Flows (C+D+E)	3248	3437	3658	4325	7171	4343	4957	5086	5176	4408	797	-1810
Memo item:												
Total NRI Net Flows	814	1579	1825	1992	2328	2295	1536	290	2120	1097	818	945

Source: Derived from Tables 3.1(b) and 3.1(c).

Table A3.1(e)
External Debt Summary: Interest Payments
(US$ million at current prices)

	1984-85	1985-86	1986-87	1987-88	1988-89	1989-90	1990-91	1991-92	1992-93	1993-94	1994-95	1995-96
A. Public & Publicly Guar. LT	834	1118	1504	1844	2002	3174	3660	3416	3324	3422	3324	3526
1. Official Creditors	444	558	694	812	941	1352	1493	1510	1629	1684	1826	1889
a. Multilateral	239	282	388	479	581	640	738	796	899	943	1014	1059
aa. of which IBRD	169	209	295	378	474	529	615	643	708	721	768	1059
ab. of which IDA	68	71	91	98	98	90	97	101	109	114	121	131
b. Bilateral	204	275	306	333	360	712	755	714	730	741	812	830
2. Private Creditors	390	561	810	1032	1060	1822	2167	1906	1695	1738	1498	1636
a. Commercial Banks	339	442	615	779	788	1520	1754	1430	1200	1142	874	985
b. Suppliers Credits	8	48	64	67	61	53	43	31	31	39	64	87
c. Bonds (including IDB)	3	17	54	83	108	147	187	200	234	342	214	195
d. Other Private	39	55	77	104	104	102	183	246	230	215	347	370
B. Private Non-Guaranteed L	138	154	158	147	127	140	135	126	123	139	391	531
C. Total LT Interest (A+B)	972	1272	1662	1992	2128	3314	3795	3542	3448	3561	3715	4057
D. IMF Service Charges	374	360	317	297	233	184	134	203	271	271	228	182
E. Interest Paid on ST Debt	389	326	356	429	437	570	899	826	399	367	312	385
F. Total Interest Paid (C+D+E	1734	1959	2335	2717	2799	4068	4828	4572	4118	4200	4255	4624
Memo item:												
Total NRI Interest Payments	291	400	524	715	609	1076	1282	1036	918	905	1014	1262

Source: World Bank, DRS data.

Table A3.2
External Reserves
(US$ million)

	Foreign Exchange	SDRs	Reserve Position in the Fund	Reserves excluding Gold	Gold[a]	Reserves including Gold	Use of IMF Credit	Net Reserves
1980-81	5850	603	405	6858	370	7228	327	6901
1981-82	3582	473	405	4460	335	4795	964	3831
1982-83	4281	291	393	4965	324	5289	2876	2413
1983-84	5099	230	518	5847	320	6167	4150	2017
1984-85	5482	145	483	6110	325	6435	3932	2503
1985-86	5972	131	554	6657	416	7073	4290	2783
1986-87	5924	179	626	6729	470	7199	4291	2908
1987-88	5618	97	676	6391	507	6898	3653	3246
1988-89	4226	103	630	4959	473	5432	2364	3067
1989-90	3368	107	634	4109	487	4596	1493	3102
1990-91	2236	102	--	2338	504	2842	2623	219
1991-92	5631	90	1	5722	542	6264	3451	2812
1992-93	6434	18	297	6749	557	7306	4798	2508
1993-94	15068	108	300	15476	583	16059	5040	11019
1994-95	20809	19	332	21160	695	21855	4312	17543
1995-96	17044	82	311	17436	654	18090	2374	15715
1996-97	22367	2	947	23316	620	23936	1313	22623
End of the Month								
1994								
March	15068	108	300	15476	583	16059	5040	11019
June	16372	45	308	16725	598	17323	4002	13321
September	18856	3	312	19171	606	19777	4055	15722
December	19386	2	310	19698	603	20301	4034	16267
1995								
March	20809	19	332	21160	695	21855	4312	17543
June	19601	95	334	20030	702	20732	3933	16799
September	19064	49	320	19433	674	20107	3377	16729
December	17467	139	316	17922	665	18587	2923	15664
1996								
March	17044	82	311	17436	654	18090	2374	15715
June	17526	128	307	17961	646	18607	2079	16527
September	18433	57	306	18796	644	19440	1755	17685
December	19742	122	306	20170	643	20813	1560	19253
1997								
March	22367	2	295	22664	620	23284	1313	21971

-- Not available.

Note: IMF Credit refers to Use of IMF credit within the General Resources Account (GRA) excluding Trust Fund, Structural Adjustment Facility (SAF), and Enhanced Structural Adjustment Facility (ESAF) loans.

a. Valued at 35 SDR's per fine troy ounce.

Source: IMF, International Financial Statistics, various issues.

Table A4.1
Central Government Finances Summary
(Rs billion at current prices)

	1991-92	1992-93	1993-94	1994-95	1995-96	1996-97 B.E.	1996-97 R.E.	1997-98 B.E.
Revenue[a]	690.68	760.89	754.05	966.90	1115.27	1353.46	1313.58	1579.42
Tax Revenue	500.69	540.44	534.49	674.54	819.39	973.10	972.12	1133.93
Customs	222.57	237.76	221.93	267.89	357.57	444.35	441.35	525.50
Union Excise[b]	160.17	163.67	172.24	210.64	221.76	250.73	246.12	276.37
Income Tax[b]	16.27	18.31	13.46	34.68	43.16	48.19	53.14	60.09
Corporate Tax	78.53	88.99	100.60	138.22	164.87	196.00	190.10	218.60
Other	23.15	31.71	26.26	23.11	32.03	33.83	41.41	53.37
Non-Tax Revenue	189.99	220.45	219.56	292.36	295.88	380.36	341.46	445.49
Interest Receipts	109.33	124.87	150.62	157.97	184.19	213.93	219.45	240.92
Asset Sales	30.38	19.61	-0.48	56.07	13.97	50.01	5.75	48.00
Other	50.28	75.97	69.42	78.32	97.72	116.42	116.26	156.57
Expenditure[c]	1053.93	1162.62	1356.62	1543.94	1717.70	1976.12	1944.89	2233.97
Non-Plan Expenditure	804.53	859.58	981.91	1133.61	1319.01	1499.75	1474.04	1693.24
Interest Payments	265.63	310.35	366.95	440.49	500.31	600.00	585.00	680.00
Defense	163.47	175.82	218.45	232.45	268.56	277.98	294.98	356.20
Subsidies	122.53	119.95	126.82	129.32	133.05	163.20	166.94	182.51
Other Non-Plan Expenditure	252.90	253.47	269.69	331.35	417.09	458.57	427.12	474.53
Plan Expenditure	309.61	366.60	436.62	473.78	463.74	546.85	548.94	628.52
Less: Recovery of Loans	60.21	63.56	61.91	63.45	65.05	70.48	78.09	87.79
Gross Fiscal Deficit	363.41	401.74	602.57	577.04	602.44	622.66	631.31	654.56
Financed by:								
Reserve Bank of India (net)[d]	59.04	32.73	13.48	9.17	190.89	n.a.	37.95	n.a.
Marketable Securities (net)[e]	114.22	181.80	387.19	183.43	191.71	301.38f	258.24	344.25f
Other Domestic Borrowing (net)	135.94	134.01	151.16	332.98	98.79	216.66	216.66	598.05
External Borrowing (net)	54.21	53.19	50.74	51.46	3.18	24.61	25.89	24.35
Memo:								
GDPmp	6167.99	7059.18	8097.66	9536.80	10985.76	12453.20	12626.20	14545.33
Fiscal Deficit / GDP	5.9	5.7	7.4	6.1	5.5	5.0	5.0	4.5
Revenue / GDP	11.2	10.8	9.3	10.1	10.2	10.9	10.4	10.9
Expenditure / GDP	17.1	16.5	16.8	16.2	15.6	15.9	15.4	15.4

Note: BE = Budget estimates; RE = Revised estimates.

a. Including sale of public assets (disinvestment).
b. Net of states' share.
c. Net of loan recoveries.
d. Monetized deficit (equal to net RBI credit to Central Government).
e. T-Bills and dated securities, excluding those issued to RBI.
f.   Includes RBI (net) figure.

Source: Ministry of Finance, Union budget documents.

Table A4.2
Budgetary Classification of Central Government Finances
(Rs. billion at current prices)

	1988-89	1989-90	1990-91	1991-92	1992-93	1993-94	1994-95	1995-96	1996-97 B.E.	1996-97 R.E.	1997-98 B.E.
Revenue receipts	435.91	499.96	549.54	660.30	741.28	754.53	910.83	1101.30	1303.45	1307.83	1531.42
Tax revenue	337.51	383.49	429.78	500.69	540.44	534.49	674.54	819.39	973.10	972.12	1133.93
Non-tax revenue	98.40	116.47	119.76	159.61	200.84	220.04	236.29	281.91	330.35	335.71	397.49
of which: Interest from states	37.70	44.24	51.74	65.22	77.54	95.53	111.83	130.02	151.13	152.34	180.32
Revenue expenditure (A+B+C+D)	541.06	642.07	735.15	823.08	927.02	1081.69	1221.11	1398.62	1618.20	1589.88	1834.09
A. Developmental	140.36	184.15	196.01	198.17	208.60	243.68	301.50	355.92	414.27	405.57	459.53
1. Social services	22.43	24.99	27.53	30.57	34.30	40.97	47.43	66.29	93.36	85.05	113.44
2. Economic services	117.93	159.17	168.48	167.60	174.30	202.71	254.07	289.63	320.91	320.52	346.09
B. Non-developmental	287.69	335.47	391.00	450.34	521.58	613.17	708.20	816.78	958.55	932.90	1129.63
Defence services	95.58	101.94	108.74	114.42	121.09	149.77	164.26	188.41	188.55	209.94	267.13
Interest payments	142.61	177.57	214.71	265.63	310.35	366.95	440.49	500.31	600.00	585.00	680.00
C. Grants-in-aid and contributions	102.08	109.36	134.39	159.53	180.54	211.11	204.83	218.28	237.43	242.82	236.53
of which: Grants to states	100.15	107.44	132.02	157.00	178.30	208.30	200.47	212.87	231.31	236.26	230.27
D. Revenue expenditure of UTs	10.92	13.09	13.75	15.05	16.30	13.73	6.59	7.63	7.95	8.59	8.41
Net current balance	-105.15	-142.11	-185.61	-162.78	-185.74	-327.16	-310.28	-297.32	-314.75	-282.05	-302.67
Capital expenditure (A+B+C+D-E)	204.08	237.18	260.88	200.63	215.99	275.41	266.75	305.12	307.91	349.25	351.89
A. Developmental	60.03	70.95	69.23	58.26	73.82	55.60	73.96	50.49	47.24	49.55	82.21
1. Social services	3.51	3.21	2.47	2.39	2.59	3.32	7.26	5.48	6.41	6.53	9.06
2. Economic services	56.52	67.74	66.77	55.87	71.23	52.28	66.70	45.01	40.83	43.02	73.14
B. Non-developmental	40.76	45.27	49.56	52.32	58.88	73.92	72.51	88.26	100.87	94.92	100.94
of which: Defence services	37.83	42.22	45.52	49.05	54.73	68.67	68.19	80.15	89.44	85.05	89.07
C. Capital expenditure of UTs	1.76	1.87	2.68	3.42	3.50	2.78	2.44	2.24	2.41	2.12	2.66
D. Loans and advances (net)	101.53	119.09	139.40	117.01	99.41	142.63	173.91	178.10	207.40	208.42	214.09
to States & UTs	67.30	79.55	98.69	94.18	86.97	100.72	143.13	142.67	148.37	148.37	170.76
to Others	34.23	39.55	40.71	22.83	12.44	41.92	30.78	29.73	36.64	30.79	28.24
E. Disinvestment of equity in PSEs	0.00	0.00	0.00	30.38	19.61	-0.48	56.07	13.97	50.01	5.75	48.00
Gross fiscal deficit (GOI Defn.)	309.22	379.30	446.50	363.41	401.74	602.57	577.04	602.44	622.66	631.31	654.56
Finance by instruments											
Market loans	84.18	74.04	80.01	75.10	36.76	289.28	203.26	330.87	254.98	199.90	344.25
Small savings	58.35	85.75	91.04	66.40	57.17	91.00	165.78	127.90	140.00	150.00	140.00
Provident funds	71.12	90.86	89.37	79.56	87.55	93.58	102.65	75.56	117.98	112.54	125.56
External loans	24.60	25.95	31.81	54.21	53.19	50.74	51.46	3.18	24.61	25.89	24.35
Treasury bills	62.44	109.11	117.69	68.87	117.73	119.82	-2.68	114.63	65.78	41.21	0.00
Other	8.53	-6.41	36.58	19.27	49.33	-41.85	56.57	-49.70	19.31	101.77	20.40

Note: BE = Budget estimates; RE = Revised estimates.

Source: Ministry of Finance, Union budget documents; Department of Expenditure, Finance Accounts; World Bank Staff Estimates.

Table A4.3
Budgetary Classification of State Government Finances
(Rs. billion at current prices)

	1988-89	1989-90	1990-91	1991-92	1992-93	1993-94	1994-95	1995-96 R.E.	1996-97 B.E.
Revenue receipts	507.09	589.08	673.19	813.59	911.04	1050.65	1222.82	1364.29	1474.31
Tax revenue	330.70	392.27	448.80	529.53	603.90	686.66	805.75	931.04	1065.75
Direct tax	24.13	30.06	33.75	39.59	42.28	49.73	70.05	80.27	88.74
Indirect tax	199.88	229.89	269.70	317.98	356.40	414.51	487.29	557.79	628.66
State share in central taxes	106.69	132.32	145.35	171.97	205.22	222.42	248.40	292.98	348.35
Non-tax revenue	176.38	196.81	224.39	284.06	307.14	363.99	417.07	433.25	408.56
of which: Grants from centre	100.15	107.44	132.02	157.00	178.30	208.30	200.47	212.87	231.31
Revenue expenditure [A+B+C]	522.96	602.53	717.73	861.86	962.05	1093.76	1284.40	1483.72	1620.44
A. Developmental (1+2)	362.37	407.81	488.55	585.05	634.65	708.38	786.37	921.93	983.45
1. Social services	205.74	240.17	279.62	310.92	345.65	389.61	449.02	552.86	593.71
2. Economic services	156.63	167.64	208.92	274.13	288.99	318.78	337.36	369.06	389.74
B. Non-developmental	155.06	188.69	221.34	266.66	315.06	373.67	484.99	545.59	617.87
of which: Interest payments	59.33	71.86	86.55	109.44	132.10	158.00	192.02	217.43	262.98
To centre	37.70	44.24	51.74	65.22	77.54	95.53	111.83	130.02	151.13
To others	21.63	27.62	34.81	44.23	54.56	62.47	80.19	87.41	111.85
C. Other expenditure[a]	5.53	6.03	7.84	10.16	12.35	11.71	13.03	16.20	19.11
Net current balance	-15.87	-13.45	-44.54	-48.27	-51.01	-43.11	-61.58	-119.43	-146.13
Capital expenditure [A+B+C]	98.66	117.52	134.78	132.49	157.77	167.84	215.41	251.07	267.73
A. Developmental (1+2)	68.53	77.28	89.61	98.61	103.44	120.51	169.31	169.97	178.33
1. Social services	11.28	11.71	12.57	16.47	16.64	18.31	23.04	28.21	35.07
2. Economic services	57.25	65.57	77.03	82.14	86.80	102.21	146.27	141.76	143.25
B. Non-developmental	2.25	2.36	2.63	2.34	3.10	3.99	4.20	6.72	8.37
C. Loans and advances (net)	27.88	37.88	42.55	31.54	51.22	43.33	41.90	74.38	81.03
Gross fiscal deficit	114.53	130.96	179.32	180.77	208.78	210.95	276.99	370.50	413.86
Finance by instrument:									
Market loans	22.46	25.95	25.60	33.10	38.50	42.28	41.05	51.11	52.99
Loans from centre (Net)	67.07	79.30	98.39	93.75	86.60	99.01	137.61	139.98	158.68
Small savings & Provident funds	20.01	23.07	30.69	29.09	36.22	43.30	47.79	48.63	51.57
Other	4.98	2.65	24.63	24.82	47.45	26.36	50.55	130.78	150.61

Note: BE = Budget estimates; RE = Revised estimates.

a. Other expenditure include compensation and assignments to local bodies and panchayat raj institutions and reserve with the finance department.

Source: Ministry of Finance, Union budget documents; Reserve Bank of India, RBI bulletins on state finances.

Table A4.4
Budgetary Classification of General Government Finances
(Rs. billion at current prices)

	1988-89	1989-90	1990-91	1991-92	1992-93	1993-94	1994-95	1995-96[a]	1996-97 B.E.
Revenue receipts	805.15	937.36	1038.97	1251.67	1396.48	1501.35	1821.35	2118.75	2413.76
Tax revenue	668.21	775.76	878.58	1030.22	1144.34	1221.15	1480.29	1750.43	2038.85
Non tax revenue	136.94	161.60	160.39	221.45	252.13	280.20	341.06	368.32	374.91
Revenue expenditure [A+B+C+D]	926.17	1092.92	1269.12	1462.73	1633.23	1871.62	2193.21	2539.45	2856.20
A. Developmental	502.73	591.96	684.56	783.22	843.24	952.06	1087.87	1277.85	1397.72
1. Social services	228.17	265.15	307.16	341.49	379.95	430.58	496.45	619.15	687.07
2. Economic services	274.55	326.80	377.40	441.72	463.29	521.48	591.42	658.69	710.65
B. Non-developmental	405.05	479.92	560.60	651.78	759.10	891.30	1081.36	1232.34	1425.29
C. Revenue disbursements of UTs	10.92	13.09	13.75	15.05	16.30	13.73	6.59	7.63	7.95
D. Other expenditure[b]	7.46	7.95	10.21	12.68	14.59	14.53	17.39	21.62	25.23
Net current balance	-121.02	-155.56	-230.15	-211.05	-236.75	-370.28	-371.87	-420.70	-442.44
Capital expenditure [A+B+C+D-E]	227.16	277.58	293.64	235.71	291.60	342.11	344.55	416.22	416.95
A. Developmental (1+2)	128.56	148.23	158.84	156.87	177.26	176.11	243.28	220.46	225.57
1. Social services	14.79	14.92	15.04	18.86	19.23	21.63	30.30	33.69	41.48
2. Economic services	113.76	133.31	143.80	138.00	158.03	154.49	212.97	186.77	184.08
B. Non-Developmental	43.01	47.63	52.19	54.67	61.98	77.90	76.71	94.99	109.24
C. Loans and advances (net)	53.82	79.85	79.93	51.13	68.47	84.83	78.20	112.50	129.75
D. Capital disbursements of UTs	1.76	1.87	2.68	3.42	3.50	2.78	2.44	2.24	2.41
E. Disinvestment of equities in PSEs.	0.00	0.00	0.00	30.38	19.61	56.07	56.07	13.97	50.01
Gross fiscal deficit	348.17	433.14	523.80	446.76	528.35	712.38	716.42	836.91	859.40
Finance by Instrument:									
Market Loans	106.64	99.99	105.61	108.20	75.26	331.56	244.31	381.98	307.97
Small Savings	58.35	85.75	91.04	66.40	57.17	91.00	165.78	127.90	140.00
Provident Funds	91.13	113.93	120.06	108.65	123.77	136.88	150.44	124.19	169.55
External Loans	24.60	25.95	31.81	54.21	53.19	50.74	51.46	3.18	24.61
Treasury Bills	62.44	109.11	117.69	68.87	117.73	119.82	-2.68	114.63	65.78
Other	5.01	-1.59	57.58	40.43	101.23	-17.62	107.12	85.03	151.49

Note: BE = Budget estimates; RE = Revised estimates.

a. Actuals for the center and revised estimates for the states.

b. Other expenditure include compensation and assignments to local bodies and panchayat raj institutions and reserve with the finance department.

Source: Union Budget Documents; RBI bulletin on state finances; World Bank Staff Estimates.

Table A4.5
Tax Revenue - Center and States
(Rs. billion at current prices)

	1988-89	1989-90	1990-91	1991-92	1992-93	1993-94	1994-95	1995-96[a]	1996-97 B.E.	1996-97 R.E.	1997-98 B.E.
Central Government											
A. Gross tax revenue	444.74	516.36	575.76	673.61	746.37	757.44	922.94	1112.37	1321.45	1323.19	1536.47
Corporation tax	44.07	47.29	53.35	78.53	88.99	100.60	138.22	164.87	196.00	190.10	218.60
Taxes on income	42.41	50.04	53.71	67.31	78.88	91.15	120.25	156.03	178.43	188.43	217.00
Customs	158.05	180.36	206.44	222.57	237.76	221.93	267.89	357.57	444.35	441.35	525.50
Union Excise Duties	188.41	224.06	245.14	281.10	308.32	316.97	373.47	401.87	468.84	461.90	522.00
Other	11.80	14.61	17.12	24.10	32.42	26.79	23.11	32.03	33.83	41.41	53.37
B. States Share of Tax Revenue	106.69	132.32	145.35	171.97	205.22	222.42	248.40	292.98	348.35	351.07	402.54
Income Tax	27.49	39.22	41.21	51.04	60.57	77.69	85.57	112.87	130.24	135.29	156.91
Estate Duty	0.01	0.00	0.00	0.00	0.00	0.00	0.00	0.00	0.00	0.00	0.00
Union Excise Duties	79.19	93.10	104.14	120.93	144.65	144.73	162.83	180.11	218.11	215.78	245.63
C. Assignments of UT taxes to local bodies	0.54	0.55	0.63	0.95	0.71	0.53	0.00	0.00	0.00	0.00	0.00
Tax Revenue (net) [A-B-C]	337.51	383.49	429.78	500.69	540.44	534.49	674.54	819.39	973.10	972.12	1133.93
State Government											
States own Tax Revenue	224.01	259.95	303.45	357.56	398.68	464.24	557.35	638.06	717.40		
Direct Tax	24.13	30.06	33.75	39.59	42.28	49.73	70.05	80.27	88.74		
Taxes on income	3.12	4.53	6.34	6.45	6.02	6.50	7.17	8.10	9.21		
Land revenue	5.94	6.90	6.07	6.36	6.17	7.32	11.41	12.87	10.86		
Stamps and registration fees	14.86	18.45	21.12	26.54	29.78	35.55	50.91	58.79	68.07		
Other	0.21	0.19	0.22	0.24	0.31	0.36	0.56	0.53	0.59		
Indirect Tax	199.88	229.89	269.70	317.98	356.40	414.51	487.29	557.79	628.66		
Sales Tax	131.22	150.60	176.67	210.64	233.49	276.38	331.54	357.63	443.53		
State excise	30.81	38.64	47.95	54.39	62.65	71.06	77.47	83.16	88.84		
Taxes on Vehicles	12.90	14.15	15.66	18.37	21.94	25.83	30.81	36.45	39.79		
Other	24.96	26.49	29.41	34.58	38.32	41.25	47.47	80.56	56.50		
State's Share of Central Taxes	106.69	132.32	145.35	171.97	205.22	222.42	248.40	292.98	348.35		
Tax revenue retained by states	330.70	392.27	448.80	529.53	603.90	686.66	805.75	930.72	1065.75		

Note: BE = Budget estimates; RE = Revised estimates.

a. Actuals for the center and revised estimates for the states.

Source: Ministry of Finance, Union budget documents; Reserve Bank of India, RBI bulletins on state finances; World Bank Staff Estimates.

Table A4.6
Non-Tax Revenue - Center and States
(Rs. billion at current prices)

	1988-89	1989-90	1990-91	1991-92	1992-93	1993-94	1994-95	1995-96[a]	1996-97 B.E.	1996-97 R.E.	1997-98 B.E.
Central Government											
Non-tax revenue	98.40	116.47	119.76	159.61	200.84	220.04	236.29	281.91	330.35	335.71	397.49
Interest receipts	69.81	84.66	87.30	109.33	124.87	150.62	157.97	184.19	213.93	219.45	240.92
from state governments	37.70	44.24	51.74	65.22	77.54	95.53	111.83	130.02	151.13	152.34	180.32
Dividends and profits	4.75	7.16	7.74	10.58	24.93	24.48	27.16	32.48	40.51	40.77	60.13
Other general services	3.95	4.05	5.06	5.72	10.14	10.46	11.87	12.42	13.53	17.38	17.76
Social services	0.80	0.57	0.65	0.90	0.79	1.01	0.95	1.09	1.40	1.37	1.41
Economic services	8.93	5.45	8.60	21.46	17.86	13.26	18.60	32.45	46.73	38.22	60.32
Grants-in-aid and contributio	6.00	7.54	5.86	9.47	9.19	9.93	10.38	11.38	8.09	11.99	11.00
Other	4.16	7.04	4.55	2.15	13.06	10.28	9.36	7.90	6.16	6.53	5.95
State Government											
States own Non-tax revenue	76.24	89.37	92.37	127.06	128.84	155.69	216.60	216.43	195.69		
Interest receipts	23.87	26.34	24.03	53.20	39.38	47.25	53.65	55.77	55.78		
General services	9.51	11.40	19.13	17.28	18.44	29.47	72.22	68.11	40.45		
Social services	5.73	6.76	5.86	7.74	8.48	9.12	9.65	10.52	11.14		
Economic services	36.64	44.59	43.01	48.39	61.48	69.21	80.35	81.06	87.38		
Forestry and wild life	10.08	11.96	11.37	12.71	12.72	14.94	16.40	17.15	17.04		
Industries	12.08	14.31	12.23	15.37	23.17	25.09	30.51	33.35	36.56		
Other Economic Services	14.48	18.32	19.41	20.31	25.59	29.19	33.44	30.56	33.78		
Other	0.49	0.28	0.34	0.45	1.06	0.63	0.74	0.96	0.94		
Grants from centre	100.15	107.44	132.02	157.00	178.30	208.30	200.47	212.87	231.31		
Non-tax revenue retained by s	176.38	196.81	224.39	284.06	307.14	363.99	417.07	433.25	408.56		

Note: BE = Budget estimates; RE = Revised estimates.

a. Actuals for the center and revised estimates for the states.

Source: Ministry of Finance, Union budget documents; Reserve Bank of India, RBI bulletins on state finances; World Bank Staff Estimates.

Table A4.7
Revenue Expenditure of the Central Government
(Rs. billion at current prices)

	1988-89	1989-90	1990-91	1991-92	1992-93	1993-94	1994-95	1995-96	1996-97 B.E.	1996-97 R.E.	1997-98 B.E.
Revenue expenditure (A+B+C+D)	541.06	642.07	735.15	823.08	927.02	1081.69	1221.11	1398.62	1618.20	1589.88	1834.09
A. Developmental	140.36	184.15	196.01	198.17	208.60	243.68	301.50	355.92	414.27	405.57	459.53
1. Social services	22.43	24.99	27.53	30.57	34.30	40.97	47.43	66.29	93.36	85.05	113.44
Education, Sports, Art and Culture	11.12	11.41	12.74	13.72	14.97	18.37	22.30	29.70	39.86	33.33	46.39
Health and Family welfare	3.11	3.48	3.97	4.50	5.59	6.47	7.82	8.33	10.55	11.24	14.17
Information and Broadcasting	2.36	3.23	3.60	4.43	4.61	4.15	5.08	5.49	5.35	5.85	6.04
Water supply and Sanitation	0.51	0.78	0.93	0.64	0.63	0.84	0.84	3.80	3.63	3.28	4.90
Labour and labour welfare	2.43	2.64	2.78	3.00	3.29	5.11	4.14	4.88	5.88	5.69	6.57
Social security and welfare	1.96	2.36	2.25	2.81	3.44	3.71	4.47	8.73	14.43	10.91	15.40
Other	0.94	1.09	1.27	1.47	1.77	2.33	2.77	5.36	13.65	14.74	19.97
2. Economic services	117.93	159.17	168.48	167.60	174.30	202.71	254.07	289.63	320.91	320.52	346.09
Agriculture and allied services	7.45	7.75	22.92	19.25	21.26	11.11	16.92	13.45	15.03	14.37	15.40
Fertilizer Subsidy	32.01	45.42	43.89	51.85	61.36	51.94	57.69	67.35	83.72	77.67	91.90
Food Subsidy	22.00	24.76	24.50	28.50	28.00	55.37	51.00	53.77	58.84	60.66	75.00
Export Subsidy	13.86	20.14	27.42	17.58	8.18	6.65	6.58	0.16	4.60	4.00	4.40
Irrigation and Flood Control	0.85	0.81	0.89	1.20	1.07	1.68	1.35	1.64	2.20	2.14	2.24
Rural Development	3.61	3.70	3.77	3.57	4.06	16.25	41.56	56.29	48.42	44.25	52.94
Special Areas Programmes	0.05	0.07	0.12	0.19	0.17	0.20	7.92	7.87	8.11	8.04	8.37
Energy	5.59	6.90	7.49	5.37	2.67	5.48	3.97	5.48	5.61	6.92	7.36
Industry and Minerals	12.20	17.96	12.26	12.03	17.98	17.93	12.88	17.20	26.84	31.50	21.94
Transport and Communications	6.79	15.62	8.05	9.19	9.68	14.45	17.80	20.44	19.94	23.04	24.78
Science, Technology and Environment	9.34	10.40	11.27	12.87	13.68	15.86	17.20	18.76	21.24	22.34	25.98
General Economic Services	4.18	5.62	5.90	6.00	6.20	5.78	19.19	25.62	27.22	25.60	15.77
B. Non-developmental	287.69	335.47	391.00	450.34	521.58	613.17	708.20	816.78	958.55	932.90	1129.63
Defence services	95.58	101.94	108.74	114.42	121.09	149.77	164.26	188.41	188.55	209.94	267.13
Interest payments	142.61	177.57	214.71	265.63	310.35	366.95	440.49	500.31	600.00	585.00	680.00
on Internal Debt	69.13	82.73	96.22	109.09	129.89	154.83	193.91	233.64	267.30	273.10	315.85
on External Debt	12.42	14.94	17.78	25.69	34.51	37.92	41.10	39.02	52.74	45.51	47.46
on Small Savings, PFs. etc.	58.01	75.73	96.37	124.20	138.83	168.42	198.91	220.64	270.75	257.99	308.38
Other	3.06	4.17	4.34	6.66	7.12	5.78	6.57	7.01	9.21	8.41	8.31
Administrative Services	17.91	20.71	25.24	27.98	37.83	38.27	42.14	48.48	95.52	59.48	103.03
Fiscal Services	11.00	12.78	12.12	17.69	20.48	21.37	23.55	25.90	26.70	25.61	25.55
Pensions and misc. services	20.60	22.46	30.19	24.63	31.84	36.80	37.76	53.67	47.78	52.87	53.91
C. Grants-in-aid and contributions	102.08	109.36	134.39	159.53	180.54	211.11	204.83	218.28	237.43	242.82	236.53
Grants to State Governments	100.15	107.44	132.02	157.00	178.30	208.30	200.47	212.87	231.31	236.26	230.27
a. Non Plan	24.11	23.69	42.19	45.16	31.77	27.22	24.79	59.39	64.13	62.24	49.51
b. State Plan Schemes	35.59	36.00	38.78	56.51	79.76	102.39	107.93	86.74	95.63	106.21	108.71
c. Central and Centrally sponsored schemes	40.46	47.75	51.05	55.32	66.78	78.69	67.75	66.74	71.54	67.81	72.06
Grants to UTs. and Others	1.93	1.92	2.37	2.53	2.24	2.81	4.36	5.42	6.12	6.56	6.26
D. Revenue Disbursments of UTs (net)	10.92	13.09	13.75	15.05	16.30	13.73	6.59	7.63	7.95	8.59	8.41
Memo Items:											
Total Subsidies	77.32	104.74	121.58	122.53	119.95	126.82	129.32	133.05	163.20	166.94	182.51
Major Subsidies	67.87	90.32	95.81	97.93	94.15	107.64	115.27	121.28	147.16	142.33	171.30
Other Subsidies	9.45	14.42	25.77	24.60	25.80	19.18	14.05	11.77	16.04	24.61	11.21
Rural Employment Programme	12.44	21.00	20.00	18.17	25.46	39.06	46.75	46.42	38.35	34.95	40.48
of which: Jawahar Rojgar Yojana	0.00	20.96	20.00	18.17	25.26	33.06	35.35	28.73	18.65	16.55	20.78

Note: BE = Budget estimates; RE = Revised estimates.

Source: Ministry of Finance, Union budget documents; Department of Expenditure, Finance Accounts; World Bank Staff Estimates.

Table A4.8
Revenue Expenditure of State Governments
(Rs. billion at current prices)

	1988-89	1989-90	1990-91	1991-92	1992-93	1993-94	1994-95	1995-96 R.E.	1996-97 B.E.
Revenue expenditure (A+B+C)	522.96	602.53	717.73	861.86	962.05	1093.76	1284.40	1483.72	1620.44
A. Developmental (1+2)	362.37	407.81	488.55	585.05	634.65	708.38	786.37	921.93	983.45
1. Social services	205.74	240.17	279.62	310.92	345.65	389.61	449.02	552.86	593.71
Education, Sports, Art and Culture.	109.43	135.71	155.28	170.77	192.61	215.94	249.77	296.50	325.10
Health and Family Welfare.	34.77	39.64	45.86	50.54	56.62	66.69	74.29	85.38	94.42
Water supply and Sanitation	13.94	14.77	16.38	18.45	20.95	24.24	29.80	30.93	32.20
Welfare of SC, ST and BCs	13.18	14.69	17.90	20.71	23.01	25.70	30.12	37.57	41.23
Social security and welfare	9.70	11.07	13.62	14.77	16.63	18.65	21.44	27.35	28.18
Other	24.72	24.29	30.59	35.68	35.83	38.38	43.60	75.12	72.58
2. Economic services	156.63	167.64	208.92	274.13	288.99	318.78	337.36	369.06	389.74
Agriculture and Allied Services	42.65	48.29	62.67	69.81	84.34	88.93	90.64	101.42	106.21
Crop Husbandry	11.06	12.65	16.97	20.82	29.37	29.12	28.88	28.72	29.59
Food Storage and Warehousing	1.23	1.56	1.88	2.38	4.16	3.81	4.36	8.07	8.95
Forestry and Wild Life	9.46	10.28	11.75	13.42	14.90	15.74	17.22	19.26	21.35
Other	20.90	23.80	32.06	33.19	35.91	40.25	40.19	45.38	46.32
Rural Development	36.54	28.27	46.75	52.87	63.62	72.77	67.79	83.03	82.39
Special Areas Programmes	3.09	3.54	3.57	4.11	3.96	4.88	4.96	7.10	7.48
Irrigation and Flood Control	33.19	33.94	34.56	41.40	48.68	54.28	64.44	67.29	75.08
Energy	7.74	10.92	9.89	50.30	26.15	31.68	29.89	27.43	24.19
Industry and Minerals	8.69	12.17	11.65	12.71	13.56	14.18	16.85	20.99	25.11
Transport and Communications	17.35	19.22	23.36	27.59	31.28	35.12	37.55	42.59	45.82
Science, Technology and Environ	0.23	0.26	0.29	0.36	0.39	0.53	0.53	0.84	1.17
General Economic Services	7.15	11.02	16.18	14.98	17.01	16.40	22.68	18.37	22.30
B. Non-Developmental	155.06	188.69	221.34	266.66	315.06	373.67	484.99	545.59	617.87
Interest Payments	59.33	71.86	86.55	109.44	132.10	158.00	192.02	217.43	262.98
On loans from the centre	37.70	44.24	51.74	65.22	77.54	95.53	111.83	130.02	151.13
On the Internal Debt	10.42	13.41	15.68	21.70	24.67	27.77	31.41	32.27	45.96
On Small Savings, PFs.	10.58	12.70	17.03	21.17	24.73	30.87	31.27	36.08	40.72
Other	5.41	6.34	7.76	1.36	11.71	11.28	9.38	8.90	37.74
Administrative Services	50.31	59.74	70.18	78.10	93.44	104.73	116.64	135.71	169.15
Pensions and Miscellaneous Servic	23.92	29.31	35.93	44.79	52.72	69.99	119.27	127.15	118.15
Other	16.72	22.96	23.01	34.33	30.24	33.51	45.72	54.35	53.81
C. Other expenditure[a]	5.53	6.03	7.84	10.16	12.35	11.71	13.03	16.20	19.11

Note: BE = Budget estimates; RE = Revised estimates.

a. Other expenditure include compensation and assignments to local bodies and panchayat raj institutions and reserve with the finance department.

Source: Reserve Bank of India, RBI bulletins on state finances; World Bank Staff Estimates..

Table A4.9
Capital Expenditure: Center and States
(Rs. billion at current prices)

	1988-89	1989-90	1990-91	1991-92	1992-93	1993-94	1994-95	1995-96[a]	1996-97 B.E.	1996-97 R.E.	1997-98 B.E.
Central Government											
Capital expenditure [A+B+C+D-E]	204.08	237.18	260.88	200.63	215.99	275.41	266.75	305.12	307.91	349.25	351.89
A. Developmental (1+2)	60.03	70.95	69.23	58.26	73.82	55.60	73.96	50.49	47.24	49.55	82.21
1. Social services	3.51	3.21	2.47	2.39	2.59	3.32	7.26	5.48	6.41	6.53	9.06
Education, Sports, Art etc.	0.13	0.08	0.06	0.04	0.05	0.06	2.25	0.14	0.11	0.17	0.22
Health and Family welfare	0.15	0.20	0.00	0.20	0.07	0.03	0.69	0.12	0.41	0.41	0.43
Housing	0.99	0.98	1.11	1.26	1.78	1.87	1.86	2.37	2.82	2.29	3.01
Information and Broadcasting	1.71	1.78	1.06	0.35	0.07	0.24	0.25	0.47	0.57	0.64	0.79
Other	0.52	0.18	0.24	0.53	0.62	1.12	2.23	2.39	2.52	3.02	4.61
2. Economic services	56.52	67.74	66.77	55.87	71.23	52.28	66.70	45.01	40.83	43.02	73.14
Agriculture and allied	0.55	0.45	0.45	0.49	0.47	0.48	2.83	3.60	3.45	3.42	4.24
Energy	19.05	26.07	27.09	19.91	16.21	17.69	22.68	20.58	9.86	11.06	14.50
Industry and Minerals	13.10	11.52	7.71	6.70	8.82	9.87	8.04	6.32	5.48	4.74	7.23
Transport & Communications	21.51	26.15	26.45	24.72	33.81	19.45	22.14	20.61	25.34	27.29	40.08
General Economic Services	0.00	1.26	2.52	2.57	9.07	1.58	6.86	-10.68	-8.21	-8.40	2.79
Other	2.31	2.28	2.56	1.48	2.85	3.21	4.14	4.59	4.91	4.92	4.30
B. Non-developmental	40.76	45.27	49.56	52.32	58.88	73.92	72.51	88.26	100.87	94.92	100.94
Defence Services	37.83	42.22	45.52	49.05	54.73	68.67	68.19	80.15	89.44	85.05	89.07
Other	2.93	3.05	4.04	3.27	4.14	5.24	4.32	8.11	11.43	9.87	11.87
C. Capital Expenditure of UTs	1.76	1.87	2.68	3.42	3.50	2.78	2.44	2.24	2.41	2.12	2.66
D. Loans and Advances(Net)	101.53	119.09	139.40	117.01	99.41	142.63	173.91	178.10	207.40	208.42	214.09
To State Governments & UTs.	67.30	79.55	98.69	94.18	86.97	100.72	143.13	148.37	170.76	177.63	185.85
To Others	34.23	39.55	40.71	22.83	12.44	41.92	30.78	29.73	36.64	30.79	28.24
E. Disinvestment of equity in PSEs	0.00	0.00	0.00	30.38	19.61	-0.48	56.07	13.97	50.01	5.75	48.00
State Government											
Capital expenditure [A+B+C]	98.66	117.52	134.78	132.49	157.77	167.84	215.41	251.07	267.73		
A. Developmental (1+2)	68.53	77.28	89.61	98.61	103.44	120.51	169.31	169.97	178.33		
1. Social Services	11.28	11.71	12.57	16.47	16.64	18.31	23.04	28.21	35.07		
Education, Sports, Art etc.	1.68	2.64	2.84	2.78	3.02	3.14	3.97	4.66	5.01		
Health and Family welfare	2.04	1.84	2.37	2.76	2.63	2.80	3.24	3.99	4.59		
Water supply and Sanitation	4.04	3.37	3.54	4.99	5.49	6.77	8.94	9.63	10.66		
Housing	1.90	1.99	1.82	2.09	1.88	2.01	2.65	3.36	4.54		
Other	1.63	1.87	2.00	3.86	3.62	3.57	4.24	6.57	10.27		
2. Economic Services	57.25	65.57	77.03	82.14	86.80	102.21	146.27	141.76	143.25		
Agriculture and allied	2.69	5.91	6.11	8.32	7.85	7.26	8.82	13.98	13.38		
Irrigation and Flood control	32.66	32.91	36.56	38.52	42.93	49.68	58.62	64.07	67.37		
Transport	10.27	11.59	13.42	13.92	15.90	20.47	24.20	27.61	28.35		
Other	11.63	15.16	20.94	21.38	20.13	24.80	54.64	36.09	34.15		
B. Non-developmental	2.25	2.36	2.63	2.34	3.10	3.99	4.20	6.72	8.37		
C. Loans and advances(Net)	27.88	37.88	42.55	31.54	51.22	43.33	41.90	74.38	81.03		

Note: BE = Budget estimates; RE = Revised estimates.

a. Actuals for the center and revised estimates for the states.

Source: Ministry of Finance, Union budget documents; Reserve Bank of India, RBI bulletins on state finances; World Bank Staff Estimates.

Table A4.10
Transfers between Center and States
(Rs. billion at current prices)

	1988-89	1989-90	1990-91	1991-92	1992-93	1993-94	1994-95	1995-96	1996-97 B.E.	1996-97 R.E.	1997-98 B.E.
States' share in central taxes	106.69	132.32	145.35	171.97	205.22	222.42	248.40	292.98	348.35	351.07	402.54
Union excise duties	79.19	93.10	104.14	120.93	144.65	144.73	162.83	180.11	218.11	215.78	245.63
Income tax	27.49	39.22	41.21	51.04	60.57	77.69	85.57	112.87	130.24	135.29	156.91
Estate duty	0.01	0.00	0.00	0.00	0.00	0.00	0.00	0.00	0.00	0.00	0.00
Grants to States	100.15	107.44	132.02	157.00	178.30	208.30	200.47	212.87	231.31	236.26	230.27
Non-plan grants	24.11	23.69	42.19	45.16	31.77	27.22	24.79	59.39	64.13	62.24	49.51
State plan schemes	35.59	36.00	38.78	56.51	79.76	102.39	107.93	86.74	95.63	106.21	108.71
Central and Centrally sponsored schemes	40.46	47.75	51.05	55.32	66.78	78.69	67.75	66.74	71.54	67.81	72.06
Loans to States & UTs	99.15	109.16	135.66	123.30	121.41	139.85	188.04	192.96	224.36	234.13	252.59
Loan Repayments by States and UTs	31.85	29.62	36.97	29.12	34.44	39.13	44.91	44.58	53.60	56.50	66.74
Interest Payments by States	37.70	44.24	51.74	65.22	77.54	95.53	111.83	130.02	151.13	152.34	180.32
NET TRANSFER (Center to States)	236.43	275.07	324.32	357.93	392.94	435.91	480.17	524.20	599.28	612.62	638.34

Note: BE = Budget estimates; RE = Revised estimates.

Source: Union budget documents; RBI bulletins on state finances; Finance Accounts; World Bank Staff Estimates.

Table A4.11
Explicit Subsidies in the Central Government Budget
(Rs. billion at current prices)

	1988-89	1989-90	1990-91	1991-92	1992-93	1993-94	1994-95	1995-96	1996-97 B.E.	1996-97 R.E.	1997-98 B.E.
A. Major Subsidies	67.87	90.32	95.81	97.93	94.15	107.64	115.27	121.28	147.16	142.33	171.30
1. Food	22.00	24.76	24.50	28.50	28.00	55.37	51.00	53.77	58.84	60.66	75.00
2. Indegenious Fertilizers	30.00	37.71	37.30	35.00	48.00	38.00	40.75	43.00	45.00	47.43	52.40
3. Imported Fertilizers	2.01	7.71	6.59	13.00	9.96	7.62	11.66	19.35	16.48	13.50	19.50
4. Other Fertilizer Subsidy	0.00	0.00	0.00	3.85	3.40	6.32	0.00	0.00	0.00	0.00	0.00
5. Export Promotion and Market Development.	13.86	20.14	27.42	17.58	8.18	6.65	6.58	0.16	4.60	4.00	4.40
6. Sale of decontrolled fertilis with concession to farmers	...	...	...	...	...	...	5.28	5.00	22.24	16.74	20.00
B. Debt relief to farmers	...	...	15.02	14.25	15.00	5.00	3.41	3.41	0.00	0.00	0.00
C. Other Subsidies	9.45	14.42	10.75	10.35	10.81	14.18	10.64	11.77	16.04	24.61	11.21
5. Railways	2.07	2.33	2.83	3.12	3.53	4.12	4.20	4.18	4.69	4.66	5.37
6. Mill-made cloth	0.27	0.10	0.10	0.15	0.15	0.16	0.00	0.01	0.01	0.00	0.00
7. Handloom Cloth	1.46	1.81	1.85	1.87	1.61	1.74	1.48	1.43	1.39	0.98	0.84
8. Import/Export of Sugar, Edible Oils etc.	0.40	0.00	..	0.00	0.00	0.00	0.00	1.00	0.00	0.50	0.50
9. Interest Subsidies	4.06	8.81	3.79	3.16	1.13	1.13	0.76	0.34	4.34	12.57	0.34
10. Other Subsidies	1.19	1.37	2.18	2.05	0.99	1.86	4.20	4.81	4.81	5.90	4.16
TOTAL - Subsidies	77.32	104.74	121.58	122.53	119.95	126.82	129.32	133.05	163.20	166.94	182.51

... Not available.

Note: BE = Budget estimates; RE = Revised estimates.

Source: Minstry of Finance, Union Budget Documents.

Table A4.12
Outstanding Debt of Central Government
(Rs. billion at current prices)

	1980-81	1985-86	1986-87	1987-88	1988-89	1989-90	1990-91	1991-92	1992-93	1993-94	1994-95[a]
1. To Reserve Bank of India	152.78	380.47	451.38	516.97	582.00	720.13	884.44	943.48	976.21	989.69	998.86
a. Treasury bills	118.44	242.49	185.61	70.91	123.18	235.73	49.80	61.59	167.17	238.38	251.67
b. CG Securities	38.58	104.23	82.26	88.43	110.89	141.02	174.50	171.47	86.43	33.11	34.47
c. Special securities	5.85	51.87	198.67	371.77	369.87	368.81	671.02	720.46	720.46	720.46	720.46
d. Other liabilities	-2.92	-16.64	-6.95	-6.12	-11.69	-25.43	-10.88	-10.04	2.15	-2.26	-7.74
e. Cash balances and Dpts.	7.17	1.48	8.21	8.02	10.25	n.a.	n.a.	n.a.	n.a.	n.a	n.a
2.To commercial banks	73.64	151.90	202.10	241.46	287.66	333.85	388.13	460.46	531.12	795.85	925.00
a. Treasury bills	5.21	0.46	0.16	0.14	0.03	0.06	0.10	0.11	3.06	0.72	0.00
b. CG Securities	68.43	151.44	201.94	241.32	287.63	333.79	388.03	460.35	528.06	795.13	925.00
To Banking system	226.42	532.37	653.48	758.43	869.66	1053.98	1272.57	1403.94	1507.33	1785.54	1923.86
3.To Private Sector	258.09	660.94	808.99	964.95	1170.59	1344.52	1557.76	1773.20	2089.21	2519.70	2952.97
a. Small savings	79.76	214.49	247.25	283.58	338.33	417.91	501.00	557.55	601.28	672.85	817.10
b. Others	178.33	446.45	561.74	681.37	832.26	926.61	1056.76	1215.65	1487.93	1846.85	2135.87
4. External Debt	112.98	181.53	202.99	232.23	257.46	283.43	315.25	369.48	422.69	473.45	509.28
5. Total outstanding debt	597.49	1374.84	1665.46	1955.61	2297.71	2681.93	3145.58	3546.62	4019.24	4778.68	5386.11

n.a. Not available.

Note: End of year stocks are used to calculated outstanding debt and External Debt as shown in the central budget.
a. Provisional.

Source: RBI, <u>Report on Currency and Finance</u>, various issues; Ministry of Finance, Union Budget & Indian Economic Statistics
(Public Finance); Ministry of Finance, <u>Economic Survey</u>, various issues; World Bank Staff estimates.

Table A4.13
Outstanding Debt of State Government
(Rs. billion at current prices)

	1980-81	1985-86	1986-87	1987-88	1988-89	1989-90	1990-91	1991-92	1992-93	1993-94	1994-95[a]
1. To Reserve Bank of India	11.65	6.31	11.47	9.90	14.14	16.70	20.90	17.50	19.26	25.17	25.65
a. Gross	12.11	10.65	14.58	10.09	14.29	n.a.	n.a.	n.a.	n.a.	n.a.	n.a.
b. Cash balances and Dpts.	0.46	4.34	3.11	0.19	0.15	n.a.	n.a.	n.a.	n.a.	n.a.	n.a.
2.To commercial banks	19.11	44.53	55.25	75.37	89.92	100.83	125.32	182.01	246.77	250.34	284.38
a. SG Securities	16.81	47.74	56.18	69.47	85.02	103.49	122.90	150.12	171.82	231.08	267.12
b. Others	2.30	-3.21	-0.93	5.90	4.90	-2.66	2.42	31.89	74.95	19.26	267.12
To Banking System (1)+(2)	30.76	50.84	66.72	85.27	104.06	117.53	146.22	199.51	266.03	275.51	310.03
3.To Private Sector	44.82	133.53	118.92	130.75	164.07	201.30	237.11	254.24	252.46	328.78	427.88
a. Provident Fund	25.36	68.25	79.55	95.83	115.85	138.91	169.61	198.70	234.92	278.22	326.01
b. Others	19.46	65.28	39.37	34.92	48.22	62.39	67.50	55.54	17.54	50.55	101.87
4.To Central Govt. (a-b-c)	164.01	352.23	421.58	483.69	542.06	623.41	719.56	809.63	903.29	996.49	1107.36
a. Loans from Center	170.71	369.84	437.02	495.34	562.22	641.39	741.17	834.90	924.12	1019.45	1167.05
b. States' holding of Trs.Bill	4.35	15.20	12.68	8.88	17.38	15.18	18.80	24.95	20.83	22.96	59.69
c. States' holding of CG Sec.	2.35	2.41	2.76	2.77	2.78	2.80	2.81	0.32	0.00	0.00	0.00
5. Total outstanding debt	239.59	536.60	607.22	699.71	810.20	942.24	1102.89	1263.38	1421.78	1600.77	1845.27

n.a. Not available.

Note: End of year stocks are used to calcualte outstanding debt.

a. Provisional.

Source: RBI, Report on Currency and Finance, various issues; Ministry of Finance, Union Budget & Indian Economic Statistics
            (Public Finance); Ministry of Finance, Economic Survey, various issues; World Bank Staff estimates.

Table A4.14
Outstanding Debt of Central and State Governments
(Rs. billion at current prices)

	1980-81	1985-86	1986-87	1987-88	1988-89	1989-90	1990-91	1991-92	1992-93	1993-94	1994-95[a]
1. To Reserve Bank of India	164.43	386.78	462.85	526.87	596.14	736.83	905.34	960.98	995.47	1014.86	1024.51
a. Center	152.78	380.47	451.38	516.97	582.00	720.13	884.44	943.48	976.21	989.69	998.86
b. State	11.65	6.31	11.47	9.90	14.14	16.70	20.90	17.50	19.26	25.17	25.65
2.To commercial banks	92.75	196.43	257.35	316.83	377.58	434.68	513.45	642.47	777.89	1046.18	1209.38
a. Center	73.64	151.90	202.10	241.46	287.66	333.85	388.13	460.46	531.12	795.85	925.00
b. State	19.11	44.53	55.25	75.37	89.92	100.83	125.32	182.01	246.77	250.34	284.38
To Banking System (1)+(2)	257.18	583.21	720.20	843.70	973.72	1171.51	1418.79	1603.45	1773.36	2061.04	2233.89
3.To Private Sector	289.51	759.25	897.03	1072.40	1294.35	1509.86	1751.65	1976.89	2300.02	2802.55	3261.47
a. Small savings	79.76	214.49	247.25	283.58	338.33	417.91	501.00	557.55	601.28	672.85	817.10
b. Others	209.75	544.76	649.78	788.82	956.02	1091.95	1250.65	1419.34	1698.74	2129.71	2444.37
4. External Debt	112.98	181.53	202.99	232.23	257.46	283.43	315.25	369.48	422.69	473.45	509.28
5. Total outstanding debt	659.67	1523.99	1820.22	2148.33	2525.53	2964.80	3485.69	3949.83	4496.07	5337.04	6004.64
Loans to States from Center	170.71	369.84	437.02	495.34	562.22	641.39	741.17	834.90	924.12	1019.45	1167.05

Note: End of year stocks are used to calculated outstanding debt and External Debt as shown in the central budget.
a. Provisional.

Source: RBI, Report on Currency and Finance, various issues; Ministry of Finance, Union Budget & Indian Economic Statistics
(Public Finance); Ministry of Finance, Economic Survey, various issues; World Bank Staff estimates.

Table A4.15(a)
Projected and Actual Plan Outlays by Sectors
(Rs. billion)

	Seventh Plan (85-86 - 89-90)		Annual Plans		Eighth Plan					
			90-91	91-92	(92-93 - 96-97)	92-93	93-94	94-95	95-96	96-97
	Proj.	Actuals	Actuals	Actuals	Projected	Actuals	Actuals	Actuals	Revised	Proj.
A Agriculture & Allied Programs	222.34	315.10	85.44	90.59	636.43	105.91	126.60	157.12	173.08	198.33
Agriculture	105.24	127.93	33.96	38.51	224.67	42.16	42.64	53.50	60.94	69.26
Rural Development	89.06	152.46	41.21	41.42	344.25	50.91	70.33	87.17	94.74	110.42
Special Area Program	28.04	34.70	10.27	10.67	67.50	12.84	13.64	16.45	17.40	18.65
B Irrigation & Flood Control	169.79	165.91	38.37	42.32	325.25	47.05	53.71	61.04	65.47	97.60
Minor Irrigation	28.05	31.92	8.35	8.44	59.77	9.95	10.48	11.85	12.17	17.16
Major Irrigation	115.56	110.20	25.01	28.24	224.15	30.47	35.71	41.59	45.00	70.81
Flood Control	9.47	9.45	2.08	2.64	16.23	3.30	3.66	3.08	3.57	5.31
Command Area Development	16.71	14.33	2.93	3.00	25.10	3.33	3.85	4.52	4.74	4.31
C Industry and Minerals	221.08	290.99	82.40	65.64	469.22	74.44	84.81	90.88	128.62	142.24
Village & Small Scale	27.53	32.49	9.07	9.41	63.34	9.95	11.52	15.12	17.66	19.26
Large & Medium Industries	193.55	258.50	73.33	56.23	405.88	64.49	73.29	75.76	110.96	122.97
D Energy	551.29	618.20	179.98	197.34	1155.61	202.90	269.09	274.82	300.67	354.01
Power	342.74	378.95	113.34	145.18	795.89	121.57	147.73	163.46	171.35	190.85
Petroleum	129.35	161.31	41.30	33.40	240.00	56.98	95.89	86.44	106.19	126.22
Coal	74.01	71.22	23.92	17.10	105.07	22.77	22.93	22.39	18.53	30.46
E Transport	229.71	297.70	86.96	93.14	559.26	106.63	119.77	120.97	141.31	208.51
Railways	123.34	165.50	49.16	53.93	272.02	61.62	59.01	54.72	75.00	81.30
Roads & Road Transport	71.90	84.59	21.32	24.82	169.52	28.48	32.49	38.44	26.36	10.61
Ports & Shipping[a]	23.13	26.07	10.97	8.45	76.14	7.28	16.20	13.13	18.24	26.27
Civil Aviation	7.58	18.99	4.92	5.47	40.83	8.82	11.46	14.44	21.00	41.39
F Communication & Broadcasting	61.14	98.93	33.54	36.14	289.66	51.51	62.02	72.74	97.79	97.56
G Science & Technology	24.63	30.23	7.87	8.62	90.42	9.30	11.53	14.07	16.32	18.42
H Social Services	295.78	332.61	87.90	102.99	751.55	113.23	140.16	174.09	231.79	304.91
Education	63.83	76.85	20.63	23.75	196.00	26.19	31.47	35.66	58.53	33.87
Health & Family Welfare	64.49	68.09	17.46	19.48	140.76	22.22	26.13	33.11	35.16	23.49
Housing & Urban Development	42.30	48.36	12.53	13.52	105.50	14.42	21.47	20.81	38.12	20.50
Water Supply & Sanitation	65.22	70.92	18.45	22.46	167.11	22.84	27.20	32.60	41.51	12.57
Other Social Services	59.94	68.38	18.84	23.77	142.19	27.55	33.89	51.92	58.46	214.47
I Others	24.24	57.94	12.72	10.74	63.60	17.56	13.11	15.94	44.50	39.50
J TOTAL	1800.00	2207.60	615.18	647.51	4341.00	728.52	880.81	981.67	1199.54	1461.07

Note: The Plan totals are at base year prices for projections and at current prices for actuals.

a. Covers Major and Minor ports, Shipping, Lighthouses and Inland Water.

Source: Planning Commission.

Table A4.15(b)
Projected and Actual Plan Outlays by Sectors
(Annual averages at constant 1980-81 prices - Rs. billion)

| | Seventh Plan (85-86 - 89-90) | | Annual Plans | | Eighth Plan | | | | | |
	Proj.	Actuals	90-91 Actuals	91-92 Actuals	(92-93 - 96-97) Projected	92-93 Actuals	93-94 Actuals	94-95 Actuals	95-96 Revised	96-97 Proj.
A Agriculture & Allied Programs	30.3	33.7	36.0	32.7	46.0	35.5	40.0	46.6	48.1	51.5
Agriculture	14.3	13.7	14.3	13.9	16.2	14.1	13.5	15.9	16.9	18.0
Rural Development	12.1	16.3	17.3	15.0	24.9	17.1	22.2	25.9	26.3	28.7
Special Area Program	3.8	3.7	4.3	3.9	4.9	4.3	4.3	4.9	4.8	4.8
B Irrigation & Flood Control	23.1	17.7	16.2	15.3	23.5	15.8	17.0	18.1	18.2	25.3
Minor Irrigation	3.8	3.4	3.5	3.1	4.3	3.3	3.3	3.5	3.4	4.5
Major Irrigation	15.8	11.8	10.5	10.2	16.2	10.2	11.3	12.3	12.5	18.4
Flood Control	1.3	1.0	0.9	1.0	1.2	1.1	1.2	0.9	1.0	1.4
Command Area Development	2.3	1.5	1.2	1.1	1.8	1.1	1.2	1.3	1.3	1.1
C Industry and Minerals	30.1	31.1	34.7	23.7	33.9	25.0	26.8	27.0	35.7	36.9
Village & Small Scale	3.8	3.5	3.8	3.4	4.6	3.3	3.6	4.5	4.9	5.0
Large & Medium Industries	26.4	27.6	30.9	20.3	29.3	21.6	23.1	22.5	30.8	31.9
D Energy	75.2	66.0	75.8	71.3	83.5	68.0	84.9	81.5	83.5	91.9
Power	46.7	40.5	47.7	52.5	57.5	40.8	46.6	48.5	47.6	49.6
Petroleum	17.6	17.2	17.4	12.1	17.4	19.1	30.3	25.6	29.5	32.8
Coal	10.1	7.6	10.1	6.2	7.6	7.6	7.2	6.6	5.1	7.9
E Transport	31.3	31.8	36.6	33.7	40.4	35.8	37.8	35.9	39.2	54.1
Railways	16.8	17.7	20.7	19.5	19.7	20.7	18.6	16.2	20.8	21.1
Roads & Road Transport	9.8	9.0	9.0	9.0	12.3	9.6	10.3	11.4	7.3	2.8
Ports & Shipping[a]	3.2	2.8	4.6	3.1	5.5	2.4	5.1	3.9	5.1	6.8
Civil Aviation	1.0	2.0	2.1	2.0	3.0	3.0	3.6	4.3	5.8	10.7
F Communication & Broadcasting	8.3	10.6	14.1	13.1	20.9	17.3	19.6	21.6	27.2	25.3
G Science & Technology	3.4	3.2	3.3	3.1	6.5	3.1	3.6	4.2	4.5	4.8
H Social Services	40.3	35.5	37.0	37.2	54.3	38.0	44.2	51.7	64.4	79.2
Education	8.7	8.2	8.7	8.6	14.2	8.8	9.9	10.6	16.3	8.8
Health & Family Welfare	8.8	7.3	7.3	7.0	10.2	7.5	8.2	9.8	9.8	6.1
Housing & Urban Development	5.8	5.2	5.3	4.9	7.6	4.8	6.8	6.2	10.6	5.3
Water Supply & Sanitation	8.9	7.6	7.8	8.1	12.1	7.7	8.6	9.7	11.5	3.3
Other Social Services	8.2	7.3	7.9	8.6	10.3	9.2	10.7	15.4	16.2	55.7
I Others	3.3	6.2	5.4	3.9	4.6	5.9	4.1	4.7	12.4	10.3
J TOTAL	245.4	235.9	258.9	234.1	313.8	244.3	278.0	291.3	333.2	379.4
Memo Item: Investment Deflator	146.7	187.2	237.6	276.6	276.6	298.2	316.8	337.0	360.0	385.1

a. Covers Major and Minor ports, Shipping, Lighthouses and Inland Water.

Source: Planning Commission.

Table A4.15(c)
Projected and Actual Plan Outlays by Sectors
(percentage distribution and achievement rates)

	Seventh Plan (85-86 - 89-90)		Annual Plans		Eighth Plan (92-93 - 96-97)				
			90-91	91-92		92-93	93-94	94-95	95-96
	% share[a]	Achieve-ment[b]	Achieve-ment[b]	Achieve-ment[b]	% share[a]	Achieve-ment[b]	Achieve-ment[b]	Achieve-ment[b]	Achieve-ment[b]
A Agriculture & Allied Programs	12.4	111.1	93.4	90.1	14.7	94.2	97.3	97.9	94.3
Agriculture	5.8	95.3	89.6	86.1	5.2	83.0	78.8	91.5	91.5
Rural Development	4.9	134.2	96.5	93.2	7.9	104.1	113.7	101.0	95.5
Special Area Program	1.6	97.0	95.1	93.4	1.6	100.9	96.3	104.5	97.8
B Irrigation & Flood Control	9.4	76.6	96.7	90.1	7.5	88.5	91.7	94.0	87.6
Minor Irrigation	1.6	89.2	94.5	87.1	1.4	84.8	86.2	83.9	80.0
Major Irrigation	6.4	74.7	99.3	91.8	5.2	90.4	93.0	97.1	89.2
Flood Control	0.5	78.2	84.3	91.6	0.4	85.0	107.5	95.9	96.2
Command Area Development	0.9	67.2	91.0	81.9	0.6	86.3	84.3	95.0	88.4
C Industry and Minerals	12.3	103.1	75.4	76.2	10.8	69.9	74.6	72.3	92.7
Village & Small Scale	1.5	92.5	89.2	79.3	1.5	79.8	89.3	94.9	94.6
Large & Medium Industries	10.8	104.7	73.6	75.7	9.3	68.6	72.8	69.0	92.4
D Energy	30.6	87.9	90.6	92.6	26.6	79.8	87.0	83.5	85.3
Power	19.0	86.6	91.3	106.1	18.3	75.5	90.0	88.6	87.3
Petroleum	7.2	97.7	94.7	67.9	5.5	87.3	83.2	75.9	89.0
Coal	4.1	75.4	81.1	67.8	2.4	87.8	84.2	80.5	57.8
E Transport	12.8	101.6	86.8	93.9	12.9	84.1	85.9	81.1	78.1
Railways	6.9	105.1	97.9	101.3	6.3	100.3	85.5	76.5	97.5
Roads & Road Transport	4.0	92.2	97.9	91.2	3.9	90.7	93.7	95.9	57.9
Ports & Shipping[c]	1.3	88.3	37.5	62.0	1.8	32.9	84.5	65.9	94.4
Civil Aviation	0.4	196.3	61.7	124.2	0.9	77.9	71.0	84.0	54.6
F Communication & Broadcasting	3.4	126.8	92.2	92.3	6.7	97.7	99.3	101.1	117.5
G Science & Technology	1.4	96.2	85.0	84.7	2.1	87.0	87.6	98.1	93.5
H Social Services	16.4	88.1	100.3	91.5	17.3	81.8	90.8	96.5	103.5
Education	3.5	94.4	93.3	91.2	4.5	82.5	86.5	81.0	109.5
Health & Family Welfare	3.6	82.7	104.6	100.7	3.2	89.3	90.3	101.9	93.7
Housing & Urban Development	2.4	89.6	128.2	77.3	2.4	66.5	93.6	77.4	105.1
Water Supply & Sanitation	3.6	85.2	95.9	89.3	3.8	89.6	92.3	90.8	96.0
Other Social Services	3.3	89.4	90.8	96.6	3.3	79.5	92.5	126.0	109.3
I Others	1.3	187.3	86.1	70.2	1.5	111.0	64.6	61.6	144.7
J TOTAL	100.0	96.1	90.2	89.5	100.0	83.7	88.0	87.5	93.3

Note: Derived from Table 4.15(b).

a. Percentage share in total plan outlay.

b. Actual outlay as a percentage of target outlay for the Plan.

c. Covers Major and Minor ports, Shipping, Lighthouses and Inland Water.

Source: Planning Commission.

Table A5.1
Money Supply and Sources of Change, 1985-86 - 1995-96
(Rs. billion)

	1986-87	1987-88	1988-89	1989-90	1990-91	1991-92	1992-93	1993-94	1994-95	1995-96
BROAD MONEY SUPPLY (M3)	1416.42	1642.79	2002.41	2309.48	2658.28	3170.49	3668.25	4344.07	5314.26	6040.07
Narrow Money Supply (M1)	515.22	585.59	711.01	810.58	928.92	1144.06	1240.66	1507.78	1922.54	2143.63
Currency with Public	283.82	335.59	380.71	463.00	530.48	610.98	682.73	823.01	1006.81	1181.61
Deposit Money (total)	228.30	246.00	323.40	341.60	391.70	524.23	544.80	659.52	881.93	928.62
Time Deposits with Banks	901.20	1057.20	1291.40	1498.90	1729.36	2026.43	2427.59	2836.29	3391.69	3896.44
SOURCES OF CHANGE										
Net Bank Domestic Credit	1667.61	1918.57	2300.36	2688.57	3119.62	3462.56	3963.73	4416.92	5151.39	5983.12
To Government	720.20	843.70	973.73	1171.53	1401.93	1582.63	1762.38	2039.18	2224.16	2574.10
From Reserve Bank of India (RBI)	462.85	526.87	596.15	736.83	888.48	940.16	984.49	993.00	1014.78	1213.49
From Other Banks	257.35	316.83	377.58	434.70	513.45	642.47	777.89	1046.18	1209.38	1360.61
To Commercial Sector	947.41	1074.87	1326.63	1517.04	1717.69	1879.93	2201.35	2377.74	2927.23	3409.02
From Reserve Bank of India	33.94	37.90	55.24	63.49	63.42	72.60	62.20	64.45	65.93	68.55
From Other Banks	913.47	1036.97	1271.39	1453.55	1654.27	1807.33	2139.15	2313.29	2861.30	3340.47
Net Foreign Exchange Assets of Banking Sector	48.15	56.72	68.00	66.51	105.81	212.26	244.43	526.26	777.85	771.97
Government's Currency Liabilities to the Public	11.92	13.80	14.75	15.55	16.21	17.04	18.24	19.90	23.79	23.86
Net Non-Monetary Liabilities	311.26	346.30	380.70	461.15	583.36	521.37	558.15	619.01	638.77	738.88
of Reserve Bank of India	134.44	142.25	169.36	175.36	270.22	274.15	282.46	260.37	293.58	323.01
of Other Banks	176.82	204.05	211.34	285.79	313.14	247.22	275.69	358.64	345.19	415.87
Broad Money Supply (M3)	1416.42	1642.79	2002.41	2309.48	2658.28	3170.49	3668.25	4344.07	5314.26	6040.07
GDP at market prices	2929.49	3332.01	3957.82	4568.21	5355.34	6167.99	7059.18	8097.66	9536.80	10985.76

Note: 1995-96 figures are as of March 31 on the basis of the closure of government accounts.

Source: Ministry of Finance, Economic Survey, various issues; Reserve Bank of India, RBI Bulletin (Weekly Statistical Supplement).

Table A5.2
Base Money Supply and Sources of Change, 1985-86 - 1995-96
(Rs. billion)

	1986-87	1987-88	1988-89	1989-90	1990-91	1991-92	1992-93	1993-94	1994-95	1995-96
TOTAL BASE MONEY SUPPLY	448.08	534.90	629.59	775.91	877.79	995.05	1107.79	1386.71	1691.71	1943.60
Currency with Public	283.82	335.59	380.71	463.00	530.48	610.98	682.73	823.01	1006.81	1181.61
Other Deposits with RBI	3.09	3.97	6.94	5.98	6.74	8.85	13.13	25.25	33.80	33.44
Cash with Banks	15.31	15.63	19.72	19.86	22.34	26.40	30.53	30.94	38.92	43.11
Bank Deposits with RBI	145.86	179.71	222.22	287.07	318.23	348.82	381.40	507.51	612.18	685.44
SOURCES OF CHANGE										
RBI Claims	524.39	609.18	722.18	875.03	1051.97	1063.78	1145.54	1112.96	1214.30	1501.43
On Government (net)	462.85	526.87	596.15	736.83	888.48	940.16	984.49	993.00	1014.78	1213.49
On Banks	27.60	44.41	70.79	74.71	100.07	51.02	98.85	55.51	133.59	219.39
On Commercial Sector	33.94	37.90	55.24	63.49	63.42	72.60	62.20	64.45	65.93	68.55
Net Foreign Exchange Assets of RBI	46.21	54.17	62.02	60.69	79.83	188.38	226.47	514.22	747.20	741.32
Government's Currency Liabilities to the Public	11.92	13.80	14.75	15.55	16.21	17.04	18.24	19.90	23.79	23.86
Net Non-Monetary Liabilities of Reserve Bank of India	134.44	142.25	169.36	175.36	270.22	274.15	282.46	260.37	293.58	323.01
Total Base Money Supply	448.08	534.90	629.59	775.91	877.79	995.05	1107.79	1386.71	1691.71	1943.60
GDP at market prices	2929.49	3332.01	3957.82	4568.21	5355.34	6167.99	7059.18	8097.66	9536.80	10985.76

Note: 1995-96 figures are as of March 31 on the basis of the closure of government accounts.

Source: Ministry of Finance, Economic Survey, various issues; Reserve Bank of India, RBI Bulletin (Weekly Statistical Supplement).

Table A5.3
Selected Monetary Policy Instruments

Year & Month	Bank Rate	Minimum Cash Reserve[a] Ratio	Statutory Liquidity[b] Ratio
1982 January 29	10	7.8	35.0
April 10	10	7.3	35.0
June 11	10	7.0	35.0
1983 May 28	10	7.5	35.0
July 30	10	8.0	35.0
August 27	10	8.5	35.0
November 12	10	Incremental CRR of 10% over November 11, 1983	35.0
1984 February 4	10	9.0	35.0
July 28	10	9.0	35.5
September 1	10	9.0	36.0
October 30	10	9.0	36.0
1985 June 8	10	9.0	36.5
July 6	10	9.0	37.0
1987 February 28	10	9.5	37.0
April 25	10	9.5	37.5
October 24	10	10.0	37.5
1988 January 2	10	10.0	38.0
July 2	10	10.5	38.0
July 30	10	11.0	38.0
1989 July 1	10	15.0	38.0
1990 September 22	10	15.0	38.5
1991 July 4	11	15.0	38.5
October 9	12	15.0	38.5
1992 April 1	12	15.0	30.0
1993 April 17	12	14.5	30.0
May 15	12	14.0	30.0
September 17	12	14.0	25.0
1994 June 11	12	14.5	25.0
July 9	12	14.8	25.0
August 6	12	15.0	25.0
1995 November 11	12	14.5	25.0
December 9	12	14.0	25.0
1996 April 27	12	13.5	25.0
May 11	12	13.0	25.0
July 6	12	12.0	25.0
October 26	12	11.5	25.0
November 9	12	11.0	25.0
1997 January 4	12	10.5	25.0
January 18	12	10.0	25.0
April 16	11	10.0	25.0
June 26	10	10.0	25.0

Note: Dates given are those on which the announced measures take effect.

a. Minimum cash reserves to be deposited with the RBI as % of net demand and time liabilities (NDTL).
b. The ratio of liquid assets, exclusive of those under (a), to aggregate demand and time liabilities
upto March 28, 1985 and net demand and time liabilities with effect from March 29, 1985.

Sources: Reserve Bank of India, Report of the Committee to Review the Working of the Monetary
System, 1985; Reserve Bank of India, Annual Report, various issues.

Table A5.4
Structure of Short-term and Long-term Interest Rates
(percent per annum)

	1980-81	1985-86	1990-91	1991-92	1992-93	1993-94	1994-95	1995-96
A. SHORT-TERM RATES								
Reserve Bank Rate	9.0	10.0	10.0	12.0	12.0	12.0	12.0	12.0
Treasury Bills:								
91-day [a]	4.6	4.6	4.6	4.6	8.8-10.7	7.1-11.1	7.2-11.9	11.4-13.0
182-day			10.0-10.1	8.8-10.1	7.8-8.4			
364-day					9.9-10.3	10.0-11.4	9.4-11.9	12.1-13.2
Call Money Rate (Bombay)	7.1	10.0	15.9	19.6	14.4	7.0	9.4	17.7
Commercial Bank Rates:								
Maximum Deposit Rate [b]	10.0	11.0	11.0	13.0	11.0	10.0	11.0	12.0
Minimum Lending Rate	13.5		16.0	19.0	17.0	14.0	Free	Free
B. LONG-TERM RATES								
I.D.B.I. Prime Lending Rate	14.0	14.0	14.0-15.0	18.0-20.0	17.0-19.0	14.5-17.5	15.0	16.0-19.0
Company Deposit Rates: [c]								
Private Sector Companies [d]								
(i) 1 year	9.0-13.5	10.0-15.0	10.5-14.0	10.5-15.0	12.0-15.0	12.0-14.0	13.0-14.0	12.0-15.0
(ii) 2 years	10.0-14.5	12.0-15.0	12.0-14.0	12.0-15.0	13.0-15.0	13.0-14.0	14.0-15.0	13.0-15.0
(iii) 3 years	13.0-15.5	13.0-15.0	13.5-14.0	14.0-15.0	15.0	14.0	14.0-15.0	14.0-15.0
Public Sector Companies								
(i) 1 year	11.0	11.5-12.0	10.5-12.0	10.5-15.0	13.0	12.0-15.0	12.0-15.0	13.0-15.0
(ii) 2 years	12.0	12.0-13.0	11.5-13.0	11.5-15.0	14.0	13.0-15.0	13.0-15.0	14.0-15.0
(iii) 3 years	13.5	13.5-14.5	13.0-14.0	13.0-15.0	15.0	14.0-15.0	14.0-15.0	15.0
Average Yield - Ordinary Shares	5.9	3.2	2.6	2.1	1.7	2.2	1.8	3.1
Redemption Yield - Government of India Securities								
(i) Short-term (1-5 years)	4.7-6.0	5.4-9.8	7.0-21.7	8.4-26.3	9.1-23.8	11.9-12.9	9.8-11.8	6.0-14.3
(ii) Medium-term (5-15 years)	5.8-6.8	6.5-9.5	9.4-12.7	9.5-13.4	9.5-14.8	12.7-13.3	11.3-13.9	5.8-14.1
(iii) Long-term (above 15 years)	6.4-7.5	8.4-11.5	10.9-12.0	9.9-12.4	8.8-12.5	12.9-13.4	11.8-13.5	11.8-13.0

Note: 1995-96 is preliminary.

a. Effective 8 January, 1993, a new auction system for 91-day Treasury Bills was introduced.

b. Effective 22 April, 1992, a single 'maximum deposit rate' has been for deposits of various maturities.
   Earlier different rates were prescribed for different deposit maturities.

c. Deposits accepted from the public.

d. Well-established private sector companies.

Source: Reserve Bank of India, Report on Currency and Finance, various issues.

Table A5.5
Sectoral Deployment of Gross Bank Credit
(Rs billion - change during year)

	1986-87	1987-88	1988-89	1989-90	1990-91	1991-92	1992-93	1993-94	1994-95	1995-96	Apr-Sep 1995-96	Apr-Sep 1996-97
Gross Bank Credit	73.56	76.91	154.68	169.43	153.48	79.86	211.34	97.18	401.28	347.12	75.94	-38.65
Public Food Procurement Credit	-4.31	-29.14	-14.21	12.37	25.00	1.64	20.73	41.64	13.68	-24.84	3.31	-13.55
Gross Non-Food Credit	77.87	106.05	168.89	157.06	128.48	78.22	190.61	55.54	387.60	371.96	72.63	-25.10
Priority Sectors	34.84	40.20	51.49	61.64	25.32	25.10	44.07	40.48	102.81	92.30	21.43	6.97
Agriculture	15.12	14.39	19.41	25.76	2.24	14.07	18.06	12.45	27.75	31.02	9.05	8.49
Small Scale Industries	12.92	17.12	23.15	24.08	16.38	9.69	18.76	25.91	50.21	42.46	5.06	-10.10
Other Priority Sectors	6.80	8.69	8.93	11.80	6.70	1.34	7.25	2.12	24.85	18.82	6.78	8.58
Industry (Medium & Large)	29.34	37.97	70.32	60.87	62.46	25.82	115.46	-7.71	168.07	184.36	39.52	-16.26
Wholesale Trade (other than food procurement)	0.14	5.18	11.69	7.05	4.38	2.44	8.15	3.61	24.19	22.44	5.68	-13.28
Other Sectors	13.55	22.70	35.39	27.60	36.32	24.86	22.93	19.16	92.53	72.86	6.00	-2.53
Export Credit (included in Gross Non-Food Credit)	7.37	7.71	22.24	21.04	9.41	11.08	50.62	17.30	79.65	46.41	5.70	-40.22
Priority Sector advances as percent of net bank credit [a]	42.20	44.10	43.20	42.40	39.20	38.70	35.10	35.30	33.20			

a. In the last month of each period, advances include Participation Certificates.

Source: Ministry of Finance, Economic Survey, various issues.

Table A6.1
Production of Major Crops

	1980-81	1984-85	1985-86	1986-87	1987-88	1988-89	1989-90	1990-91	1991-92	1992-93	1993-94	1994-95	1995-96
Total Foodgrains	129.6	145.5	150.4	143.4	140.4	169.9	171.0	176.4	168.4	179.5	184.3	191.5	185.1
Kharif	77.6	84.5	85.2	80.2	74.6	95.6	101.0	99.4	91.6	101.5	100.4	101.1	98.2
Rabi	51.9	61.0	65.2	63.2	65.8	74.3	70.0	77.0	76.8	78.0	83.9	90.4	86.9
Total Cereals	119.0	133.6	137.1	131.7	129.4	156.1	158.2	162.1	156.4	166.6	170.9	177.5	171.9
Kharif	73.9	79.8	80.7	76.0	70.2	90.0	95.5	94.0	87.2	95.8	95.0	96.4	93.4
Rabi	45.1	53.8	56.4	55.7	59.2	66.1	62.7	68.1	69.2	70.8	75.9	81.1	78.5
Rice	53.6	58.3	63.8	60.6	56.9	70.5	73.6	74.3	74.7	72.9	80.3	81.8	79.6
Kharif	50.1	53.8	59.4	53.6	49.0	63.4	65.9	66.3	66.4	65.3	70.7	72.6	70.1
Rabi	3.5	4.6	4.4	7.0	7.8	7.1	7.7	8.0	8.3	7.6	9.6	9.2	9.5
Wheat	36.3	44.1	47.1	44.3	46.2	54.1	49.8	55.1	55.7	57.2	59.8	65.8	62.6
Barley (Jowar)	10.4	11.4	10.2	9.2	12.2	10.2	12.9	11.7	8.1	12.8	11.4	9.0	9.6
Kharif	7.5	7.8	7.3	6.5	8.6	7.1	9.2	8.3	5.7	9.4	7.3	5.9	5.9
Rabi	2.9	3.6	2.9	2.7	3.6	3.1	3.7	3.4	2.4	3.4	4.1	3.1	3.7
Maize	7.0	8.4	6.6	7.6	5.7	8.2	9.7	9.0	8.1	10.0	9.6	8.9	9.4
Bajra	5.3	6.0	3.7	4.5	3.3	7.8	6.6	6.9	4.7	8.9	5.0	7.2	5.4
Total Pulses	10.6	12.0	13.4	11.7	11.0	13.8	12.8	14.3	12.0	12.8	13.3	14.1	13.2
Kharif	3.8	4.8	4.6	4.2	4.4	5.6	5.5	5.4	4.4	5.6	5.4	4.7	4.8
Rabi	6.8	7.2	8.8	7.5	6.6	8.2	7.3	8.9	7.6	7.2	7.9	9.4	8.4
Gram	4.3	4.6	5.8	4.5	3.6	5.1	4.2	5.4	4.1	4.4	5.0	6.4	5.0
Tur	2.0	2.6	2.4	2.3	2.3	2.7	2.7	2.4	2.1	2.3	2.7	2.1	2.4
Total Oilseeeds [a]	9.4	12.9	10.8	11.3	12.6	18.0	16.9	18.6	18.6	20.1	21.5	21.3	22.4
Kharif	5.0	7.0	6.0	6.4	6.4	10.5	9.6	9.8	9.3	12.0	12.3	11.9	12.7
Rabi	4.4	5.9	4.8	4.9	6.2	7.5	7.3	8.8	9.3	8.1	9.2	9.4	9.7
Groundnut	5.0	6.4	5.1	5.9	5.8	9.7	8.1	7.5	7.1	8.6	7.8	8.1	7.8
Kharif	3.7	4.7	3.7	4.4	4.2	7.5	6.1	5.1	5.0	6.7	5.7	6.1	5.8
Rabi	1.3	1.7	1.4	1.4	1.7	2.2	2.0	2.4	2.1	1.9	2.1	2.0	2.0
Rapeseed & Mustard	2.3	3.1	2.7	2.6	3.4	4.4	4.1	5.2	5.9	4.8	5.3	5.8	6.1
Sugarcane	154.2	170.3	170.7	186.1	196.7	203.0	225.6	241.0	254.0	228.0	229.7	275.5	282.9
Cotton	7.0	8.5	8.7	6.9	6.4	8.7	11.4	9.8	9.7	11.4	10.7	11.9	13.1
Jute & Mesta	8.2	7.8	12.6	8.6	6.8	7.9	8.3	9.2	10.3	8.6	8.4	9.1	8.9
Jute	6.5	6.5	10.9	7.3	5.8	6.7	7.1	7.9	8.9	7.5	7.3	8.0	7.7
Mesta	1.7	1.3	1.8	1.3	1.0	1.2	1.2	1.3	1.4	1.1	1.1	1.1	1.2
Potato	9.7	12.6	10.4	12.7	14.1	14.9	14.8	15.2	16.4	15.2	17.4	17.4	19.2

Notes: Units of measurement of all commodities is million tonnes, except in the case of cotton, jute and mesta where production is in terms of millions of bales. Figures for 1995-96 are provisional.

a. Includes groundnuts, rapeseeds and mustard, sesame, linseed, castorseed, nigerseed, safflower, sunflower and soybean.

Source: Ministry of Finance, Economic Survey, various issues.

Table A6.2
Irrigated Area Under Different Crops
(million hectares)

	1980-81	1984-85	1985-86	1986-87	1987-88	1988-89	1989-90	1990-91	1991-92	1992-93	1993-94
Total Foodgrains	37.8	40.1	40.4	41.8	40.5	43.9	44.3	44.9	45.8	46.9	48.2
Total Cereals	35.8	38.4	38.3	39.5	38.4	41.8	41.9	42.3	43.4	44.4	45.6
Rice	16.4	17.7	17.7	18.1	17.0	19.1	19.4	19.4	20.2	20.1	20.7
Jowar	0.8	0.7	0.7	0.8	0.8	0.8	0.9	0.8	0.8	0.8	0.8
Bajra	0.6	0.6	0.6	0.7	0.8	0.6	0.7	0.5	0.7	0.6	0.7
Maize	1.2	1.0	1.1	1.3	1.2	1.2	1.2	1.2	1.3	1.3	1.4
Wheat	15.6	17.5	17.3	17.7	17.8	19.1	18.8	19.5	19.6	20.8	21.4
Barley	0.9	0.6	0.7	0.6	0.6	0.6	0.5	0.5	0.6	0.6	0.5
Total Pulses	2.0	1.8	2.1	2.3	2.0	2.2	2.3	2.6	2.4	2.5	2.6
Other Crops											
Oilseeds [a]	2.3	3.5	3.4	3.4	4.3	5.0	5.2	5.8	6.8	6.4	6.5
Cotton	2.1	1.9	2.3	2.2	2.1	2.4	2.6	2.5	2.6	2.7	2.6
Sugarcane	2.4	2.6	2.6	2.8	3.0	3.0	3.1	3.4	3.6	3.5	3.4

a. Oilseeds include groundnuts, rapeseed and mustard, linseed, sesame, and others.

Source: Ministry of Finance, Economic Survey, various issues.

Table A6.3
Yield Per Hectare of Major Crops
(kgs. per hectare)

	1980-81	1984-85	1985-86	1986-87	1987-88	1988-89	1989-90	1990-91	1991-92	1992-93	1993-94	1994-95	1995-96
Total Foodgrains	1023	1149	1175	1128	1173	1331	1349	1380	1382	1457	1501	1548	1499
Kharif	933	1041	1042	985	996	1166	1241	1231	1174	1302	1324	1341	1318
Rabi	1195	1341	1410	1382	1468	1628	1544	1635	1751	1725	1787	1864	1774
Total Cereals	1142	1285	1323	1266	1315	1493	1530	1571	1574	1654	1701	1763	1727
Kharif	1015	1129	1140	1074	1082	1270	1366	1357	1305	1440	1465	1486	1460
Rabi	1434	1617	1718	1673	1763	1964	1875	2010	2126	2068	2132	2260	2207
Rice	1336	1417	1552	1471	1465	1689	1745	1740	1751	1744	1888	1911	1855
Kharif	1303	1374	1514	1393	1368	1627	1677	1670	1676	1676	1807	1841	1776
Rabi	2071	2274	2329	2563	2640	2548	2678	2671	2720	2720	2816	2731	2761
Wheat	1630	1870	2046	1916	2002	2244	2121	2281	2394	2327	2380	2559	2493
Barley (Jowar)	660	715	633	576	762	697	869	814	655	982	898	779	834
Kharif	737	820	761	665	892	789	1053	969	757	1230	1065	988	1014
Rabi	520	563	447	437	568	550	604	582	496	632	704	555	651
Maize	1159	1456	1146	1282	1029	1395	1632	1518	1376	1676	1602	1448	1570
Bajra	458	519	344	401	378	646	610	658	465	836	521	700	575
Total Pulses	473	526	547	505	515	598	549	578	533	573	598	610	552
Kharif	361	453	412	392	435	504	480	471	393	495	492	351	354
Rabi	571	589	658	604	587	686	616	672	672	654	701	589	540
Gram	657	661	742	649	629	753	652	712	739	684	783	853	697
Tur	689	819	767	722	685	779	763	673	588	652	762	644	662
Total Oilseeds [a]	532	684	570	605	629	824	742	771	719	797	799	843	851
Kharif	492	633	516	554	559	805	691	698	604	804	759	797	814
Rabi	588	758	651	687	720	851	822	872	886	786	860	910	906
Groundnut	736	898	719	841	855	1132	930	904	818	1049	941	1027	1014
Kharif	629	779	602	733	737	1066	824	751	687	969	813	913	884
Rabi	1444	1518	1549	1540	1425	1442	1532	1611	1501	1473	1624	1650	1772
Rapeseed & Mustard	560	771	674	700	748	906	831	904	895	776	847	950	912
Sugarcane	57844	57673	60000	60000	60000	61000	65000	65000	66000	64000	67000	71000	68000
Cotton	152	196	197	169	168	202	252	225	216	257	249	257	246
Jute & Mesta	1130	1242	1524	1454	1274	1540	1646	1634	1662	1658	1713	1760	1733
Jute	1245	1411	1710	1647	1496	1748	1879	1833	1837	1857	1907	1949	1889
Mesta	828	764	910	865	680	909	956	988	1019	955	1008	1023	1114
Potato	13256	14806	12000	15000	16000	16000	16000	16000	16000	15000	17000	16000	17000

Note: Figures for 1995-96 are provisional.

a. Includes groundnuts, rapeseeds and mustard, sesame, linseed, castorseed, nigerseed, safflower, sunflower and soybean.

Source: Ministry of Finance, Economic Survey, various issues.

Table A6.4
Net Availability, Procurement and Public Distribution of Foodgrains
(million tonnes)

	1980-81	1984-85	1985-86	1986-87	1987-88	1988-89	1989-90	1990-91	1991-92	1992-93	1993-94	1994-95	1995-96
Net Production	113.4	127.3	131.6	125.5	122.8	148.7	149.7	154.3	147.3	157.5	161.2	167.2	161.9
Net Imports	0.7	-0.4	0.5	-0.2	3.8	1.2	1.3	-0.1	-0.4	3.1	1.1	0.4	-1.3
Change in Government Stocks	-0.2	2.7	-1.6	-9.5	-4.6	2.6	6.2	-4.4	-1.5	10.8	7.5	-1.8	-8.8
Net Availability	114.3	124.3	133.8	134.8	130.8	147.2	144.8	158.6	148.4	149.8	154.8	169.4	169.4
Procurement	13.0	20.1	19.7	15.7	14.1	18.9	24.0	19.6	17.9	28.1	26.0	22.5	19.8
Public Distribution	13.0	15.8	17.3	18.7	18.6	16.4	16.0	20.8	18.8	16.4	14.0	15.3	20.5

Note: Production figures relate to agricultural year. Figures for procurement and public distribution relate to calendar years.

Source: Ministry of Finance, Economic Survey, various issues.

Table A6.5
New Index of Industrial Production
(1980-81=100)

	Weight	1987-88	1988-89	1989-90	1990-91	1991-92	1992-93	1993-94	1994-95	1995-96	1994-95 over 1993-94	1995-96 over 1994-95
General Index	100.0	166.4	180.9	196.4	212.6	213.9	218.9	232.0	253.7	283.3	9.4	11.7
Mining and Quarrying	11.5	184.6	199.1	211.6	221.2	222.5	223.7	231.5	248.8	266.4	7.5	7.1
Electricity Generated	11.4	181.0	198.2	219.7	236.8	257.0	269.9	290.0	314.6	340.3	8.5	8.2
Manufacturing Index	77.1	161.5	175.6	190.7	207.8	206.2	210.7	223.5	245.4	277.3	9.8	13.0
Food products	5.3	139.0	148.5	150.9	169.8	178.0	175.3	160.0	181.7	207.5		14.2
Beverages, tobacco, etc.	1.6	84.9	92.1	103.0	104.8	107.3	113.7	137.8	134.8	160.8	-2.2	19.3
Cotton textiles	12.3	111.2	107.8	112.3	126.6	139.0	150.1	160.5	155.8	159.6	-2.9	2.4
Jute textiles	2.0	91.0	101.9	97.4	101.6	90.8	87.0	103.2	91.5	92.6	-11.3	1.2
Textile products	0.8	91.7	134.2	151.7	103.2	97.2	75.8	73.4	78.6	89.7	7.1	14.1
Wood & wood products	0.5	161.7	171.7	176.0	197.2	185.0	190.5	199.3	205.5	239.9	3.1	16.7
Paper & paper products	3.2	166.3	171.3	181.5	198.0	203.0	210.9	224.8	258.1	286.4	14.8	11.0
Leather & leather products	0.5	185.5	177.4	188.3	194.3	181.3	187.7	204.3	211.9	227.5	3.7	7.4
Rubber, plastic & petroleum prod.	4.0	155.1	168.3	173.5	174.0	172.0	174.6	176.4	182.1	196.4	3.2	7.9
Chemical & chemical products	12.5	200.9	233.4	247.6	254.1	261.2	276.9	297.9	326.3	360.9	9.5	10.6
Non-metallic mineral products	3.0	158.1	184.6	189.9	193.1	205.2	208.9	218.5	236.0	264.3	8.0	12.0
Basic metal & alloy products	9.8	135.6	144.9	143.7	158.8	167.8	168.4	224.2	214.5	225.0	-4.3	4.9
Metal products	2.3	129.6	133.5	142.6	143.1	133.1	124.6	126.5	148.7	175.3	17.5	17.9
Machinery & machine tools	6.2	139.2	161.2	171.9	186.9	183.3	181.1	189.2	206.9	252.2	9.4	21.9
Electrical machinery	5.8	335.2	346.0	459.2	563.6	493.7	483.6	460.1	609.9	730.5	32.6	19.8
Transport equipment	6.4	151.9	171.3	181.1	192.5	191.1	200.6	211.2	239.2	295.9	13.3	23.7
Miscellaneous products	0.9	272.1	306.3	333.2	321.8	269.9	281.3	267.0	269.6	299.3	1.0	11.0

Note: Figures for 1995-96 are provisional.

Source: Ministry of Finance, <u>Economic Survey</u>, various issues.

Table A6.6
Production, Imports and Consumption of Fertilizers
(000' nutrient tons)

(Apr-Mar)	Nitrogenous [a]			Phosphatic [b]			Potassic		Total		
	Production	Imports	Consumption	Production	Imports	Consumption	Imports	Consumption	Production	Imports	Consumption
1980-81	2163.9	1510.2	3678.1	841.5	452.1	1213.6	796.8	623.9	3005.4	2759.1	5515.6
1981-82	3143.3	1055.1	4068.7	950.0	343.2	1322.9	643.8	676.2	4093.3	2042.1	6067.8
1982-83	3429.7	424.6	4242.5	983.7	63.4	1432.7	643.7	726.3	4413.4	1131.7	6401.5
1983-84	3491.5	656.1	5204.4	1064.1	142.6	1730.3	556.4	775.4	4555.6	1355.1	7710.1
1984-85	3917.3	2008.6	5486.1	1317.9	745.2	1886.4	871.0	838.5	5235.2	3624.8	8211.0
1985-86	4328.0	1680.0	5661.0	1428.0	816.0	2005.0	903.0	808.0	5756.0	3399.0	8474.0
1986-87	5410.0	1103.0	5716.0	1660.0	255.0	2079.0	952.0	850.0	7070.0	2310.0	8645.0
1987-88	5466.0	175.0	5717.0	1665.0	0.0	2187.0	809.0	880.0	7131.0	984.0	8784.0
1988-89	6712.0	219.0	7251.0	2252.0	407.0	2721.0	982.0	1068.0	8964.0	1608.0	11040.0
1989-90	6747.0	523.0	7386.0	1796.0	1311.0	3014.0	1280.0	1168.0	8543.0	3114.0	11568.0
1990-91	6993.0	414.0	7997.0	2052.0	1016.0	3221.0	1328.0	1328.0	9045.0	2758.0	12546.0
1991-92	7301.0	566.0	8046.0	2562.0	967.0	3321.0	1236.0	1361.0	9863.0	2769.0	12728.0
1992-93	7430.0	1160.0	8426.0	2306.0	746.0	2842.0	1082.0	884.0	9736.0	2988.0	12152.0
1993-94	7231.0	1564.0	8789.0	1816.0	722.0	2669.0	880.0	908.0	9047.0	3166.0	12366.0
1994-95	7948.0	1476.0 [d]	9507.0	2493.0	380.0 [d]	2932.0	1109.0 [d]	1125.0	10438.0	2965.0 [d]	13564.0
1995-96 [c]	8777.0	1938.0	9823.0	2558.0	647.0	2898.0	1423.0	1156.0	11335.0	4008.0	13877.0
1996-97 [c]	9023.0	--	--	2680.0	--	3709.0	--	1465.0	11703.0	--	16422.0

-- Not available.

a. Excludes nitrogen meant for non-agricultural purposes.

b. Excludes data in respect of bonemeal and rockphosphate.

c. Anticipated.

d. Incorporates import of Urea in nutrient terms, the only controlled fertiliser imported on Government account.

Source: The Fertilizer Association of India, Fertilizer Statistics, various issues; Ministry of Finance, Economic Survey, various issues.

Table A6.7
Indian Railways: Freight and Passenger Traffic

| | | | | Passenger Traffic | | | | | |
| | Revenue Earning Freight Traffic | | | Non-Suburban | | | Suburban [a] | | |
Year	Originating tonnage (mln.tons)	Net tons-kilometers (million)	Average lead (kilometers)	Passenger originating (million)	Passenger-kilometers (million)	Average lead (kilometers)	Passenger originating (million)	Passenger-kilometers (million)	Average lead (kilometers)
1980-81	195.9	147652	754	1613	167472	103.9	2000	41086	20.5
1981-82	221.2	164253	743	1640	176822	107.8	2064	43965	21.3
1982-83	228.8	167781	733	1626	181142	111.4	2029	45789	22.6
1983-84	230.1	168849	734	1491	180808	121.3	1834	42127	23.0
1984-85	236.4	172632	730	1449	182318	125.8	1884	44264	23.5
1985-86	258.5	196600	760	1549	195175	126.0	1884	45439	24.1
1986-87	277.8	214100	771	1610	208057	129.0	1970	48411	24.6
1987-88	290.2	222528	767	1637	217632	133.0	2171	51859	23.9
1988-89	302.1	222374	736	1495	211819	141.6	2022	52023	25.7
1989-90	310.0	229602	741	1544	226045	76.9	2129	54933	25.8
1990-91	318.4	235785	741	1599	236066	147.6	2281	59724	26.2
1991-92	338.0	250238	740	1637	251174	153.4	2436	63543	26.1
1992-93	350.1	252388	721	1467	239655	163.3	2298	60547	26.4
1993-94	358.7	252411	704	1406	233200	165.9	2318	63147	27.2
1994-95	373.0	259810	697	1451	243798	168.0	2359	63275	26.8
1995-96	390.7	270489	692	1534	268708	175.2	2527	73651	29.1
1996-97	410.0	281227	686	1554	272101	175.1	2560	74624	29.1

Note: Figures for 1996-97 are revised estimates.

a. Passengers booked between stations within the suburban areas of Bombay; from 1988/89 onwards suburban passenger traffic include Metro Railway, Calcutta.

Source: Ministry of Railways, Railway Budget.

Table A6.8
Petroleum Summary
Commodity Balance of Petroleum and Petroleum Products
(million tons)

	1980-81	1984-85	1985-86	1986-87	1987-88	1988-89	1989-90	1990-91	1991-92	1992-93	1993-94	1994-95	1995-96 [a]
A. CRUDE PETROLEUM													
1.Refinery Throughput	25.8	35.6	42.9	45.7	47.7	48.8	51.9	51.8	51.4	53.5	54.3	56.3	58.6
2.Domestic Production	10.5	29.0	30.2	30.5	30.4	32.0	34.1	33.0	30.4	27.0	27.0	32.2	35.1
(a) On-shore	5.5	8.9	9.4	9.9	10.2	10.9	12.4	11.8	11.4	11.2	11.6	12.0	11.9
(b) Off-shore	5.0	20.1	20.8	20.6	20.2	21.1	21.7	21.2	19.0	15.8	15.4	20.2	22.7
3.Imports	16.2	13.7	15.1	15.5	18.0	17.8	19.5	20.7	24.0	29.2	30.8	27.3	27.3
4.Exports	--	6.5	0.5	--	--	--	--	--	--	--	--	--	--
5.Net Imports (3-4)	16.2	7.2	14.6	15.5	18.0	17.8	19.5	20.7	24.0	29.2	30.8	27.3	27.3
B. PRODUCTS													
1.Domestic Consumption [b] of which:	30.9	38.5	40.8	43.4	46.4	50.1	54.1	55.0	57.0	58.9	60.8	65.5	72.6c
(a) Naphtha	2.3	3.1	3.1	3.2	2.9	3.4	3.4	3.4	3.5	3.4	3.2	3.4	3.7
(b) Kerosene	4.2	6.0	6.2	6.6	7.2	7.7	8.2	8.4	8.4	8.5	8.7	9.0	9.4
(c) High Speed Diesel	10.3	13.7	14.9	16.0	17.7	18.8	20.7	21.1	22.7	24.3	25.9	28.3	32.3
(d) Fuel oils	7.5	7.9	7.9	7.9	8.1	8.5	8.8	9.0	9.2	9.3	9.2	9.9	10.7
2.Domestic Production	24.1	33.2	39.9	42.8	44.7	45.7	48.7	48.6	48.3	50.4	51.1	52.9	55.1
(a) Naphtha	2.1	3.5	5.0	5.6	5.5	5.4	5.2	4.9	4.5	4.6	4.7	5.7	6.0
(b) Kerosene	2.4	3.4	4.0	4.9	5.1	5.2	5.7	5.5	5.3	5.2	5.3	5.3	5.3
(c) High Speed Diesel	7.4	11.1	14.6	15.5	16.3	16.7	17.7	17.2	17.4	18.3	18.8	19.6	20.7
(d) Fuel oils	6.1	7.9	8.0	8.0	8.5	8.9	9.0	9.4	9.6	10.4	10.3	9.8	9.6
3.Imports	7.3	6.1	3.9	3.1	3.9	6.5	6.6	8.7	9.4	11.3	12.1	14.0	20.3
4.Exports [c]	--	0.9	2.0	2.5	3.4	2.3	2.6	2.6	2.9	3.7	4.0	3.3	3.4
5.Net Imports	7.3	5.2	1.9	0.6	0.5	4.2	4.0	6.1	6.5	7.6	8.1	10.7	16.9

-- Not available.

a. Provisional.

b. Excludes refinery fuel consumption.

c. Excludes supplies of POL products to Nepal.

Source: Ministry of Finance, Economic Survey, various issues.

Table A6.9
Generation and Consumption of Electricity
(000 GWH)

	1980-81	1985-86	1986-87	1987-88	1988-89	1989-90	1990-91	1991-92	1992-93	1993-94	1994-95 [a]	1995-96 [a]
A. GENERATION OF ELECTRICITY BY SOURCE AND REGION												
1. Thermal [b]												
Northern	13.69	25.73	29.80	37.74	41.24	48.82	52.13	60.44	66.17	71.45	72.43	81.76
Western	25.37	48.94	54.58	61.80	63.39	73.08	76.95	84.33	88.50	96.27	102.93	115.73
Southern	9.22	20.45	24.10	28.07	30.53	34.03	35.76	40.39	44.31	51.03	54.80	65.20
Eastern	12.53	18.37	19.31	20.77	21.40	21.55	20.39	22.40	24.56	28.36	30.54	34.67
North-Eastern	0.50	0.87	1.06	1.24	1.15	1.22	1.31	1.19	1.23	1.08	1.43	1.95
All-India	61.30	114.35	128.85	149.61	157.71	178.70	186.55	208.75	224.77	248.19	262.13	299.31
2. Hydro												
Northern	15.08	19.49	22.02	20.86	23.57	25.01	27.16	27.21	25.45	24.34	30.24	29.25
Western	7.81	6.18	6.15	5.06	7.54	6.87	8.31	8.16	7.27	8.72	10.30	7.55
Southern	20.28	21.15	21.08	17.35	21.64	24.54	29.17	29.63	30.70	30.72	35.06	28.46
Eastern	2.96	3.17	3.67	3.19	3.76	4.11	5.34	5.87	4.52	4.48	5.26	5.51
North-Eastern	0.41	1.03	0.92	0.97	1.36	1.58	1.66	1.89	1.93	2.20	1.85	1.83
All-India	46.54	51.02	53.84	47.44	57.87	62.12	71.64	72.76	69.87	70.46	82.71	72.60
3. Nuclear												
Northern	1.23	1.28	1.32	1.39	1.87	1.73	2.16	1.66	2.77	1.50	1.34	2.75
Western	1.77	1.96	2.00	1.61	1.90	1.55	1.90	1.71	1.97	2.43	1.83	3.82
Southern	..	1.74	1.70	2.04	2.05	1.35	2.07	2.16	1.98	1.39	2.43	1.41
All-India	3.00	4.98	5.02	5.04	5.82	4.63	6.14	5.53	6.72	5.32	5.60	7.98
4. Utilities- All India (1 + 2 + 3)	110.84	170.35	187.71	202.09	221.40	245.44	264.33	287.03	301.36	323.97	350.44	379.89
5. Self-Generation in Industry and Railways	8.42	13.04	13.57	16.89	19.91	23.23	25.11	28.60	31.35	32.28	35.07	37.35
6. Total- All India (4 + 5)	119.26	183.39	201.28	218.98	241.31	268.66	289.44	315.63	332.71	356.25	385.51	417.24
B. CONSUMPTION OF ELECTRICITY BY SECTORS												
1. Mining & Manufacturing [c]	55.35	78.30	81.98	82.97	92.05	100.40	105.38	110.62	116.17	121.38	129.86	
2. Transport	2.31	3.08	3.23	3.62	3.77	4.07	4.11	4.52	5.07	5.62	5.89	
3. Domestic	9.25	17.26	19.32	22.12	24.77	29.58	31.98	35.85	39.72	43.34	47.91	
4. Agriculture	14.49	23.42	29.44	35.27	38.88	44.06	50.32	58.56	63.33	70.70	79.30	
5. Others	8.30	12.26	13.66	15.42	17.02	17.01	19.74	21.42	22.38	24.41	26.40	
6. Total	89.70	134.32	147.64	159.40	176.49	195.12	211.53	230.97	246.67	265.45	289.36	

a. Provisional Data.
b. Includes steam, diesel, wind and gas.
c. Includes industrial power from utilities plus net generation in the non-utilities.

Source: Central Electricity Authority, Power Data Bank & Information Directorate.

Table A6.10
New Index Numbers of Wholesale Prices - by Years
(Base 1981-82=100)

	Weights	87-88	88-89	89-90	90-91	91-92	92-93	93-94	94-95	95-96	percent change[a]
TOTAL FOOD ARTICLES	17.386	161.1	177.1	179.3	200.6	241.1	271.0	284.4	313.8	334.6	6.6
Food Grains	7.917	141.3	161.8	165.4	179.2	216.4	242.4	260.8	293.0	313.7	7.1
Other Food	9.469	177.7	189.9	190.9	218.5	261.8	294.9	304.2	331.1	352.1	6.3
INDUSTRIAL RAW MAT.	14.909	142.8	140.3	145.3	166.6	192.3	192.2	211.8	247.1	267.6	8.3
Non-Food Articles	10.081	163.0	160.2	166.0	194.2	229.2	228.7	249.1	297.0	322.8	8.7
Minerals	4.828	100.5	98.6	102.2	109.0	113.5	116.1	133.9	142.9	152.4	6.7
FUEL, POWER & LUB.	10.663	143.3	151.2	156.6	175.8	199.0	227.1	262.4	280.4	284.4	1.4
MANUF. PRODUCTS	57.042	138.5	151.5	168.6	182.8	203.4	225.6	243.2	268.8	292.4	8.8
Food Products	10.143	140.5	147.8	165.4	181.7	206.3	223.8	246.7	269.9	279.3	3.5
Beverage & Tobacco	2.149	155.0	180.7	207.7	242.1	265.7	293.7	306.6	341.2	372.5	9.2
Textiles	11.545	126.6	139.6	158.2	171.2	188.0	201.3	219.9	255.4	293.1	14.8
Chemicals and Chemical Products	7.355	131.9	135.8	140.1	147.9	168.4	192.6	207.8	231.5	247.9	7.1
Basic metals and Products	7.632	149.7	176.4	205.6	219.9	234.8	256.6	276.6	298.7	326.3	9.3
Machinery and Machine Tools	6.268	132.3	150.8	166.2	180.2	208.3	230.6	237.9	260.7	281.9	8.1
Transport Eqpt.	2.705	135.5	148.9	166.2	181.3	202.5	218.1	223.9	238.2	253.2	6.3
ALL COMMODITIES	100.0	143.6	154.3	165.7	182.7	207.8	228.7	247.8	274.7	294.8	7.3

Note: This WPI series based 1981-82 was introduced as of July 1989. Data for 1995-96 are provisional.

a. Refers to percent change in fiscal year 1995-96 over 1994-95.

Source: Ministry of Industry, Office of the Economic Adviser.

Table A6.11
Contribution of Selected Commodities to
Increase in WPI in Calendar Year 1996

	Weights	1995	1996	1996 over 1995 Percent Change	percent contribution to change in WPI
Agriculture	27.47	327.2	349.6	6.4	36.3
Food	17.39	330.0	361.5	8.7	32.3
Cereals	6.82	297.6	323.9	8.1	10.6
Pulses	1.09	389.7	437.2	10.9	3.1
Others	9.47	346.4	379.9	8.8	18.7
Non-Food	10.08	322.4	329.1	2.0	4.0
Minerals	4.83	150.3	156.0	3.6	1.6
Fuel and Power	10.66	284.1	308.0	7.8	15.1
Coal	1.26	367.8	387.0	5.0	1.4
Mineral oils	6.67	235.0	257.5	8.7	8.8
Electricity	2.74	363.2	394.9	8.0	5.1
Manufactured Products	57.04	288.1	301.3	4.4	44.5
Food products	10.14	278.4	288.8	3.6	6.2
Sugar	4.06	223.0	230.8	3.4	1.9
Edible oils	2.45	301.9	301.3	-0.2	-0.1
Other food products	3.64	324.3	345.1	6.0	4.5
Textiles	11.55	285.4	302.7	5.7	11.8
Cement	0.92	263.1	289.0	8.9	1.4
Iron and Steel	2.44	285.9	300.0	4.7	2.0
Capital goods	6.27	--	--	--	--
Others	25.73	364.3	379.5	4.0	23.1
ALL COMMODITIES of which	100.00	291.3	308.3	5.5	100.0
Agriculture-based	37.61	314.0	333.2	5.8	42.5
Non-Agricultural	62.39	277.6	293.3	5.3	57.5

-- Not available.

Note: Weighted share of each commodity in total absolute change in Wholesale Price.

Source: Ministry of Industry, Office of the Economic Adviser.

Table A 6.12
Consumer Price Index Numbers for Industrial Workers, Urban Non-Manual
Employees and Agricultural Laborers

Year (April-March)	Industrial Workers		Urban Non-Manual Employees (1984-85=100)	Agricultural Laborers [a] General Index (1960-61=100)
	Food Index (1982=100)	General Index (1982=100)		
1989-90	177.0	173.0	145.0	746.0
1990-91	199.0	193.0	161.0	803.0
1991-92	230.0	219.0	183.0	958.0
1992-93	254.0	240.0	202.0	1076.0
1993-94	272.0	258.0	216.0	1114.0
1994-95	297.0	279.0	237.0	1204.0
1995-96	337.0	313.0	248.0	1378.3
Average of weeks				
1994				
March	281	267	222	1175.0
June	294	277	230	1189.0
September	309	288	238	1251.0
December	311	289	240	1297.0
1995				
March	311	293	244	1300.0
June	331	306	254	1337.0
September	345	317	261	1413.0
December	344	317	262	1401.8
1996				
March	339	319	264	1395.9
June	361	333	--	1454.8
September	372	344	--	1525.5
December	--	350	--	1549.1
Percentage Change in Index over the corresponding month of previous year				
1994				
March	11.5	9.9	8.3	11.6
June	12.2	10.8	9.5	12.5
September	12.4	11.2	9.7	12.4
December	10.7	9.5	8.6	11.2
1995				
March	10.7	9.7	9.9	10.6
June	12.6	10.5	10.4	12.4
September	11.7	10.1	9.7	12.9
December	10.6	9.7	9.2	8.1
1996				
March	9.0	8.9	8.2	7.4
June	9.1	8.8	--	8.8
September	7.8	8.5	--	8.0
December	--	10.4	--	10.5

-- Not available.

a. Indices relate to Agricultural Years (July-June).

Source: Ministry of Labor, Labor Bureau, Simla; Central Statistical Organization; Ministry of Finance, Economic Survey, various issues; CMIE, Monthly Review of the Indian Economy.

Table A 6.13
Evolution of the Wholesale Price Index, 1991-96
(index and twelve months point-to-point increase)

	Weight	June 1991		June 1994		June 1995		June 1996		Dec 1996		%
		Index	percent	Index	percent	Index	percent	Index	percent	Index	percent	Contrib.
WPI	100.00	100.0	11.2	135.1	11.8	146.3	8.3	154.3	5.4	160.84	6.9	60.8
Primary Articles	32.30	100.0	8.3	133.8	14.6	144.2	7.8	155.4	7.8	162.13	8.8	20.1
Food	17.39	100.0	0.6	136.7	12.4	145.5	6.4	160.1	10.1	170.75	14.1	12.3
Food grains	7.92	100.0	18.6	146.1	17.0	159.8	9.4	173.9	8.9	192.02	16.8	7.3
Non-Food	10.08	100.0	10.1	131.2	22.0	145.3	10.7	151.8	4.4	152.72	1.0	5.3
Minerals	4.83	100.0	6.4	126.4	3.5	133.5	5.6	139.9	4.8	142.07	2.1	2.0
Fuel, Power, Lubricants	10.66	100.0	9.2	146.7	9.8	150.2	2.4	155.7	3.7	175.73	17.1	8.1
Manufactured Products	57.04	100.0	9.4	133.7	10.6	146.8	9.8	153.1	4.3	157.27	3.9	32.7
Food products	10.14	100.0	12.0	134.3	10.2	139.0	3.5	141.1	1.6	151.60	7.7	5.2
Textiles	11.55	100.0	5.1	137.2	18.0	160.1	16.7	167.9	4.9	169.48	1.8	8.0
Chemicals	7.36	100.0	6.5	141.1	9.2	154.9	9.8	163.4	5.5	165.48	4.1	4.8
Metal and Metal Products	7.63	100.0	8.7	126.8	9.3	139.6	10.2	145.7	4.3	148.97	3.2	3.7
Machinery	6.27	100.0	9.5	128.0	7.4	141.3	10.3	146.7	3.8	150.81	4.6	3.2
Memo Items												
Administered Prices:	15.93	100.0		143.9		147.1		151.5		167.83		10.8
Petroleum crude & natural gas	4.27	100.0		127.1		130.3		130.3		133.03		1.4
Petroleum products	6.67	100.0		138.5		138.3		139.6		165.08		4.3
Coal	1.26	100.0		154.1		158.1		158.4		190.20		1.1
Electricity	2.74	100.0		160.4		169.3		185.5		189.16		2.4
Urea	0.99	100.0		148.4		155.3		155.2		155.05		0.5
Decontrolled Prices:												
Iron and steel	2.44	100.0		128.3		139.1		142.4		148.94		1.2
Phosphatic fertilizers	0.18	100.0		302.7		306.0		317.5		313.56		0.4
Super phosphate	0.06	100.0		282.2		290.9		320.9		310.54		0.1
Ammonium phosphate	0.12	100.0		315.4		315.4		315.4		315.44		0.3
Lubricating oil	0.45	100.0		171.0		168.7		184.8		189.55		0.4

Note: The last column indicates each item contribution to the WPI increase, that is the index item percentage change in Dec 1996 times the weight of the item in the WPI.

Source: Ministry of Finance, Economic Survey, various issues; CMIE, Monthly Review of the Indian Economy, various issues.

Distributors of World Bank Publications

Prices and credit terms vary from country to country. Consult your local distributor before placing an order.

ARGENTINA
Oficina del Libro Internacional
Av. Cordoba 1877
1120 Buenos Aires
Tel: (54 1) 815-8354
Fax: (54 1) 815-8156

AUSTRALIA, FIJI, PAPUA NEW GUINEA, SOLOMON ISLANDS, VANUATU, AND WESTERN SAMOA
D.A. Information Services
648 Whitehorse Road
Mitcham 3132
Victoria
Tel: (61) 3 9210 7777
Fax: (61) 3 9210 7788
E-mail: service@dadirect.com.au
URL: http://www.dadirect.com.au

AUSTRIA
Gerold and Co.
Weihburggasse 26
A-1011 Wien
Tel: (43 1) 512-47-31-0
Fax: (43 1) 512-47-31-29
URL: http://www.gerold.co/at.online

BANGLADESH
Micro Industries Development
Assistance Society (MIDAS)
House 5, Road 16
Dhanmondi R/Area
Dhaka 1209
Tel: (880 2) 326427
Fax: (880 2) 811188

BELGIUM
Jean De Lannoy
Av. du Roi 202
1060 Brussels
Tel: (32 2) 538-5169
Fax: (32 2) 538-0841

BRAZIL
Publicações Tecnicas Internacionais Ltda.
Rua Peixoto Gomide, 209
01409 Sao Paulo, SP
Tel: (55 11) 259-6644
Fax: (55 11) 258-6990
E-mail: postmaster@pti.uol.br
URL: http://www.uol.br

CANADA
Renouf Publishing Co. Ltd.
5369 Canotek Road
Ottawa, Ontario K1J 9J3
Tel: (613) 745-2665
Fax: (613) 745-7660
E-mail: order.dept@renoufbooks.com
URL: http://www.renoufbooks.com

CHINA
China Financial & Economic
Publishing House
8, Da Fo Si Dong Jie
Beijing
Tel: (86 10) 6333-8257
Fax: (86 10) 6401-7365

COLOMBIA
Infoenlace Ltda.
Carrera 6 No. 51-21
Apartado Aereo 34270
Santafé de Bogotá, D.C.
Tel: (57 1) 285-2798
Fax: (57 1) 285-2798

COTE D'IVOIRE
Center d'Edition et de Diffusion Africaines
(CEDA)
04 B.P. 541
Abidjan 04
Tel: (225) 24 6510;24 6511
Fax: (225) 25 0567

CYPRUS
Center for Applied Research
Cyprus College
6, Diogenes Street, Engomi
P.O. Box 2006
Nicosia
Tel: (357 2) 44-1730
Fax: (357 2) 46-2051

CZECH REPUBLIC
National Information Center
prodejna, Konviktska 5
CS – 113 57 Prague 1
Tel: (42 2) 2422-9433
Fax: (42 2) 2422-1484
URL: http://www.nis.cz/

DENMARK
SamfundsLitteratur
Rosenoerns Allé 11
DK-1970 Frederiksberg C
Tel: (45 31) 351942
Fax: (45 31) 357822

ECUADOR
Libri Mundi
Libreria Internacional
P.O. Box 17-01-3029
Juan Leon Mera 851
Quito
Tel: (593 2) 521-606; (593 2) 544-185
Fax: (593 2) 504-209
E-mail: librimu1@librimundi.com.ec
E-mail: librimu2@librimundi.com.ec

EGYPT, ARAB REPUBLIC OF
Al Ahram Distribution Agency
Al Galaa Street
Cairo
Tel: (20 2) 578-6083
Fax: (20 2) 578-6833

The Middle East Observer
41, Sherif Street
Cairo
Tel: (20 2) 393-9732
Fax: (20 2) 393-9732

FINLAND
Akateeminen Kirjakauppa
P.O. Box 128
FIN-00101 Helsinki
Tel: (358 0) 121 4418
Fax: (358 0) 121-4435
E-mail: akatilaus@stockmann.fi
URL: http://www.akateeminen.com/

FRANCE
World Bank Publications
66, avenue d'Iéna
75116 Paris
Tel: (33 1) 40-69-30-56/57
Fax: (33 1) 40-69-30-68

GERMANY
UNO-Verlag
Poppelsdorfer Allee 55
53115 Bonn
Tel: (49 228) 212940
Fax: (49 228) 217492

GREECE
Papasotiriou S.A.
35, Stournara Str.
106 82 Athens
Tel: (30 1) 364-1826
Fax: (30 1) 364-8254

HAITI
Culture Diffusion
5, Rue Capois
C.P. 257
Port-au-Prince
Tel: (509) 23 9260
Fax: (509) 23 4858

HONG KONG, MACAO
Asia 2000 Ltd.
Sales & Circulation Department
Seabird House, unit 1101-02
22-28 Wyndham Street, Central
Hong Kong
Tel: (852) 2530-1409
Fax: (852) 2526-1107
E-mail: sales@asia2000.com.hk
URL: http://www.asia2000.com.hk

HUNGARY
Euro Info Service
Margitszgeti Europa Haz
H-1138 Budapest
Tel: (36 1) 111 6061
Fax: (36 1) 302 5035
E-mail: euroinfo@mail.matav.hu

INDIA
Allied Publishers Ltd.
751 Mount Road
Madras - 600 002
Tel: (91 44) 852-3938
Fax: (91 44) 852-0649

INDONESIA
Pt. Indira Limited
Jalan Borobudur 20
P.O. Box 181
Jakarta 10320
Tel: (62 21) 390-4290
Fax: (62 21) 390-4289

IRAN
Ketab Sara Co. Publishers
Khaled Eslamboli Ave., 6th Street
Delafrooz Alley No. 8
P.O. Box 15745-733
Tehran 15117
Tel: (98 21) 8717819; 8716104
Fax: (98 21) 8712479
E-mail: ketab-sara@neda.net.ir

Kowkab Publishers
P.O. Box 19575-511
Tehran
Tel: (98 21) 258-3723
Fax: (98 21) 258-3723

IRELAND
Government Supplies Agency
Oifig an tSoláthair
4-5 Harcourt Road
Dublin 2
Tel: (353 1) 661-3111
Fax: (353 1) 475-2670

ISRAEL
Yozmot Literature Ltd.
P.O. Box 56055
3 Yohanan Hasandlar Street
Tel Aviv 61560
Tel: (972 3) 5285-397
Fax: (972 3) 5285-397

R.O.Y. International
PO Box 13056
Tel Aviv 61130
Tel: (972 3) 5461423
Fax: (972 3) 5461442
E-mail: royil@netvision.net.il

Palestinian Authority/Middle East
Index Information Services
P.O.B. 19502 Jerusalem
Tel: (972 2) 6271219
Fax: (972 2) 6271634

ITALY
Licosa Commissionaria Sansoni SPA
Via Duca Di Calabria, 1/1
Casella Postale 552
50125 Firenze
Tel: (55) 645-415
Fax: (55) 641-257
E-mail: licosa@ftbcc.it
URL: http://www.ftbcc.it/licosa

JAMAICA
Ian Randle Publishers Ltd.
206 Old Hope Road, Kingston 6
Tel: 809-927-2085
Fax: 809-977-0243
E-mail: irpl@colis.com

JAPAN
Eastern Book Service
3-13 Hongo 3-chome, Bunkyo-ku
Tokyo 113
Tel: (81 3) 3818-0861
Fax: (81 3) 3818-0864
E-mail: orders@svt-ebs.co.jp
URL: http://www.bekkoame.or.jp/~svt-ebs

KENYA
Africa Book Service (E.A.) Ltd.
Quaran House, Mfangano Street
P.O. Box 45245
Nairobi
Tel: (254 2) 223 641
Fax: (254 2) 330 272

KOREA, REPUBLIC OF
Daejon Trading Co. Ltd.
P.O. Box 34, Youida, 706 Seoun Bldg
44-6 Youido-Dong, Yeongchengo-Ku
Seoul
Tel: (82 2) 785-1631/4
Fax: (82 2) 784-0315

MALAYSIA
University of Malaya Cooperative
Bookshop, Limited
P.O. Box 1127
Jalan Pantai Baru
59700 Kuala Lumpur
Tel: (60 3) 756-5000
Fax: (60 3) 755-4424

MEXICO
INFOTEC
Av. San Fernando No. 37
Col. Toriello Guerra
14050 Mexico, D.F.
Tel: (52 5) 624-2800
Fax: (52 5) 624-2822
E-mail: infotec@rtn.net.mx
URL: http://rtn.net.mx

NEPAL
Everest Media International Services (P) Ltd.
GPO Box 5443
Kathmandu
Tel: (977 1) 472 152
Fax: (977 1) 224 431

NETHERLANDS
De Lindeboom/InOr-Publikaties
P.O. Box 202, 7480 AE Haaksbergen
Tel: (31 53) 574-0004
Fax: (31 53) 572-9296
E-mail: lindeboo@worldonline.nl
URL: http://www.worldonline.nl/~lindeboo

NEW ZEALAND
EBSCO NZ Ltd.
Private Mail Bag 99914
New Market
Auckland
Tel: (64 9) 524-8119
Fax: (64 9) 524-8067

NIGERIA
University Press Limited
Three Crowns Building Jericho
Private Mail Bag 5095
Ibadan
Tel: (234 22) 41-1356
Fax: (234 22) 41-2056

NORWAY
NIC Info A/S
Book Department, Postboks 6512 Etterstad
N-0606 Oslo
Tel: (47 22) 97-4500
Fax: (47 22) 97-4545

PAKISTAN
Mirza Book Agency
65, Shahrah-e-Quaid-e-Azam
Lahore 54000
Tel: (92 42) 735 3601
Fax: (92 42) 576 3714

Oxford University Press
5 Bangalore Town
Sharae Faisal
PO Box 13033
Karachi-75350
Tel: (92 21) 446307
Fax: (92 21) 4547640
E-mail: oup@oup.khi.erum.com.pk

Pak Book Corporation
Aziz Chambers 21, Queen's Road
Lahore
Tel: (92 42) 636 3222; 636 0885
Fax: (92 42) 636 2328
E-mail: pbc@brain.net.pk

PERU
Editorial Desarrollo SA
Apartado 3824, Lima 1
Tel: (51 14) 285380
Fax: (51 14) 286628

PHILIPPINES
International Booksource Center Inc.
1127-A Antipolo St, Barangay, Venezuela
Makati City
Tel: (63 2) 896 6501; 6505; 6507
Fax: (63 2) 896 1741

POLAND
International Publishing Service
Ul. Piekna 31/37
00-677 Warzawa
Tel: (48 2) 628-6089
Fax: (48 2) 621-7255
E-mail: books%ips@ikp.atm.com.pl
URL: http://www.ipscg.waw.pl/ips/export/

PORTUGAL
Livraria Portugal
Apartado 2681, Rua Do Carmo 70-74
1200 Lisbon
Tel: (1) 347-4982
Fax: (1) 347-0264

ROMANIA
Compani De Librarii Bucuresti S.A.
Str. Lipscani no. 26, sector 3
Bucharest
Tel: (40 1) 613 9645
Fax: (40 1) 312 4000

RUSSIAN FEDERATION
Isdatelstvo <Ves Mir>
9a, Lolpachniy Pereulok
Moscow 101831
Tel: (7 095) 917 87 49
Fax: (7 095) 917 92 59

SINGAPORE, TAIWAN, MYANMAR, BRUNEI
Asahgate Publishing Asia Pacific Pte. Ltd.
41 Kallang Pudding Road #04-03
Golden Wheel Building
Singapore 349316
Tel: (65) 741-5166
Fax: (65) 742-9356
E-mail: ashgate@asianconnect.com

SLOVENIA
Gospodarski Vestnik Publishing Group
Dunajska cesta 5
1000 Ljubljana
Tel: (386 61) 133 83 47; 132 12 30
Fax: (386 61) 133 80 30
E-mail: repansekj@gvestnik.si

SOUTH AFRICA, BOTSWANA
International Subscription Service
P.O. Box 41095
Craighall
Johannesburg 2024
Tel: (27 11) 880-1448
Fax: (27 11) 880-6248
E-mail: iss@is.co.za

SPAIN
Mundi-Prensa Libros, S.A.
Castello 37
28001 Madrid
Tel: (34 1) 431-3399
Fax: (34 1) 575-3998
E-mail: libreria@mundiprensa.es
URL: http://www.mundiprensa.es/

Mundi-Prensa Barcelona
Consell de Cent, 391
08009 Barcelona
Tel: (34 3) 488-3492
Fax: (34 3) 487-7659
E-mail: barcelona@mundiprensa.es

SRI LANKA, THE MALDIVES
Lake House Bookshop
100, Sir Chittampalam Gardiner Mawatha
Colombo 2
Tel: (94 1) 32105
Fax: (94 1) 432104
E-mail: LHL@sri.lanka.net

SWEDEN
Wennergren-Williams AB
P.O. Box 1305
S-171 25 Solna
Tel: (46 8) 705-97-50
Fax: (46 8) 27-00-71
E-mail: mail@wwi.se

SWITZERLAND
Librairie Payot Service Institutionnel
Côtes-de-Montbenon 30
1002 Lausanne
Tel: (41 21) 341-3229
Fax: (41 21) 341-3235

ADECO Van Diemen EditionsTechniques
Ch. de Lacuez 41
CH1807 Blonay
Tel: (41 21) 943 2673
Fax: (41 21) 943 3605

TANZANIA
Oxford University Press
Maktaba Street, P.O. Box 5299
Dar es Salaam
Tel: (255 51) 29209
Fax: (255 51) 46822

THAILAND
Central Books Distribution
306 Silom Road
Bangkok 10500
Tel: (66 2) 235-5400
Fax: (66 2) 237-8321

TRINIDAD & TOBAGO, AND THE CARRIBBEAN
Systematics Studies Unit
9 Watts Street
Curepe
Trinidad, West Indies
Tel: (809) 662-5654
Fax: (809) 662-5654
E-mail: tobe@trinidad.net

UGANDA
Gustro Ltd.
P.O. Box 9997, Madhvani Building
Plot 16/4 Jinja Rd.
Kampala
Tel: (256 41) 254 763
Fax: (256 41) 251 468

UNITED KINGDOM
Microinfo Ltd.
P.O. Box 3, Alton, Hampshire GU34 2PG
England
Tel: (44 1420) 86848
Fax: (44 1420) 89889
E-mail: wbank@ukminfo.demon.co.uk
URL: http://www.microinfo.co.uk

VENEZUELA
Tecni-Ciencia Libros, S.A.
Centro Cuidad Comercial Tamanco
Nivel C2, Caracas
Tel: (58 2) 959 5547; 5035; 0016
Fax: (58 2) 959 5636

ZAMBIA
University Bookshop, University of Zambia
Great East Road Campus
P.O. Box 32379
Lusaka
Tel: (260 1) 252 576
Fax: (260 1) 253 952

ZIMBABWE
Longman Zimbabwe (Pvt.)Ltd.
Tourle Road, Ardbennie
P.O. Box ST125
Southerton
Harare
Tel: (263 4) 6216617
Fax: (263 4) 621670

06/19/97